THE BIG SHIP

AN AUTOBIOGRAPHY BY HENRY A. LARSEN

IN CO-OPERATION WITH

FRANK R. SHEER AND EDVARD OMHOLT-JENSEN

McCLELLAND AND STEWART LIMITED

Toronto/Montreal

THE BIG SHIP

The Canadian Publishers

McClelland and Stewart Limited
25 Hollinger Road, Toronto 16

Printed and bound in Canada

All Eskimo names and place names are spelt in keeping with the new orthography which has been developed to give a uniform spelling to Eskimo words. We are greatly indebted for this to the Administrator of the Arctic A. Stevenson and to Joanassie Salomonie of the Orthography Section of the Northern Administration Branch of the Department of Indian Affairs and Northern Development.

ACKNOWLEDGEMENTS

NOTE ON TITLE: *"Hanorie Umiarjuag" is Eskimo for "Henry With the Big Ship," a term of respect and endearment. Hence the title* The Big Ship.

While the following is based on the exhaustive notes provided by the late Henry Larsen and his almost total recall of days gone by, we are greatly indebted to a number of people who have given generously of their time and experience in reading the manuscript.

In addition to Commissioner L. H. Nicholson, the following must also be mentioned: Sqn. Ldr. Scott Alexander (Ret.) (Larsen's old shipmate from the *St. Roch*), Cmdr. M. Barrow, RCN, Mr. Wm. Dunstan, Department of Transport, Assistant Commissioner C. N. K. Kirk, RCM Police, Mr. A. Stevenson, Administrator of the Arctic, Department of Indian Affairs and Northern Development, and members of the Larsen family.

Frank Sheer *Edvard Omholt-Jensen.*

CONTENTS

FOREWORD

At the Festival of Britain in 1951, there was a remarkably complete and well-designed Polar section. Separate illuminated large-type listings carried the names of Arctic and Antarctic explorers in the order of their appearance on the stage of history. At the top of the Arctic list was the name "Henry Hudson"; at the bottom the name "Henry Larsen." I recall the thrill I experienced when I realized that this sturdy, quiet member of our Force had earned inclusion in such a notable company.

The story of the life and accomplishments of my friend and former associate Henry Larsen is one that cried for recording, and that has been well done in the following pages. He may be said to have closed the book on the old style of Arctic exploration, and his service experience stretched from sailing-ships to high-speed aircraft.

Henry Larsen was a modest man with a deep love of the North and its people. Perhaps one of the greatest compliments paid him has been by the Eskimos themselves in the affection they still express for this man who lived with them and knew them so well. Eyes light up in Eskimo settlements when his name is spoken.

The *St. Roch* under Larsen faced many dangers in her northern voyages and these are described here simply and without embellishment. Readers will sense, however, that she would almost certainly have met her fate in these Arctic seas, as did many stout ships before her, had it not been for the judgment, seamanship and knowledge of ice possessed by her Master. Ship and skipper together made a combination that was able, time after time, to win through.

While he did not like administrative and office work, Larsen had knowledge and a practical approach to problems which were of great value, and I pay tribute to the sound advice he gave on many matters touching the work of the Force in the North. In particular, his philosophy on the situation and treatment of our Eskimo citizens warrants careful reflection.

In all respects Henry Larsen was a worthy product of his homeland and an outstanding Canadian.

L. H. NICHOLSON

Commissioner

Royal Canadian Mounted Police

THE BIG SHIP

1 THE FIRST DAY IN THE MOUNTED POLICE

The date was April 16, 1928, and the rain was pouring down as I walked to the Mounted Police Barracks in Vancouver, but nothing could dampen my spirit. It mattered little that I had to wait in Sergeant-Major Jock Binning's office now that I was nearing my dreams' fulfilment—to become a member of the Royal Canadian Mounted Police. Dazzled by the impressive figure of the serious Scotsman Binning in his blue uniform, I forgot all about the long road I had behind me. All I could see was the Sergeant-Major, his riding boots and Sam Browne belt polished to a high gloss.

The Sergeant-Major had not talked much, only asked my name and advised me to walk straight-backed into the office of the Officer Commanding and to answer all his questions briefly and precisely.

The Officer Commanding of the Force in Vancouver was Superintendent A. W. Duffus, an elderly grey-haired gentleman with a pear-shaped nose. He turned out to be very pleasant and asked me a number of personal questions. Then I was duly sworn in as a member of the Royal Canadian Mounted Police.

Afterwards I was asked to sit down with the Sergeant-Major while the Superintendent questioned me in detail about what I had done before, and I told him that I had spent most of my life at sea. When he asked me if I knew anything about horses or riding, I had to say no, and to my great surprise he said that this was perfect. The Force had more than its share of people who knew horses, and yet only managed to break their arms and legs and ruin the horses, he added.

"Sergeant-Major," Superintendent Duffus said near the end of the interview, "make sure that this man doesn't get near a horse for a while. He's too valuable to us to become hospitalized just now."

With the interview over I was issued uniform and equipment. First of all it was the famous scarlet tunic, the broad-brimmed Stetson, a red toque for winter use and a fur cap. Then followed fatigues, boots and breeches, blankets, sheets, underwear and countless brushes and other polishers. I also got a .303 rifle and a .45 Colt, as well as twelve rounds of ammunition and a Sam Browne belt. With all this, I was taken to the barracks, given a bunk and shown how to make it up.

It happened that I was the only recruit enrolled just then, as the last intake had been around New Year's, and they had already left for the training centre at Regina, Saskatchewan. The course was now half over, so it was decided that I was to get my basic training in Vancouver.

My first day in the Force was a long one. When I finally went to bed, I remained awake a long time after the lights had been turned off. Had I made the right decision? Was it wise to attempt to realize a boyhood dream, and a romantic one at that? There were so many unanswered questions. But two of my greatest wishes had come true. At the age of twenty-eight I had been to the Arctic and was now a member of the RCMP.

That night my thoughts went back over the years. I had come a long way, not only in time, but also in distance since I had left my childhood home at the age of fifteen early in World War I.

2 THE EARLY YEARS

I was born and raised in Norway near the mouth of the Oslo Fiord, where the sea not only provided most people's livelihood, but was also the main highway. The sea became my great love from the moment when I first set out with the pilot boats during my summer holidays. Then followed small jobs on all kinds of pleasure vessels and an occasional adventure with the fishing boats. But I was still only a boy and the school bell was still stronger than those of the many ships in the harbour.

History and geography became my favourite subjects and I developed an early yearning for new lands and a curiosity for the history of the past. Our teachers encouraged and helped me to further reading in the small school library, where I soon had read every book on geography, particularly those dealing with the polar regions. I was immediately fascinated by the books written by such people as Fridtjof Nansen, Roald Amundsen and Otto Sverdrup, and, of course, Vilhjalmur Stefansson. When I read about the courage of Frobisher and the tragedy that was Franklin's, I wished that I could follow in the footsteps of these brave men, over the sea to unknown lands in the northern ice.

I was barely fifteen when I went to sea. My first run was with lumber to Swedish and Danish ports. The skipper was an uncle of mine, but the work was very hard and anything but exciting, so after a year of this I left and signed on the bark *Baunen* bound for Pensacola, Florida, from the French port of Brest.

Together with five or six others, I left for Brest via London and Paris under the watchful eye of Captain Olsen, also known as the "Devil of Bengal," which had been the name of one of the ships he had commanded. We arrived in London in the middle of a German Zeppelin raid, but in spite of the war the city was an adventure for a young boy, even though I did not get much of a chance to take in the sights. The Mate had entrusted me with an enormous world atlas, which I had to carry around no matter where I went. Today I am pretty sure that this was done on purpose to keep me out of trouble, and that it did. After all, what trouble can a young fellow get into with an atlas under his arm!

My first big ship was a sight to behold, but we did not have much time to stand around admiring the bark. While German prisoners of war were unloading her, we started to scrape and paint the hull before we were finally towed out of the Bay of Biscay, three weeks later, heading for Barbados.

No sooner had the tug left us than two French girls appeared on deck. Two crew members, a Norwegian and an American, had smuggled them on board; but when the ship started to heave, the girls were unable to stay in hiding any more. When the skipper spied the girls, he let out a roar that could be heard for miles. He ordered the ship to be turned about and had a signal flag hoisted to recall the tug. We had to lower some of the sails, and soon French cruisers and patrol vessels came steaming at us at top speed. They were convinced that we had been attacked by a German submarine. The skipper used his entire repertoire of trilingual curses while the girls were put on board the tug, much to the amusement of the crews on the warships. The two sailors got an English-Norwegian tongue-lashing they probably never forgot.

On the Atlantic I experienced my first storm, but our 1,200-ton ship came through with flying colours. We did not have time to think about the weather anyway. One watch followed another and quite often we would be working sixteen to twenty hours a day. Sixteen men was not much of a crew for a ship that size, especially when all the sails had to be raised manually. Even when the weather was calm, we were kept busy fixing the sails and the rigging, scraping rust and painting.

To a young, growing boy the food was not much to brag about. The margarine was stale, so we used canned milk on bread instead. However, we had to remember to plug the hole in the can each time we had taken some milk in order to keep the cockroaches out of it. They seemed to be all over the place, and once in a while we would find a few floating around the bottom of a can when we had finished it. The meals generally consisted of hard biscuits, sugar, salted meat and dried fish. Fortunately, we were able to do some fishing once in a while, mostly for bonitos. All we had to do was to fasten a piece of white cloth to a hook and drop the line over the side with the hook dangling just above the water. The bonitos, mistaking the cloth for a flying fish, soon were leaping at the bait and thus provided us with a welcome change at mealtimes.

In the Gulf ports we took on a load of planks and set off for Buenos Aires, where we were met, not only by the pilot and the ship chandlers, but also by all sorts of beggars, procurers and swindlers. One man towered head and shoulder above them all, the giant Norwegian parson in charge of the Sailors' Mission. Johan Nielsen was one of the finest men I have ever met, and should be given credit for having looked after countless Norwegian sailors who came to Buenos Aires. At that time the port was one of the wildest in the world and the dock area was full of human derelicts of all nationalities. They drifted about and lived on hand-outs from the hundreds of ships calling on the busy port. As soon as they spotted a fellow-countryman, they tried to hit him for some money. A floating body was quite common in the water around the ships, and we took great care never to go ashore alone, but stayed together in groups.

When I finally returned to my home in Norway it was near the end of January 1917.

Strutting around in my blue, double-breasted suit and with almost eighteen years behind me, I felt that nobody could mistake me for anything but a true sailor.

3 THE INDIAN GIRL, THE SEA DEVIL AND "THE GENERAL"

It was an exceptionally cold winter that year and practically impossible to find any work ashore, so I ended up signing on the bark *Indian Girl* together with a friend of mine. We kept close to the Norwegian coast as we worked our way up north before heading west for Norfolk, Virginia. In this way we hoped to avoid submarines as well as mines, and apart from a blizzard the days were fairly quiet until we reached a point north of Scotland. Three British destroyers hailed us and ordered the *Indian Girl* to go to Kirkwall where we were to be searched. We quickly realized that it was the Sea Devil himself, the German Count von Luckner, they were after. His speciality was to sail under the Norwegian flag in a ship which strongly resembled ours, raiding any Allied ship he encountered. The British Navy had been fooled time and time again, and he had sunk a great number of ships. It was obvious that the British were not going to let themselves be fooled this time. But they had not counted on Captain Andersen, a stubborn old salt from the town of Tonsberg. Captain Andersen, a deeply religious man, feared the Lord, but was determined that the British Navy was not going to stand in his way.

That very night he assembled the entire crew—we were eighteen—in his cabin for his usual religious service. For some reason he chose to speak about Jesus who had walked the waters. Then followed some hymns which he played on his old-fashioned phonograph, while he joined in the singing with his deep voice. Soon we were all singing, and received our earthly reward, a cigar or a few cigarettes.

Strengthened by the service, the Captain ordered us to turn about and head for our original destination, the United States. I was at the helm and at that time totally unaware, of course, that I was to meet von Luckner at an Explorers' Club dinner in New York City some forty years later. When we finally met, the charming old pirate was past eighty and expressed great interest in my story of the *Indian Girl*. He said he was sorry that he had been forced to sink so many fine ships, and proudly pointed out that not a single life had been lost as a result of his wartime activities.*

The next day we ran into another British naval vessel, which signalled to us that the United States had declared war on Germany, but we arrived safely at our destination and later continued to Buenos Aires.

In July of 1918 we sailed up the Hudson River after having completed numerous round trips to South America. By now I felt that I knew every inch of the ship. As we anchored near the Brooklyn Bridge, however, I decided to leave in spite of the fact that I had come to like both the ship and the crew. In those days, it was almost a matter of prestige to go from one ship to another.

After three weeks ashore I joined the *General Gordon*, a proud Norwegian four-master with a crew of twenty-one. Next to the impressive skipper, who was a giant of a man, I suppose the Danish cook awed me the most.

"This trip won't end well," he assured me from the very first day we met. And perhaps it was not all that strange, because his past three ships had all been sunk by German submarines.

This time we took off for Montevideo and on our way down we ran into a terrifying pampero, or hurricane. The prophecies made by the Dane were not to come true on this occasion, however, and we reached our port without any trouble.

While we were ashore all the church bells suddenly started to ring out, the traffic came to a halt and an enormous crowd of people gathered at the docks.

Viva Americano! Viva Angleterro! Viva Noruego! Just about every nation got its *viva*. It was November 11, 1918, and the Armistice had just been announced. All the ships set off their sirens and rockets were fired while the sailors streamed ashore in hordes. The wine was cheap, and here at last they finally had something to celebrate after braving submarines and mines for four years. But the feeling of brotherly love did not last too long, and soon nation was fighting nation. The drunker

*The old Count outlived Larsen by a year and a half and died in Malmo, Sweden.

the men became, the worse the fights, and after some time it was no longer possible to keep track of the citizenship of one's adversaries. All that mattered was to get into the best possible fight, regardless of whether one was fighting with or against compatriots.

The police watched all this patiently, but in the end it became too much even for the happy-go-lucky Uruguayans, who finally had to bring in mounted policemen to get the sailors back to their ships.

These fights, incidentally, were the closest I ever did get to any real battles during the First World War.

Before I said farewell to my last sailing ship, *General Gordon*— or "The General," as we affectionately called her—I experienced a shipwreck off the coast near Charleston, South Carolina. Sail after sail was blown out and both our lifeboats were smashed. Almost buried in water, the ship started to drift; and the hurricane lasted for a full twenty-four hours. We ran aground for good on the morning of February 18, 1919, with the deck barely above water. In spite of an offer to stay and work on a plantation near Port Royal, I set off for New York. Some of the other crew members signed on sailing ships in Charleston for seventy-five dollars a month, and the United States Coast Guard was also making tempting offers. But I had other plans, hoping to attend the Norwegian State Navigation School in Oslo. To get back home I signed on my first steamer, the *Vinstra*, headed for South Africa, India and, eventually, Norway.

4 STEAM

I had hardly ever been aboard a steamer and was shocked to see the entire midships in *Vinstra* full of coal, ashes, shovels and junk. When I managed to find the First Mate somewhere in between the heaps of coal, I was informed that I was to be the Boatswain. No matter how much I protested, saying that this was my first steamer and adding that I was only nineteen years old, the Mate remained firm. Boatswain it was!

As Boatswain I was to bunk with the carpenter, a Finn who was twice my age, but in spite of this difference we soon became good friends. The rest of the crew were friendly enough, but they were all older men and kept mostly to themselves. Luckily the carpenter gave me much good advice and it did not take me long to feel at home, in spite of the unfamiliar surroundings and the ubiquitous coal.

The food on the steamer was far better than anything I had been used to on the sailing-ships. We had lots of fresh meat and vegetables and a sufficient supply of fresh water to wash in, even for the occasional shower. The working hours were regular and nobody had to climb the rigging; and yet I somehow missed the close friendship that was so typical of the sailing-ships, and often wished I could be back on a square-rigger.

This time I saw parts of the world that were new to me, such as Cape Town, Java, Ceylon, Aden, Suez and Port Said. I cannot say that I was particularly impressed by these places even if they were interesting, and I was quite happy when we left the East behind us and headed for Gibraltar and Rotterdam. A few days later we were on our way up the North Sea watching carefully for drifting mines left over from the war.

Quite a few things had changed in Oslo—or Christiania, as it was still called in 1919—but then I myself had changed since I was there last. As we passed Brest on our way north, my thoughts had gone back nostalgically to my first trip on the *Baunen*. I was never to stand on the deck of a square-rigger again. The era of the sailing-ships had come to an end. At least, there were not many left by the time I graduated from the Navigation School during the summer of 1920.

After ten days of exams we were given our diplomas and were declared fully qualified to navigate steam as well as sailing-ships anywhere in the world. But like most young Norwegians I was ordered to do my duty for King and Country and had to report to the Navy for my compulsory military service. We who had started to believe what our diplomas said about our proficiencies did, however, learn a number of things in the Navy, not the least of which was that the Navy had its own ways of doing things.

5 FOURTH MATE LARSEN

In the early summer of 1922 I signed on a Fred. Olsen Line ship as Fourth Mate. The Motor Ship *Theodore Roosevelt,* one of Norway's biggest and most modern, sailed between Norway and the Pacific coast. Among our ports of call were San Francisco and Vancouver, where we took on board wheat for European ports.

We left Oslo fully loaded for Honolulu, and on Hawaii I managed to see Waikiki Beach before we went on to San Pedro, San Francisco, Seattle and Vancouver.

I made four round trips, all told, and I think it was on the second-last one that I saw the polar explorer Roald Amundsen, who had been my hero for years. He came on board in Seattle, where he had arrived from Point Barrow, Alaska. His famous ship *Maud* had been left in the ice somewhere near Wrangel Island after he tried to drift to the North Pole. He was then busy planning a flight by aeroplane from Point Barrow to Spitzbergen.

Amundsen was actually on a speaking tour just then, but the purpose of his visit to the *Theodore Roosevelt* was to arrange passage back to Norway for his pilot Oscar Omdahl. The Hudson's Bay Company had brought Omdahl down to Vancouver from Point Barrow, free of charge, on their ship *Lady Kindersley.* But when he came to us, Omdahl soon became aware of the fact that he was not going to be a tourist any more. The stern skipper, Erik Thomle, declared that Omdahl would have to work in the engine room as a greaser, and gave strict orders that he had to live and eat with the other greasers. Captain Thomle had no use for lazy-bones, tourists or explorers, who wasted their money drifting around in the Arctic ice. I had the impression that had it been Amundsen himself who had been coming with us, he would have had to work his way across if the skipper had anything to say in the matter.

Omdahl and I quickly found each other, and as I had plenty of room in my cabin, I let him store his clothing and all his strange souvenirs there. During the next weeks we spent hours talking about his various trips and his plans for the future.

He told me that Amundsen had built a small house near Wainwright in the vicinity of Point Barrow and that he had spent a full year there. An accident finally wrecked the ski-undercarriage on his plane, and that was the end of the experiment. But Omdahl was convinced that he would be flying to the North Pole some day.

Polar aviation was still in its infancy in 1922, and if it had not been for the courage and stubbornness of people like Omdahl, I suppose Amundsen never would have made it.

"We'll get there," he used to say, "even if I have to fly an old piece of board!"

Four years later, in 1926, he flew across the Pole in the dirigible *Norge*, but was killed the following year while flying across the Atlantic.

We had no crystal ball in my cabin in the *Theodore Roosevelt*, but one thing I did know: I had to get to the North. In spite of a promotion to Third Mate and the promise of a good career with the shipping line, I made up my mind to give it all up in order to realize my dreams.

It turned out to be far from easy to get north. Previously more than twelve supply ships had been sailing regularly from the west coast to the Arctic—now only three remained. Of these the *Arctic* and *Nanook* were from San Francisco and the *Lady Kindersley* belonged to the Hudson's Bay Company. It seemed almost impossible for me to get in touch with either of the owners.

In the meantime, as a result of the great earthquake in 1923, I had an opportunity to see Japan. The *Theodore Roosevelt* was sent off with food and emergency supplies for the victims. No sooner was I back in Vancouver again than I decided to take the important step. Knowing that my future was in the North, I left my ship and was on my own.

6 NORTH WITH KLENGENBERG

While in Vancouver during the spring of 1924 I happened to read a newspaper article about Christian Klengenberg from Coronation Gulf in the Canadian Arctic. He had travelled by dog team from Herschel Island in the Northwest Territories to Fairbanks, Alaska, with his two sons Andrew and Jorgen. From Fairbanks they went on with a cargo of fur to Seattle and bought a schooner, which the old man then was getting ready for the return voyage.

This was something for me, and I was off to Seattle. The *Maid of Orleans* was a fine two-masted schooner, white-painted and easy to find on the waterfront. An elderly, white-haired man was pacing the deck while two olive-skinned young fellows were sunning themselves on the hatch. The boys looked oriental, but then I noticed that the younger one had the same eagle-beaked nose as the old man and realized that these were Klengenberg and his sons.

I was asked to come aboard and was hired on the spot. It was really all pretty simple, for they were badly in need of a navigator. Klengenberg was a great talker and started to tell about Roald Amundsen and Vilhjalmur Stefansson, whom he had met on Herschel Island in 1906. He was originally from Denmark, but had sailed around the world as a cook before he ended up in the Arctic some time in the 1890's, when he left a whaling ship and married an Eskimo woman. Although he now was a naturalized American, he had applied for Canadian citizenship after having lived in the Canadian Arctic for more than twenty years. In the meantime he had to sail under the American flag.

This turned out to be his first visit to the South since 1907. The supplies he was gathering were partly for his own large family, and partly for trade with the Eskimos on Victoria Island. It was Klengenberg who first found the band of Eskimos on the island in 1905 and had interested Stefansson in them. As a result, the scientist spent an entire winter with the natives and studied these so-called "Blond Eskimos."

Before I had a chance to think, I was busy getting everything ready on board. It was my responsibility as the Mate to see to it that the schooner was properly outfitted, and a good many things remained to be done. Klengenberg told me confidentially that as a rule he was not too keen on real sailors because it was most likely that we would have to winter in the North, and then there would be nothing for that type of man to do. Consequently we did not have much of a crew. Apart from Klengenberg and his sons, we were five, all told. One of the men had never even been to sea.

It was not all work in Seattle, though. Through Klengenberg I got to know all kinds of people. There were still a good many old-timers from the North around, and they all knew "Charlie," as they called my new boss. I was made an honorary member of the "Alaska and Yukon Sourdough Club" and was even invited to the home of Mrs. Carmack, the widow of the man who made the original gold strike at Klondike. Both Mr. Carmack and his Indian friend Skookum Jim were names familiar to me from Jack London and Oliver Curwood's books, but when I read about these men as a young boy, I never thought that one day I would be having dinner with Carmack's widow and Skookum Jim's daughter, a beautiful half-breed girl.

The schooner was fully loaded when we at last headed north in late June 1924. The deck was full of coal, oil and lumber in addition to two big boats and a number of smaller ones, which the skipper hoped to sell. We also had a woman on board, Miss Alice Supplee, who was engaged to the engineer, Oliver Morris. She was to teach the younger Klengenberg children. She and Morris were married later and lived near Point Barrow where they raised a large family.

The first part of the trip went off without a hitch. When we got to Teller we stopped to visit Klengenberg's brother-in-law Albert Bernhard. He was a German who had come from one of the Baltic seaports and ended up in the North after many years at sea. He and Klengenberg had married two Eskimo sisters, and Albert had at least twelve children. Some years earlier one of his daughters had been caught in a snowstorm and had to have a leg amputated when it was frozen. Albert was far from being a wealthy man, and he could scarcely express his gratitude when Klengenberg presented him with an artificial leg for his daughter. This, no doubt, was the most popular of all the gifts he brought.

Next we came to Point Hope, some 250 miles to the north. We went through the Bering Strait and were met by a large crowd of Eskimos. They all appeared to know Charlie Charluruk, or Little Charlie, as they called him, and there was nose-rubbing and laughter all round.

While this was going on, one man kept quietly in the background. He had come aboard with the Eskimos but looked different, not the least in the way he was dressed. It was Knud Rasmussen, the famous Danish polar explorer, who had arrived that spring by dog team all the way from Greenland together with a Greenlander and his wife. He was quite a man, and I must have made a nuisance of myself with my countless questions about his adventures.

This was an occasion that called for a celebration, and the skipper invited everybody to a party. All his old friends were given gifts, and he saw to it that they all had enough to eat. The Eskimos too brought gifts such as geese, ducks and a variety of birds' eggs. Many also carried large oily sealskin bags and I wondered what these might hold, but did not get around to asking. As a newcomer I decided that the best thing was to await the developments quietly.

After a while a rather plump Eskimo woman approached me with one of these bags in her hand. It was obvious that she felt sorry for me, because I seemed to be an outsider.

With quick movements she dug her hand into the bag, pulled out what looked like a piece of bacon and cut off a bit with a knife she was carrying somewhere about her. Then she trimmed off some of the fat or blubber and cut the chunk into still smaller pieces without quite severing them from the square. She put some into her own mouth and some into mine while she with a smile was mumbling something to the effect that she hoped I liked her mattaq. It did not taste bad at all, and reminded me a little bit of coconut. The important thing was not to chew it too long, but to swallow it like raw oyster. Eaten that way it tasted every bit as good as oysters.

Mattaq is the skin of the large Bowhead whale, also called narwhal, or of any whale for that matter. The Point Hope Eskimos had hundreds of sealskin pokes full of mattaq stored away below the ground in their large ice houses. When a whale is killed, the hide or blubber is stripped off the carcass. A large portion of the blubber, which can reach almost twelve inches in thickness, is cut off and used for fuel, but the remaining two to three inches of blubber next to the outer layer, which has the texture of sponge rubber, is kept. That is the mattaq.

Klengenberg told me that it was customary to give gifts in return and gave me a few bars of soap for the woman. She apparently never forgot the soap, for each time I came to Point Hope during the many years to come, she was always on hand with a slab of mattaq.

The celebration lasted two days, and in return we were invited to an Eskimo dance. The dancers were mostly the older Eskimos. A row of old drummers chanted and beat their drums while the men and women danced in two lines opposite each other. Most of the dances were symbolic and described scenes from their daily life. The performers often ended up completely entranced as a result of the rhythmic drumming and monotonous singing, although once in a while one of them would let out some loud yells. Later I was to learn that these dances varied greatly from one area to another.

Even Eskimo parties come to an end, and at last we said goodbye to Rasmussen and all the others and continued on our way, well provided for with gifts.

We kept close to the shore and used our hand lead constantly. The weather was mostly fine and the sea calm, and I enjoyed myself greatly navigating between the ice-floes in the sunshine. Our charts were far from accurate and, of course, lacked details, but Klengenberg knew the few landmarks along the coast where he had sailed on whalers and travelled by dog team in the wintertime.

A few miles west of Point Barrow we headed into fog, which became steadily worse. In the end we could barely see half a mile ahead of us. Then all of a sudden two other ships, *Arctic* and *Lady Kindersley*, appeared, first as blurred outlines, then quite clearly. We did not waste any time getting aboard with the mail we had picked up for them at Nome. These two ships were moored to the edge of a pressure ridge of ice that had gone aground, and were waiting for it to start to move so that they could go around Cape Smythe to Point Barrow. The *Nanook* with Captain Pedersen on the bridge had managed to get through a few days earlier.

Klengenberg knew it was dangerous to remain in such an exposed position, in case a northwest wind should come up, so we continued, in spite of the fog, and practically crawled along the edge of the pressure ridge right to its very tip. From there on the ice was floating, but was still tightly packed, calling for even greater caution.

As if the ice were not bad enough, the fog grew worse, and the compass was not of any use to us now. Every time we hit the ice the compass needle would dance about in all directions, but somehow we managed to work the narrow lead. Klengenberg was in the crow's-nest while I had the wheel, but from deck level I could actually see better than he did.

Finally our soundings told us that we were past the Cape and I suppose we were some twenty miles east of Point Barrow before we were stopped by ice again. It was now impossible to get through owing to the fog, but the immediate danger of being crushed by pressure ice was over as it was fairly calm, and we moored to an ice-floe that had run aground.

I now had a pretty good idea of how to navigate a ship along this coast, which had long, very low sand-banks forming an almost ice-free lagoon from Point Barrow to Flaxman Island. It is impossible to go inside these sand islands, but by sounding continuously we managed to keep just outside the banks. As the ice always seems to be more or less in movement, it was important to be on the look-out for the slightest change or opening, so that we could take advantage of it while we slowly crept eastward.

7 HERSCHEL ISLAND FOR THE FIRST TIME

It was August when we finally reached Herschel Island and anchored in the bay. The harbour was full of Eskimo whale-boats. All the small sail- and motor-boats had been brought there either by the Hudson's Bay Company or on board Captain Pedersen's *Nanook*. These boats came from the entire Mackenzie delta and from Aklavik to trade with the big ships. There were also many white traders among the visitors, several of them married to Eskimo women.

The Royal Canadian Mounted Police had its District Headquarters on the island and the Commanding Officer, Inspector T. B. Caulkin, had been in the north for many years. It was a great disappointment to Klengenberg when Caulkin informed him that only Canadian ships were allowed to proceed east of Herschel Island to trade or to deliver freight of a non-Canadian origin. The skipper told the Inspector that he had a large family on Victoria Island, and that as far as he knew, they were without food, fuel or other supplies. Many other Eskimo families were also dependent on trading with him.

In those days Herschel Island had no wireless contact with the outside world, so Inspector Caulkin had to make his own decision. He fully understood Klengenberg's predicament, and yet he could not very well go against his own orders from Headquarters in Ottawa. However, he did allow Klengenberg to continue east on the condition that he would unload only provisions necessary to keep his own family alive for a year. There would be no trading at all. He added that the Hudson's Bay Company now had some trading posts near Coronation Gulf, and that a supply ship was expected there any day now. Klengenberg had no choice, of course, and we started to get ready for the last lap of our voyage.

In the meantime I took the opportunity to go ashore and meet the people. I was still wearing my uniform from the *Theodore Roosevelt*. It had shining brass buttons, and these threatened to cost me my bachelorhood. In one of the tents I visited with the Klengenberg brothers, we met an old woman who had come from the east to find herself a new husband. When she saw me, or rather my shining buttons, she called out to Andrew and nodded in my direction. Both Andrew and Jorgen started to howl with laughter and explained that the old woman was wondering if I wanted to marry her. I asked Andrew to thank her for the honour, but to tell her that I had decided to wait for a while before getting married. That satisfied her.

I also got to know many people with whom I was to have contact for many years to come, after I joined the Mounted Police. One of these, Ole Andreassen, was a Norwegian who had come from a place not far from where I was born. He had been a member of Stefansson's Expedition across the Beaufort Sea from Alaska and had also been with the explorer when he found the four islands north of Melville Island and Ellef Ringnes Island in 1913-18. Andreassen now had his own trading post and would have been a well-to-do man had he not been so kind-hearted that he gave away almost everything he had, both to Eskimos and to whites.

Before we left Herschel Island, Corporal Pasley of the RCMP joined us with his nine giant dogs, a sled and numerous bags of dog food. We were to put him ashore on Baillie Island where the Police had a smaller detachment, and to take on a constable who was to stay with us for the rest of the trip. I soon got to like Pasley, who was much older than I and had come to Canada from England. He had some twelve years' service in the Force.

It did not take us long to get from Herschel to Baillie, for the ice conditions were very good. We decided to take advantage of the good weather and continued as quickly as we could, after having taken Constable MacDonald on board to make sure that Klengenberg followed Inspector Caulkin's instructions.

The weather stayed fine, mostly without any ice at all, and we were grateful, because space was at a premium. MacDonald and I shared a bunk—that is, he slept while I was on deck—and we had some good chats about ships and sailing, topics he was quite familiar with, coming from Lunenburg, Nova Scotia.

8 VISIT TO KLENGENBERG'S HOME

Rymer Point is on the southern side of Victoria Island, about twenty miles past Read Island in Dolphin and Union Strait. Here we found the water sufficiently deep, with a bottom sloping gently towards the shore. We anchored and made a gangway to the shore, using our whalers as pontoons.

We were met by more than 150 Eskimos, among them Klengenberg's own family. His eldest son Patsy was in his thirties, was married and had his own family. His daughter Edna was married to an Alaskan Eskimo. A younger daughter, Lena, had taken the opportunity to get married to a local Eskimo while her father was away, something Klengenberg strongly disapproved of. His oldest daughter was married to the Norwegian Storker Storkerson, who also had been with Stefansson.

The reception these people gave us was wonderful. (Klengenberg and the boys had been away a year and a half.) All work was postponed until the next day. First the Eskimos were to come on board for a party. For most of them, this was their first visit in a big ship, and they swarmed all over. They all seemed to like Klengenberg, who had to shake hands with each and every one, and there was talking and questions and more questions without end.

The deck was cleared for the party, and as the guests arrived they were given cookies, canned meat, butter, jam and tea to their hearts' content—which was quite considerable. In the meantime Klengenberg and Constable MacDonald started to figure out what supplies would be required to keep the family alive for a year. I was free to do as I pleased and went ashore with Andrew, Jorgen and a group of Eskimos.

There were tents made of canvas or skins everywhere, and long rows of drying-stands for fish, seal and caribou meat. The people were generally dressed in elaborately made clothing of caribou skin, and the only apparent difference between the men and the women was that the women had larger hoods on their parkas for carrying their babies in.

These Eskimos were taller and had a lighter complexion than any others I had seen, and I wondered if this could have been the result of the visit made by the ships *Erebus* and *Investigator*. These two ships had been searching for Franklin seventy-three years before, and together they had a crew of more than a hundred men, who undoubtedly had been in contact with the Eskimos on Victoria Island.

As practically a member of the Klengenberg family, I was the object of a great deal of curiosity and hospitality. I was still wearing my uniform with the shining buttons, and quickly realized that this was the reason they all followed me with their eyes. One of the men had kept an eye on me for quite a while, and finally winked at me and beckoned me to come outside. He seemed harmless enough, so I left the tent I was visiting and walked along the shore until we reached some big boulders. On top of these were some things that looked like covered baskets. This puzzled me. I had heard that this particular band used to place their dead on stands made of driftwood for drying in the sun. Frequently the dogs, who were always running around looking for food, ate the bodies. My friend climbed a boulder and threw down a couple of big baskets. I was greatly relieved when he opened them and pulled out several sets of brand new caribou-skin clothing. He had stored them there for the summer, and I now understood that he wanted to trade with me for my uniform and, not the least, my cap. We traded and changed on the spot. I do not really know which of us was the prouder. His wife was all smiles, too, when her husband turned up in the uniform with the brass buttons.

In another tent, where a heavy, motherly-looking woman presided, I happened to look into a small wooden keg, which contained some oil and something else which to me looked exactly like a pair of human hands. I whispered something to Jorgen Klengenberg and pointed to the keg, and this I was soon to regret. The woman, who had been smiling at me all the time, now was really beaming. She reached into the keg and pulled out one of the objects of my curiosity, licked off the oil and handed it to me. Jorgen explained to me that it was only seal or ujjuk flippers, and that I had better eat it, as she had been wondering what to offer me until she had noticed that I was looking at the keg. The flippers had, of course, been skinned and partly boiled before they were pickled and placed in oil, but they still looked like human hands, as far as I was concerned. But I knew that this one was clean now, for the lady of the house had licked it right in front of me, so I gnawed away at it as best I could. Actually it was mostly gristle and quite tasteless, but I believe that pickled in brine as we do pigs' feet it would be quite a dish. My hostess was talking away and explaining, and as I did not understand a word, I only nodded in reply now and then, mostly at the wrong times as it turned out. The tent was full of people, among them many children, and a good-looking teen-aged boy. The woman kept talking to him and to me, and pointed to him over and over again, obviously trying to tell me that this was her son. But she must have felt that she had not really made herself understood, for to really get this point across to me, she squatted down and made a motion with her hands as if pulling something from under her parka and again pointed to the boy. I now hurriedly nodded vigorously to make her understand, this time, that I realized that she had given birth to this strapping boy, before she decided to go on to further demonstrations.

These Eskimos had hardly changed their way of life at all since Klengenberg first met them in 1905-6. His boat, the *Olga*, had frozen in the ice, and he did not know that there were any people at all in the area around Coronation Gulf. One day when he was setting his traps, he came across sled tracks and decided to investigate. After a while he came to a camp with many Eskimos. Somehow he felt anything but sure of himself, because the western Eskimos had told him that there were Eskimos in the east who were dangerous. It was too late to turn around then, however, so he drove his dog team straight into the crowd that had gathered. None of them were armed, as he had taken them completely by surprise, but it was quite clear that several of them were far from friendly. There was no time to lose, so Klengenberg ran over to the oldest and ugliest of the women, hugged her and started to rub noses. The Eskimos howled with laughter, and that broke the ice. As a rule the Eskimos have a well-developed sense of humour, and this was funny. Within a short time Klengenberg was friendly with all of them, and many of the Eskimos I had met had been in that first group he had encountered that day.

This band still had its own medicine-man, or angakkuq. He was a big man by the name of Koohah, and there was no end to what he could do. Pasty, Klengenberg's oldest son, who could both read and write and had been with people like the Canadian anthropologist Diamond Jenness, fully believed in Koohah, and told me in detail about the many magic and unbelievable tricks he could perform, as well as his other powers and his wisdom.

I was surprised to see how many good home-made tools these people had. Copper was plentiful in that area, and old Koohah had a piece of pure copper so heavy that I could barely lift it. Out of this he fashioned chisels to use on the ice and long butcher knives and snow knives, harpoon heads and fishing spears. Many of the older men had beautifully-made bows and big sealskin quivers full of arrows with copper heads. Wood was scarce, so the arrows were frequently made up of two or more pieces of wood glued together with a home-made glue made of animal blood. The workmanship was so good that it was barely possible to see where the arrows had been glued together.

9 TRAGIC VOYAGE TO THE WEST

We started to unload the supplies we had brought in. It was done under the strict supervision of Constable MacDonald, who wrote down every item taken ashore. Early in the morning of August 19 we started off on our return trip to Herschel Island. We hoped to be able to continue to the South before the passage was closed by ice for the duration of the winter.

Jorgen, the skipper and I were on deck most of the time that first day, as the lead was full of sand-bars and we had to proceed carefully. Constable MacDonald was asleep in my bunk until I was relieved in the evening, and we then had a bite to eat together with Jorgen and sat around talking for a while. But I was so tired that I almost fell asleep at the table and turned in.

A couple of hours later I woke up when I noticed that the ship went full speed ahead, stopped and then turned about. I started to run up on deck; everything was in an uproar. On the ladder I met Klengenberg running from his own cabin, where he had been asleep.

The schooner was now completely still in clear, open water. Constable MacDonald had fallen overboard. One of the men was out in a rowboat looking for him, and returned shortly after with the constable's caribou-skin parka and his notebook, which he had found floating in the water. But of MacDonald himself there had been no sign. There was not much we could do. We sailed about for a while looking for him, but without any luck.

Bror Wiik, the crew member who had been to sea and acted as the skipper's secretary and also gave us a hand on deck, told me what had happened. MacDonald had been on deck for a while after supper and talked to him and another man. Then he went below and sat in the pantry. Bror remained on deck with Fred Wolkie, the son of a German whaling skipper, who was at the helm. As Wiik went below for a moment, he met MacDonald on his way up, they exchanged a few words and then the constable went aft. When Wiik came back up on deck after a while, he asked where the policeman was and Fred answered that he was probably in the stern somewhere and they called out to him, but received no reply. Bror Wiik then started to get scared and was afraid that MacDonald might have fallen overboard and shouted to Fred that he should turn the vessel about. In the confusion they searched for a while without calling the rest of us, but it is unlikely that that would have made any difference. MacDonald could hardly have had a chance in the ice-cold water.

It was impossible to ascertain why or how the constable had fallen overboard. We thought that perhaps he had gone up forward, where there was no railing, and had lost his balance while he was standing there. With the noisy engine going it would have been practically impossible for the helmsman to hear any cries for help, and from where he was standing he could not see the bow. Even if we only made six knots, the water was so cold that not even the best swimmer could have lasted until the ship had been turned about and returned. How the constable had managed to get his parka off and put his notebook on top of it remained a mystery. However, as it turned out during the questioning later, it was fortunate for Klengenberg that he had done so.

We were all pretty gloomy, and Klengenberg was obviously greatly disturbed. I felt sorry for him. One of the many stories that were told about him now could do him a great deal of harm.

In 1905, when Klengenberg first met the Coronation Gulf Eskimos, his ship *Olga* was frozen in the ice. Some members of his crew started to make their own home brew, and the engineer was particularly active in this field. When Klengenberg asked him to stop, he was told that this was none of his business. The engineer and some of the others also refused to go out to gather driftwood or to do other work. In the end the engineer armed himself and spent most of the time in his own cabin.

One day, as Klengenberg was getting aboard, the crew was almost in full mutiny, so he grabbed a rifle to protect himself. Shortly after, some heated words were exchanged, and the engineer grabbed the gun and tried to use it. Klengenberg, however, was quicker and wounded him. The skipper then asked the others to take the rifle away from the engineer, but they refused, so he finally went into the engineer's cabin himself and demanded the rifle. But instead of giving it to Klengenberg, the engineer turned the rifle on him. Again Klengenberg fired first, and this time killed the engineer on the spot.

Not until the following year, when they reached Herschel Island, could he report to the police what had happened. The crew confirmed the skipper's explanation. As there was considerable doubt at the time as to who had the police authority in that area, the case was placed in the hands of the American authorities, since *Olga* was an American ship. The trial took place in San Francisco in 1907, and Klengenberg was acquitted.

But now he was sure that the old story would be revived. Personally I felt very bad about what had happened, for I had come to like the constable very much. In all the years I had spent at sea, I had never experienced anything similar.

With the flag at half mast we arrived at Baillie Island. Corporal Pasley and a constable came aboard immediately and Klengenberg gave them a brief report of the drowning. Then we set off for Herschel Island, where we at once reported to Inspector Caulkin, who questioned everybody on the ship and conducted a thorough investigation.

Klengenberg was well known on Herschel Island. Everybody remembered the trial of seventeen years earlier, and it was evident that many doubted his version of Constable MacDonald's accident. Those who believed that Klengenberg was responsible in some way were wondering what his motives could be. Would he have profited from the constable's death? It was natural enough for people to think that he had broken his promise to Inspector Caulkin and unloaded more supplies than he was permitted to. If so, they reasoned, MacDonald would have found out and been ready to report to his superiors. If this suspicion could have been substantiated, it would have had serious consequences for Klengenberg indeed.

Inspector Caulkin was not a man to take anything at face value. He ordered everything on board taken ashore to be checked in the police storehouse. Every single item was checked off on the list the captain had for customs purposes, and luckily for him, every item missing was found recorded in MacDonald's notebook, which we had fished out of the water. This proved that everything was in order. It took some ten days to complete the checking, and we did not take the things on board again as it was just as well to store them on land until next summer. By that time Klengenberg hoped to have everything straightened out with the authorities so that he could trade in the East again.

On Herschel Island we had some more bad news. The Hudson's Bay Company ship *Lady Kindersley* had been crushed by the ice near Point Barrow a few days after we had talked to its crew. None had gone down with the ship, but neither the cargo nor the equipment on board had been saved, so now the situation on Herschel was critical. *Lady Kindersley* had seven hundred tons of supplies destined for the island, and this was a hard blow to the traders there. Klengenberg could have sold his cargo twice over if he had only paid the duty as required, but that he refused to do. Yet he gave the Mounted Police and the locals what they needed and left one man behind to look after the rest of his supplies when we sailed again on September 10. The investigation had been satisfactorily concluded and we were free to go as we wished.

We headed westward and quickly ran into heavy ice. About two hundred miles from Point Barrow we came to a complete stop, caused by the new ice which tied together all the ice-floes.

We soon became stuck and barely managed to get free again just in time before we would have been frozen in for good. If that had happened, we would have had to go along with the drifting ice, of course, and most likely gone out to sea.

Reluctantly Klengenberg decided to return to Herschel Island, where we knew we would at least find a good harbour. There was no doubt that the pack ice had arrived for the winter.

10 FROZEN IN FOR THE WINTER

Herschel Island had a strong westerly gale when we arrived back on September 23 and made ready to freeze in for the winter. I really looked forward to spending the winter in the Arctic. This was what I had been dreaming about for years. For Klengenberg, however, it was anything but fun. He stood to lose one or perhaps two trading seasons as we now realized that we would have to go back east and leave more supplies for his people before we could proceed to the South next summer.

In preparation for the wintering we started to make a frame of lumber to place over the deck. Then we took down the sails, which I cut carefully along the seams and stretched over the frame, so that we had a roof for protection against the snow. Some of us took off for a little fresh-water lake on the northern end of the island and cut ice blocks which we pulled to the ship on sleds with dog teams. The blocks were to be our fresh-water supply.

It was during the ice-cutting that I had my first chance at driving a dog team. Klengenberg had borrowed some dogs from a number of people, so it was not a broken-in team we had at our disposal. In the beginning the dogs seemed to decide where they wanted to take me, but it was not too long before I mastered them. I also learned to respect the dogs. Eskimo dogs are good work animals if they are well treated with a reasonable mixture of love and discipline. Above all, they must have plenty of food.

In the middle of October there was still some open water to the east of the island, where the wind often came from the west and broke the ice into pieces that drifted away. One day I took off with a couple of the boys and a flat-bottomed boat which we pulled across the ice to the open water, and then started to row. The duck hunting was good and we became so absorbed by what we were doing that we completely forgot where we were. With a full load in the boat, more than three hundred ducks and a small seal, we suddenly noticed that the wind had turned, and that we were unable to get through the new ice, which was forming rapidly. It was starting to turn dark, but fortunately we could still be seen from the shore, even if the people there were unable to come to our aid. Our only way out was to scatter the ducks around on the ice. Without the load the thin ice barely carried the boat, which we carefully carried between us. We also pulled the seal. Walking on both sides of the boat, we edged our way towards land. The ice stayed overnight, so next morning we were able to go out with our dog teams and pick up the ducks. They were good and fat that year, and helped us considerably as far as the diet was concerned.

I liked the life on Herschel Island and soon made many friends among the Eskimos, and visited the police barracks often. There was never a dull moment. Every Saturday night the RCMP had a dance, for there were quite a few women there at the time, wives of policemen and others. We were all welcome, and usually the Eskimos also showed up, partaking of the refreshments that were served afterwards.

As far as the work was concerned, there was not much for me to do on board, and the engineer Morris and I were not even paid while we were frozen in the ice. This was according to our previous agreement with the skipper, and Klengenberg was going to make up for it by lending us complete trapping outfits and by paying us for all the furs we brought in.

Not knowing much about the conditions, we believed that we would get rich on fur only, because we had heard that there was an ample supply of white fox on the island. This was not so at all. More than two hundred Eskimos and white trappers had been depending on the catch for years, and white fox was now so scarce that one had to run very long trap-lines to catch anything at all. As we were neither British subjects nor residents of the Northwest Territories, we also had to buy a trapping licence, which would cost us two hundred dollars even before we could get started. The engineer was furious and claimed that we had been cheated, but personally I do not think the skipper really had counted on our freezing in and having to spend the winter in the North. Inspector Caulkin, however, was an understanding man and allowed Morris and me to run trap-lines without a licence. I guess he also knew that we would not catch much.

I got to know several Eskimo hunters who taught me much about the Arctic. A big, elderly fellow by the name of Peter Chichack appeared willing to adopt me and suggested that we should go into some sort of partnership. I never really discovered how this was to work out, but he had no children and was the best hunter in the area, so I had no objections to being treated as a kind of son.

One day early in the winter some hunters were ready to set off for the mainland to hunt for caribou, and Peter invited me to join them. Steve Kobloalook, who was something of a medicine-man, was also coming. The others were convinced that he could fly; but in spite of his abilities, we decided to use dog teams. All told we were six, and apart from myself, who was travelling with Peter, each man had his own six-dog team.

The first day we covered somewhere around twenty miles and camped for the night with a family on the mainland. I was dead tired, for I had been running most of the way to keep my feet warm. Fortunately I managed to get hold of a pair of deerskin socks, which helped. Next morning we got up early to get a good start, but spent almost three hours eating and drinking mug after mug of tea before we were ready to leave. The Eskimos must be among the greatest tea-drinkers in the world. However, we finally got under way, mostly following a dried-out river bed. Some thirty-five miles from the coast we made camp again and, of course, drank more tea. The evening meal consisted of frozen raw fish.

The hunt was on early the next day. I had only a .20-.20 rifle, so they decided that I should go out alone and try to get some ptarmigan, while they hunted caribou. It was my first time on snowshoes and I must admit I was rather clumsy. I was so intent on following some tracks that I failed to see a windfall, and before I knew it, I had stumbled over the tree trunk and found myself upside down with my head in the snow, one of my snowshoes caught in a branch, and hanging on to my rifle for dear life. I knew that if I let go of it I would never find it again in the deep snow. I worked furiously at getting myself free but without any success. As time went by I began to get scared, for my face, which was full of snow, started to freeze and I visualized myself frozen to death in the wilderness. Only after several uncomfortable hours did I manage to get free.

In the meantime my friends had shot six caribou, so that night we had an abundance of meat over our open fire. We cooked one pot of meat after another and ate and ate until well past midnight. Exhausted as I was, I still did not get much sleep as I was kept awake by a choir of snoring and burping, the like of which I had never heard. Half asleep, I managed to get on my feet the next morning when we started to eat again, this time porridge with leftover meat spiced with caribou hair, all mixed together.

We hitched up the dogs, picked up the caribou that were left and followed the edge of the forest eastward without seeing any more game. Late at night we reached an Eskimo camp. This was where Laughing Joe, Peter's father-in-law, lived. His house was a curious structure, built of large willows that had been cut and set out in a big circle, then bent towards the centre and interlocked with other willows threaded horizontally, so that the whole thing looked like an up-ended woven basket. The lower half of this frame was banked with huge slabs of sod, the upper portion covered with skins. It was certainly a comfortable house, and it had a large sheet-iron stove in the middle with the pipe going straight up through the top. The house reminded me a lot of the Siberian yurts, and was the only one of its kind I ever saw in the Arctic. Joe was a Nunamiut or Inland Eskimo, and we were well received and shown the usual Eskimo hospitality before we continued back to the ship the next day.

11 MORE ABOUT LIFE ON HERSCHEL

As I became increasingly friendly with the policemen, I told Inspector Caulkin that my dream was to join the Royal Canadian Mounted Police.

"I don't see any reason why you couldn't," he said. "You seem to be the type of man we need in the North, but you must remember that once you have joined you must be prepared to serve anywhere in Canada."

However, he was convinced that with my specialized experience I could more or less count on northern service, and that was what I wanted above all. He also explained that first of all I had to obtain Canadian citizenship, which meant waiting another four years.

The Inspector was of the opinion that the Force should have a little schooner of its own which could sail everywhere in this enormous area to act as a floating detachment in the summer and a permanent station during the winter. The idea had originated with his predecessor, Inspector S. T. Wood, who had left for the South a short while earlier after five years' service in the Arctic, mostly on Herschel Island. Both of these police officers were experienced men who knew the Arctic well, and realized that the RCMP was suffering by being dependent on civilian trading ships for transportation and supplies. The shipping season in the Arctic is very short, and now that the whaling had practically come to an end, there were fewer and fewer ships in the North every year.

Caulkin thought that one of these days the idea of a police ship would become a reality and this, of course, made me even more interested in joining the Force. It was obvious that if the Mounted Police were to have its own ship, my chances would be increased. But I still had to wait for my citizenship. Inspector Caulkin quietened my fears that I would be too late by adding that he was sure that such a ship could hardly be built and equipped in less than four years.

The northern coast of Canada and Alaska has an interesting history and I learned much about it that winter. Whaling ships from New England had been hunting in Alaskan and Siberian waters for many years. It was the Greenland whale they were after, particularly the baleen or whalebone, the huge strainers in the mouth of the whale. On a big whale, these could weigh up to a ton, and their price was about five dollars per pound. Many whalers used to winter on the Siberian coast near the Bering Strait, but as the whales moved northward, they followed and ended up on Herschel Island with its good harbour.

This all took place in the 1890's and as far as I can remember from what I was told there, no ships had been in those waters at that time since 1850-52 when the British sent out an expedition to search for Franklin. The whalers found many Eskimos on Herschel, but none of them were hunting whales. Gradually more and more whaling ships followed, and many of them had quite seamy crews.

During the winter of 1894-95 more than seven hundred men and six women from the South were up there. The local Eskimos called themselves Cogmollicks, and the white hunters were of the opinion that they were lazy and useless in comparison with the western Eskimos. They also met Inland Eskimos, the Nunamiuts, who were quite numerous at that time, and Irqiliit, which was the Eskimo name for Indians, who roamed the entire area with their dog teams.

Before long, with both natives and newcomers slaughtering them, the caribou started to get scarce, and the whalers, who were a rather rough lot, soon became a curse on the Eskimos. During the long winter months while their ships were frozen in the ice, these crews had nothing to do but to gather driftwood for fuel. Many moved in with Eskimo women, and a period of wenching and home-brewing followed that is still remembered in the North. In return for their hospitality, the natives received only the diseases of the whites. Although the old whaling skippers ruled with an iron hand, there was little they could do as far as the women were concerned, for the Eskimos themselves were more than willing to lend their wives to the sailors in return for small gifts. It often happened that a whaler simply moved in with an Eskimo family and shared not only accommodation but also the lady of the household.

After a while the people at Fort MacPherson learned what was happening on the coast and the mission sent a priest up to the North. Law and order did not follow until 1903-4 when two policemen from the then North West Mounted Police arrived and started to clean up the conditions.

One should not judge these people too harshly for the unsavoury conditions, however: to the Eskimos this was an entirely new world opening up, and the whalers themselves were often simple people who were unaware of the lasting damage they were doing. There were all kinds of races and nationalities aboard the whaling ships: whites, Kanakas from Hawaii and Negroes from the Cape Verde Islands. These Negroes were often called "Portuguese." There were even people from as far away as the Fiji Islands and Samoa, and many Eskimos along the Alaska coast and the western part of the Canadian Arctic are the descendants of these men.

Oddly enough, the Eskimos of mixed blood appeared to be the best. The infusion of new blood must have been useful. Many of the smaller groups had lived in almost total isolation for long periods of time, and a certain degeneration had followed. The newcomers brought their initiative and energy to these people. No matter where they came from, they quickly adapted themselves to the local conditions. (I believe that anyone can learn to live in the Arctic, and to do every bit as well as the Eskimos, if not better.) Newcomers also had the advantage that they were not satisfied with living from one day to the next, without any thought for the future. I have even seen white men who were better hunters and dog-team drivers than the Eskimos, and I have a very strong suspicion that there is not one single full-blooded Eskimo left in this particular area.

12 SEAL HUNT

On the northern side of Herschel Island it frequently happened that the ice opened up so we could go on a seal hunt. I was with the Eskimos and we used to take off with twelve to fifteen dog teams. Some of the people had boats with them, in case the ice they were on should tear itself loose and start to drift.

In order to exist, the Arctic seal makes breathing-holes in the ice early in the fall when it starts to freeze up. Each seal usually has a number of holes. As long as the ice does not break open, the seals will stay fairly close to their holes all winter. They can manage to get up and get a breath of fresh air even when there is snow on the ice. In fact, they seem to prefer the snow-covered holes, because these are better protected. Only dogs and polar bears can track down the holes under the snow. When the seals have their young early in the spring, the female scoops out a shelf under the snow where she gives birth, sheltered from both wind and weather, as well as from marauding bears and foxes.

It is a cold and slow job to hunt seal in the winter time. First of all the holes must be located, and this is where the dogs come in handy with their keen sense of smell. They are kept on a long leash and when they start to smell a hole they are pulled back and tied down so that they will not scare the seal away. In the meantime, though, it often happened that the seal would have become aware of the dog first and take off. Then all one could do was to sit down and wait for it to come back, which at times would take hours.

As a rule, the Eskimos pushed a thin rod with a floater attached into the hole, all the way down into the water. When the seal returned and the water rose in the hole, the rod was raised too. At that very moment the Eskimo would ram his spear or harpoon down into the hole and right into the head of the seal. They seldom missed.

It was easier to hunt seal in open water. There the seal considers himself safer and the hunters who know the habits of the animal inside out can manage to get pretty close to them without being noticed. The seal is a very curious animal, and at times will reach half out of the water to see what is going on. In addition to this, it is very fat in the winter and floats high in the water.

In order to catch a seal they had shot, the Eskimos would use a football-shaped piece of wood, with several sharply bent nails sticking out of it, fastened to a long rope. With great agility the Eskimos would swing the wood several times over their heads and then let go so that it landed on the other side of the seal. As they pulled in the rope, carefully, the hooks or nails would catch the carcass. From then on, all they had to do was to pull in. Peter and I pulled in many a seal this way, after he had shot them.

I was lucky and got the first seal I aimed at with my rifle. But then I had studied Stefansson's books in which he explained the method to use, and I had followed the instructions to the letter. Since then I have shot at and missed many seals, but the first one remained the great thrill as far as seal hunting is concerned.

On the same hunt, I also landed myself a big Ujjuk, the Big Bearded Seal. It weighed at least a thousand pounds and was worth as much as ten ordinary seals. The meat on the big seal is better than ordinary seal meat, but the most important thing is the hide, which is used for the soles of mukluks. When the hide is dried and stretched it is stronger than any other hide and far easier to shape.

But to return to my Ujjuk. It took me quite a while to crawl close enough to shoot the enormous animal. I aimed at the top of its skull, and it died on the spot. But it was so heavy and big that I could not even budge it. It is difficult enough to pull an ordinary seal onto a sled. My dogs were far off and reluctantly I left the Ujjuk in order to get them. When I found the dogs, I unhitched the sled and hung on for my life as we took off in a flying start.

Fortunately for me I had on a pair of sealskin pants, which acted as a cushion and saved me from getting too bruised from the bumps. I cut a slit in the lip of the Ujjuk and fastened the dog line in it. Then I jumped up on the animal, one leg dangling from each side, as the dogs set off at top speed for the shore. I wish I had had a photograph of that scene!

On board Edna Klengenberg skinned the Ujjuk, cut all the blubber carefully away and stretched the hide before she put it on a frame to dry.

13 NEW SUMMER IN THE NORTH

Spring returned near the end of May. Suddenly the entire island came to life again. No matter where one turned, there were children running about, day and night.

The Eskimos were hunting seal on the shore and it was a miracle that nobody was killed the way they fired off rifles and shotguns. Even small boys were allowed to try their luck with .22's, which seemed ideal for the seal hunt. I saw a mother searching the shore for her son. When she found him, a ten-year old boy running around with a rifle, she called out to him and he came over to her right away. He dropped the rifle and dived in under her parka while she bent forward. It was the most natural thing in the world for a mother to breast-feed a boy that age, it seemed, and the mother appeared happy with the boy's appetite. As soon as he had had enough, he picked up his rifle again and continued his hunt.

Shortly after, Klengenberg received permission from the Canadian authorities to supply his own trading post and to trade with the Eskimos as before. Once we had taken on board all that belonged to the skipper, we made ready to sail. The fog was still quite thick, but the sun managed to peek through once in a while, so it was not too cold. But the ice did not break up fully, and only in the beginning of July did the fog lift sufficiently so that we could leave, this time with a Corporal Belcher aboard.

It took us almost three weeks to get to Cape Bexley at the mouth of Dolphin and Union Bay, and soon we were back on Victoria Island in spite of the difficult ice conditions. This time the stay was very short and after a warm reunion we left and went back to Baillie Island on our way to the South.

It was the middle of September when we arrived back at Seattle and moored at the dock we had left in June the previous year. We had sailed from the Aleutians to Seattle in nine days, and were dead tired. I had not had much sleep since we left Unimak Pass. In addition to my turns at the wheel, I had navigated all the time and had found out that a schooner is not the same thing as a big steamer, which usually stays on course. Our ship had neither the aids that the bigger ships had nor several people on the bridge day and night. The rudder was anything but reliable, and I had only two sightings on the whole voyage.

Next morning Klengenberg went ashore to report our arrival to the port authorities and to get in touch with the Seattle Fur Exchange, as we were in a hurry to get rid of the white fox pelts. Now that we were back in civilization he needed cash right away.

Both the authorities and the press came on board. The United States Immigration officers checked to see if there were anybody on the ship trying to land illegally. When they came to me, I was informed that I could neither remain in the United States nor sign on any American ships without taking out American First Papers with the intention of becoming a United States citizen. They added that this would take years, but I replied that I was not interested in staying as I intended to go to Canada and apply for Canadian citizenship. The ship was laid up now until Klengenberg could have it refitted and transferred to Canadian registry, so I found myself without any work on board. The engineer and I were signed off at the end of September, and all I received for a year and a half's work was five hundred dollars. But then we were not paid for all those months in the ice. The pay was not all that important to me, however. I had gained invaluable experience as far as life and sailing in the Arctic was concerned and only looked forward to the following summer when I could go back north.

In the meantime, however, I had to find something else to do and ended up making a round trip to the Tropics on a tramp steamer. I then returned to Vancouver and rejoined Klengenberg and his schooner, which had been renamed *The Old Maid*, as Canada already had a ship registered under her former name, *Maid of Orleans*.

When I left Herschel Island again for Vancouver in August of that year, I was not to see the island again until 1928, when I returned as a constable in the RCMP.

14 CANADIAN CITIZEN

The winter of 1926-27 was the first I spent ashore in a good many years. I did not care much for it, for I did not know what to do with myself. I had never worked on land before.

I ended up as a road worker at a pay of fifty cents an hour and stayed with this until February. Even though I did not like that type of work I valued the experience, for at least it taught me that this kind of work was not for me.

During this time I visited Klengenberg frequently. He had bought himself a little house and had even acquired an automobile. This kind of life appeared to agree with him, but his two sons, Andrew and Jorgen, were fed up with it. I also met Corporal Pasley, my old friend from the Mounted Police, who told me that it now was fairly certain that the Force was going to build a ship of its own. He asked me to keep in touch with him.

After a brief spell of commercial fishing I returned to Vancouver in May to see Klengenberg. I was greatly surprised to learn that he had changed his mind, he was not going north this summer, as one of his other sons had written and told him that the fur catch had been very poor that year. However, I had the impression that he really preferred the more comfortable life now after all the hardships in the North. His two sons were furious. They wanted him to turn the ship over to them and asked me to come with them, but this was not to be, and they had to wait another year before they could return to their home.

I must say that I was disappointed myself. Even if fishing was more profitable, I had been looking forward to the voyage to the North; but I ended up going back fishing.

During one of my visits to Vancouver I applied for Canadian

citizenship and appeared before Judge Grant on November 18, 1927. He was an impressive old man and imbued me with the proper sense of solemnity when I took the oath of loyalty to my new King and Country. Two witnesses were required for the ceremony, and mine were Corporal Pasley and another friend. This was an important day for me. Afterwards I spent an entire week in Vancouver as a newly-made Canadian.

The best news I had during this stay was that the RCMP now had decided definitely to start building its ship the following winter. Corporal Pasley had been given command of the ship and best of all, he wanted me on board. This was just what I had been dreaming about, and we agreed that I would apply for the Force shortly after New Year's.

After a couple of anxious weeks of waiting for a reply, I was asked to report to the Officer Commanding of the Vancouver Detachment, and here I was, in my bunk at the Fairmont Barracks.

When I finally dropped off to sleep on my first day as a member of the Force, I knew that I was going to give it my best.

15 THE SHIP AND THE CREW

The next weeks were busy ones. Sergeant Paton, who had gone through the ice with a dog team in the Arctic and had both hands frozen, had been given the assignment of training me. One thing followed another with drill, practice on the firing range, and studying the rules and regulations. I did not have much to do with the horses, but did get an opportunity to admire the more than sixty beautiful animals in the stable.

Many of the men I met at Fairmont Barracks in the beginning were to serve under me in later years. I also found it helpful, later, that I had made so many friends in Vancouver.

I saw my good friend Corporal Pasley frequently. Ed was now married and lived outside the barracks. As he had served in the British

Navy before joining the Force, he was in charge of supervising the building of the new Arctic patrol schooner at the Burrard Wharf in North Vancouver. In his free time he studied navigation as he prepared to take command. An old skipper from Newfoundland, Captain Gillen, who had been a whaler in the Bering Strait, was in charge of the building, and was to go north with the ship on her maiden voyage as an instructor. The Force, of course, had no qualified seamen in its ranks.

Most of my spare time was spent at the wharf. The ship was not exactly a beauty, but she was solidly built, and that was the most important thing. I was impatiently waiting for her to be all ready. In the meantime I visited Klengenberg in my new uniform, and he looked very happy to see me again. He had been in doubt whether or not to accept an offer from the Hudson's Bay Company for the *Old Maid*, and the news that I had joined the RCMP decided him. He was not too keen on experimenting with a new crew in the Arctic and sold the ship, sent his sons back to Victoria Island and retired from the fur trade for good.

The ship was launched near the end of May and was given the name *St. Roch* after the electoral district of the then Minister of Justice, Ernest Lapointe. The crew still had not been picked and the shipbuilders worked day and night to get the schooner ready. She was getting some rather antiquated equipment: I particularly disliked the looks of the anchor windlass and the deck winch. It all looked pretty weak to me, and I mentioned this to Corporal Pasley. But old Captain Gillen, the official technical adviser, did not share my opinion. As I was not even officially picked as a crew member yet, my word did not count for much with the new Commanding Officer, who had taken over after Superintendent Duffus.

When the crew finally was picked, Captain Gillen was made skipper and a fellow by the name of Kelly became the engineer. According to the contract the shipbuilders had to provide the skipper and the company in Oakland, California, that had built the engine had to supply the engineer for the first voyage to Herschel. If nothing unforeseen happened, these two were to leave the ship there and return to the South. Corporal Pasley was then to take command. The rest of the crew consisted of Constables M. F. Foster as engineer, Sealey as wireless operator, W. J. Parry as cook, and A. F. Tudor, M. J. Olsen, T. G. Parsloe and myself as ordinary crew members. Only two of these had been to sea before—Tudor, who had served in the British Navy as an officer, and Olsen from Vancouver, who had been in the merchant marine.

At the last moment, however, some important changes in the crew took place, owing to the expressed wishes of Corporal Pasley to take along his wife. He pointed out that the old whaling skippers used to do the same, but that did not go over with the RCMP. The result was that Corporal Pasley withdrew from service on *St. Roch*, and shortly after left the Force. We got a young French-Canadian constable, A. Lamothe, on board instead. Like most of the others, he was without any sea experience, and had never been to the Arctic. I was now acting as Mate under Captain Gillen, with Frank Tudor as Second Mate.

During our trials with a number of high-ranking officers on board, we became aware of many shortcomings, not the least with the anchor gear, which I had pointed out earlier to Pasley. But in spite of the fact that it broke on the way back, Captain Gillen declared that he was satisfied. As could be expected, the police officers listened to him.

While we were taking on our supplies a number of odd things happened. Captain Gillen decided that we should take on board thirty tons of coal in bulk to save space. I was strongly opposed to this, as I knew that it would be difficult to unload again, but the skipper was unmoved. We were also the butts of many remarks down at the dock. The old tug-boat skippers and other knowledgeable people came to have a look at the ship, and none of them had a kind word for her. Some came right out and said that she would never even see the Arctic. Few of them would have signed on if they had been offered a chance. They called us "horse-sailors," as we had to wear the Mounted Police uniform as much as possible on board.

I, for my part, was glad that we had not hired professional sailors, because I was sure that such men never would have worked out on a ship like this one. I am sure that the cramped bunks, the spartan food, and the ship as a whole would never have received the approval of real sailors. Our policemen were quite different, they were used to taking orders, and above all, they were all imbued with an *esprit de corps* and were particularly proud of the fact that they had been picked for Arctic duty, which always carried some extra prestige in the RCMP.

The ship had been given so many tasks that necessarily something had to suffer for it. First of all, *St Roch* was to be a patrol ship for the RCMP in the western Arctic. But she was also to be a floating detachment of the Force, able to winter, to carry supplies to other detachments, to assist in transporting the native population from one place to another, and last but not least, to carry patients to the hospital in Aklavik and children to the school there. In addition to this, there were countless other tasks, both planned and unforeseen. The only trouble was that the Mounted Police did not have an adviser who realized all the demands that would be made on a police ship that was to be in the Arctic for years on end.

The *St. Roch* was 104 feet long and built of Douglas fir on a very heavy frame. The entire outside was sheeted with Australian gumwood, also called ironbark, which was very strong and expected to withstand the grinding of the ice-floes, which in no time would splinter and wear down our softwood planking. She had accommodation for thirteen men on board: eight forward in the foc's'le below deck, and four men aft, also below. The latter area also served as a mess. On the deck, immediately abaft the main mast, was a little pilot- or wheelhouse, divided up so that it also provided a small cabin for the skipper. The cabin was barely big enough to get undressed in.

The galley was a tiny little hole aft below, where our cook could scarcely turn around. It did not exactly help that "Dad" Parry, as we called him, was the biggest member of the crew. The engine was a 150 h.p. Union diesel, and it served us faithfully for years without the least bit of trouble, even though it was looked after by amateurs most of the time.

The ship had schooner rigging and also carried three lower sails, jib, foresail and mainsail. The mainsail was rather big with the boom hanging out several feet beyond the stern. Because of the wheel-house, the boom was placed so high up in the mast that it made it a pretty dangerous business to take in the sail. The result was that the mainsail was never used on the trial voyage. A few years later I had the whole thing changed the way I wanted it.

The rudder itself also was made of Australian gumwood, and was fitted in such a way that it could be raised up on deck through a specially constructed rudder-well similar to the one on Amundsen's *Maud*.

We also had an auxiliary 8 h.p. gas engine. It was used to start the big engine, to produce power for our wireless transmitter, to run our water pump when we wanted to wash down the deck, and for other purposes.

We had no batteries for electric light, which thus was a luxury we could have only when we were at sea and could use the power from the main generator. Otherwise we used kerosene or gas lamps. There was only one compass on board, placed in the wheel-house where it was impossible to use it for taking bearings, as one could barely see above the bow of the ship. This was a serious shortcoming for navigation in Arctic waters.

Before we left I pointed out that we had only one twenty-foot motor launch and one regulation lifeboat, both heavy and difficult to get on the water and most impractical for seal hunts and fishing. From experience I knew how important this was when it came to getting food for the dogs, and I tried to get a little skiff or jolly which could easily be pulled up on the ice if necessary. But in spite of the fact that such a boat could have been had for around thirty dollars at the time, the answer was no. The result was that I made my own little boat out of canvas and woodwork, and that was all we had for seal hunting and fishing on our first voyage. For a brand new polar ship like *St. Roch*, the equipment was surprisingly inadequate.

16 MAIDEN VOYAGE TO THE NORTH

On June 28 we were under sail. Only three months after I had joined the Force, I was on my way back to the Arctic as First Mate on the first Canadian police ship.

Outside Prince Rupert we headed for the open sea and ran right into a strong northwesterly gale. We had all sails up to steady the ship, but with her round bottom, *St. Roch* was not built for sailing. Soon she was bucking and heaving like a bronco, as one of the constables expressed it while he was still able to talk. The majority of the boys, who had never experienced anything like this before, had to give in quickly and succumb to the misery of seasickness.

Even though I was used to the sea, I must admit that this was as bad as anything I had ever seen. *St. Roch* was, and remained, the most uncomfortable ship I have ever been in. And yet I quickly came to love her and would never have traded her for any other. But just then we had our hands full, for everything was in a mess below deck. The hatches had taken in so much water that everything was floating around—crates of eggs, bags of potatoes and other supplies we had stored in our cabin together with our own personal equipment and possessions.

In the galley it was impossible to keep the stove going and those of us who were able to eat during the next few days lived on ship's biscuits, bully beef and cold ham—a diet not too unlike what we had on the old sailing-ships I had been in.

When the storm finally calmed, we headed for Unimak Pass. While the mess below was being cleaned up I had a chance to get to know Captain Gillen, who had many fantastic and yet true stories to tell about his many years at sea as a whaling skipper in the North.

In the early days, he told us, it was not unusual for the skippers to take on Indians on the west coast of Vancouver Island or on the Queen Charlotte Islands, as these men were the best hunters. They paddled quickly and noiselessly close to the seal while it was sleeping in the water. The Indians also killed the animals with harpoons, while the whites had to kill them with heavy-calibre rifles. As the ships often stayed a year or more in the North, it sometimes happened that someone on board died. If it was an Indian, the usual routine of lowering the body in the sea did not suffice. Superstitious as they were, they insisted that their dead be buried in their own soil according to their ancient rituals. Otherwise both the ship and the tribe would meet with misfortune. However, it was not quite that simple to keep a body on a ship for such a long time. But the Indians were practical people and permitted the skippers to perform some sort of embalming. It was simply done by removing all the intestines, draining the blood out of the body and then filling it up with salt and oakum, which was used for caulking the seams of the ship. Then the body was sewn up and put into a barrel full of brine, just as sealskins were. The departed Indian would keep just as well as the catch, and the Indians were very happy with this arrangement.

The weather calmed and one morning we decided to stop and try our luck at cod fishing. I had bought some cod hooks and lines in Vancouver, and soon Kelly and I had a pile of codfish gasping on the deck. Kelly, among many other things, also claimed to be an excellent cook and felt it was time that we had a good meal, so when he offered to make supper, codfish à la Kelly, Dad Parry was more than happy to relinquish the galley. The chowder was made of a dozen or two cod heads, and soon a fragrant aroma could be traced to the galley. I was on watch and only hoped that the others would not eat it all before I was relieved to go below and eat, but I need have had no fears. Cod heads, of course, make the best chowder, but Kelly had decided not to pick the meat loose, leaving that to the boys, so when they sat down at the table and the pot was brought in, it was full of whole fish, with all the mournful eyes looking at them. This was too much for the crew, who beat a hasty retreat onto the deck. But Captain Gillen, being a Newfoundlander, was sitting calmly sucking on a cod head. As a Norwegian I knew that my mother country's honour was at stake, so of course, I helped myself. In fact, I even had a second helping, which Kelly highly appreciated.

As we came to Dutch Harbor on Unalaska in the Aleutians the sun was shining, and we spruced the ship up a little. We also had some work done on the exhaust pipe of the main engine, which continuously threatened to set fire to the ship, so we anchored next to two American Coast Guard cutters. They looked pretty smart in comparison with our little *St. Roch*.

We received ample assistance with our repair work and became very friendly with the Americans, who invited us aboard the cutters for lunch and a dance. They were somewhat baffled when we arrived in full uniform, scarlet tunic, Stetson and riding boots with spurs and all. The cutters had several good musicians and one of the captains acted as band leader. There were not too many white women to dance with, but many young, and not-so-young, Aleutian beauties, dressed in their Sunday best, were more than happy to comply. One of the older ones, who was quite plump, came over to Captain Gillen and gave him a big hug. As soon as he had blushingly overcome his embarrassment, he went into action as he recognized her as his old flame from seven years previously.

It felt good to be ashore again, and we also took on fresh supplies. Our next stop was Teller, eighty miles north of Nome. This was the spot where Roald Amundsen had landed with the dirigible *Norge* two years earlier and then dismantled it. We could still see remnants of it, pipes and so on, and I also saw many Eskimos dressed in parkas made from the silk originally used for the dirigible. Some of the silk even had the aluminum coating still on.

Near Point Barrow we encountered the drift ice again, which forced us to go all the way back to Cape Smythe, where we anchored. The Eskimos had been driving huge caribou herds right down to the shore and were slaughtering some bucks. I recognized several of the Eskimos, and they all came over to shake hands, with their own still bloody from the killed animals. Constable Tudor, the former British naval officer, was the most prim among us, and I will not even try to describe his face when he was confronted with a bloodied hand, still warm from the stomach of a caribou.

When we reached Herschel Island on July 24, it had taken us five weeks from Vancouver. The voyage had disclosed many shortcomings of the ship, but we managed to straighten out most of them ourselves. On the whole, *St. Roch* had done very well. It was far from a poor ship, as it seemed to have a knack for twisting and turning in all directions.

The meeting with the Herschel Islanders again was something I had looked forward to. While we certainly had not expected a reception committee, we had counted on some interest at least. But not one solitary Eskimo turned out. We found this rather strange, as they usually were all over the place whenever a ship arrived, and we had sounded off ever since we had rounded the point. Not even Inspector V. A. M. Kemp, who was then the Commanding officer of the western Arctic, was on the beach. We could not see too well as the visibility was poor, but then we became aware of the situation. The yellow quarantine flag was flying on both the Hudson's Bay building and the mission station.

After a while a lonely, dead-tired Corporal William Chitty came out to us in a rowboat. He told us about an extensive influenza epidemic that had started far to the south months earlier and had spread along the Mackenzie River almost two hundred miles north to Herschel Island. The natives had died like flies, among them my old friend and first hunting partner, Peter Chichack, and his wife. It was a sad reunion with those who were left.

Our wireless had been out of order for days, so we had not been informed of the epidemic, but when Inspector Kemp came on board he gave us all the details. Like the rest of the people there, he had worked round the clock for more than two weeks. The dead had to be buried and the living looked after. None of the whites had been affected and thus they were able to be of assistance to the policemen and others in helping the Eskimos.

17 MY NORTHERN SERVICE STARTS

Inspector Kemp told us what to do to prevent the epidemic from spreading, and also informed us that he had decided to come with us as we continued farther east. This was an unusual event, because it had been many years since a Commanding Officer had been able to visit all the outlying detachments. At the same time Kemp wanted to get to know us better and then decide who was to have which job on board permanently. So far, the duty had been temporary. Inspector Kemp was to have the final say in the matter of the crew.

As we continued eastward, we saw sad proof of the ravages of the epidemic. Baillie Island was the first place we came to that had not been hit. The people there did not even know what had happened farther west.

Before we continued east to Bernard Harbour and Cambridge Bay, Captain Gillen asked for a local pilot, for these waters were new to him. Inspector Kemp hired an old trader, Fred Jacobson, whom I had met a couple of times when I was with Klengenberg. He had just arrived at Baillie in his small schooner together with his Eskimo wife and six children, and was very happy to get the job. His only condition was that we should tow his schooner to Inman River for him.

Inspector Kemp was satisfied with the Baillie Island detachment. It was under the command of Corporal George Wall, who had been put ashore there by Klengenberg in 1926, so again I met old friends. Many Eskimos arrived too in small boats, and they were far from poor. They had carried on lively trading all winter with polar fox and polar bear skins, and had caught lots of herring and whitefish. On the mainland they had hunted caribou, geese, ducks and other birds, and some of them had earned at least ten thousand dollars and had acquired all kinds of possessions. But as they gathered more earthly goods, the white man's luxury, they required more dogs to transport it all. This in turn meant more dog food. In the end it reached the point where they spent more time hunting for dog food than other bounty or food for their families. It was quite obvious that many of those we met had reached that point.

One evening while we were heading eastward through the Lambert Channel in calm water, I was practically thrown out of my bunk while asleep. The ship had crunched into something. First I thought we had hit an ice-floe at full speed, but what I saw when I came up on deck was worse than any ice-floe. We had run aground. Captain Gillen was astern with Jacobson and was chewing tobacco like mad. He ordered full speed aft, but to no avail.

Our pilot, who had sailed through the strait several times, had never noticed any shallow water in this spot. He had passed by here with his own schooner, but ours apparently drew more water. At our top speed, six and a half knots, we had run smack onto a shoal and there we were with the entire keel on the reef. When we went out in the motor launch we could see that there was deep water just a few feet ahead of the bow. Had we passed the reef by a few yards to either side we would have been all right. As we were sitting on a ledge we had to try to get the ship to jump off. We lowered our two boats, lashed them together and took out our kedge anchor, which we dropped as far from the ship as possible. It was attached to a long wire rope, which in turn was fastened to our anchor windlass. When we began to heave, our deck machinery was so light that it soon loosened from the deck without a great deal of strain on the cable. This was what I had expected, and, of course, the ship did not budge.

We then tried to list the ship by shifting several tons of the deck cargo from port to starboard, and again resorted to manual use of the windlass, but this did not help either. The ship was solid. The only thing that remained to do was to lighten the load, and we threw more than sixty of our oil drums overboard and lashed them together with a long rope so that they were strung out. Even this did not help any. It seemed pretty hopeless, and there was no ship in sight. The only way out appeared to be to drop our supplies overboard too.

Late in the afternoon of the next day Nature came to our aid as a strong westerly wind came up and made the water rise. I could feel the stern starting to swing a little, and suggested that we should put the engine full speed ahead. I had been out sounding around the ship and knew that with deep water only a few feet ahead and the strong current, we would soon be free. Captain Gillen accepted my suggestion and after several attempts *St. Roch* was afloat again. We all heaved a sigh of relief, not the least Inspector Kemp. When we heaved anchor, the difficult work of saving the cargo we had unloaded was started. Of the sixty oil drums, we only lost two.

Our next stop was Coppermine, where we halted briefly and from there went on to Cambridge Bay on Victoria Island. This was a new port of call for me, and I was quite surprised to see how many Eskimos there were around the Hudson's Bay Company post, the Anglican mission and the police barracks. The *Bay Maud* was still anchored out in the bay and I found it sad to see Amundsen's fine ship as just another floating radio station.

The Officer-in-Charge of the Cambridge Bay detachment was Sergeant Frederick Anderton. He was transferred to *St. Roch* and made responsible for all the police administration for the rest of our voyage. Two of his tasks were to see to it that we received sufficient rations and to look after the accounting for our supplies. The RCMP had an excellent accounting system and not a thing was misused or wasted. All worn-out equipment or parts had to be saved and shown to an officer before new items could be issued.

I took the opportunity to go ashore and I think it was the finest group of Eskimos I have ever seen. In time I came to know most of them and many became my close personal friends. They were good-looking, taller and lighter-complexioned than most Eskimos. Men as well as women were tastefully dressed in caribou-skin clothing. I was struck by the fact that these people, who had only recently come into contact with civilization, were unusually independent. Only later, after being exposed to the full influence of civilization over a long period of time, did they start to require the many things that we consider absolutely necessary in our lives.

Before we left Cambridge Bay, we took on some new guests: two Eskimo women, a man and couple of children. The winter before a murder had been committed at Bathurst Inlet, and Sergeant Anderton, who conducted the investigation, had arrested a man called Usina. It was him that we now were bringing to Herschel Island where he was to appear in court. The two women were not only witnesses in the case, but the widows of the two men Usina had killed. All three seemed pleased with the arrangement on board and enjoyed their trip. Usina was later sentenced to five years in prison for manslaughter and was set free after a couple of years, when we brought him back to where he came from. With all the gifts he had received from the police and others, he was then considered a wealthy man by Eskimo standards and was greatly admired by his tribesmen.

When we finally reached Inman River we found that a violent storm, which we also had felt, had played havoc with Jacobson's supplies. His little schooner had been blown to sea and his trading goods were buried under several feet of sand and rock. Inspector Kemp gave Jacobson as much as he could spare as compensation for what he had lost. We felt very sorry for Jacobson; this trip had not paid off for him at all. Fortunately, we did find his schooner some sixty miles farther east, resting unharmed on the shore.

18 SKIPPER IN THE MOUNTED POLICE

August 28 that year was a memorable day for me. As mentioned previously, Inspector Kemp was to make the final decision regarding the crew after our return to Baillie. That day he called us together on deck and announced that Captain Gillen and the engineer, Kelly, were about to leave us and return south with *Bay Chimo*. Kelly had trained Contable Jack Foster, who was now fully qualified to take over. As Second Engineer, the Irish-Canadian Bob Kells was picked. He had longer service with the Force than any of us, apart from Sergeant Anderton. To my great surprise Kemp's next remarks were: "As you know, Larsen, the most important decision is to pick the skipper and chief navigator. I have kept an eye on you on this trip and have decided to give the job to you. First of all, you know the waters around here better than anybody else in the crew and, secondly, you have long experience at sea."

It almost seemed that he had to apologize to himself for turning the ship over to a fresh recruit. I could hardly mumble a few words of thanks, because I had never expected this.

"There's only one thing," Kemp continued. "You are the newest member of the Force on board, but I'm sure nobody will object to your appointment; most probably they expected it. However, Sergeant Anderton will be in charge as far as police matters are concerned, while you are responsible for everything which has to do with the operation of the ship."

Sergeant Anderton grinned, and this appeared to be unanimously accepted, but then it really was an order. For five years I enjoyed excellent co-operation with Sergeant Anderton before he left the Arctic, was promoted and transferred to Rockcliffe Barracks at Ottawa as Staff Sergeant.

The rest of the crew consisted of Constable Tudor as Mate, Olsen as Second Mate, Sealey as wireless operator and Parry as cook. The crew list was completed by Constable Parsloe. Not a very impressive crew, but it turned out the fewer the better. This was an opinion I was to retain for the rest of my time on board.

I would have liked to have Inspector Caulkin with me that day when we were standing on the deck of *St. Roch*. I was sure that he had had something to do with my appointment. But I did not get to see him again before spring of 1940 in Ottawa, when he was Officer Commanding of "G" Division and told me about the planned voyage through the Northwest Passage.

Inspector Kemp also was to decide where *St. Roch* would winter for the first time, and picked Langton Bay, considerably to the east of Baillie Island at the bottom of Franklin Bay. This spot had been winter quarters for the old whaling ships ever since 1897. The harbour was, from what I heard, good, with several lakes around, well stocked with fish. This would assure us of food for our dogs, and in addition to this, the bay was on a direct line between Baillie Island and Bernard Harbour.

We now started to make ourselves ready for the winter. First we filled our oil tanks and took on new supplies, then we tried to get some good sled dogs. This was quite a problem, and the collection we finally sailed off with was none too good. The sleds, however, were the very best, made by Eskimos from Nome, Alaska. To this day I claim that these Eskimos make the best sleds in the entire Arctic.

Two days after my new appointment we sailed off to *St. Roch*'s first winter quarters and immediately encountered difficulties.

We had hardly anchored near Baillie Island before a northwesterly storm descended upon us with sleet on top of everything else. As the harbour was very shallow, I did not like to remain there too long and decided to weigh anchor and try my luck farther out to sea. *St. Roch* twisted and turned and heaved for six hours, and our poor dogs ran from one side of the deck to the other in wild panic. Finally I started up the engine, slowly in the beginning to ease the pressure on the anchor chain, but in the long run this did not work either. It was starting to get darker and the sleet now turned into a full blizzard. It was then that I decided to ride out the storm in the Amundsen Gulf. This was not a very popular decision as some of the boys felt that this would be the end of the ship and all of us, but I felt that this was our best chance.

With the sail up and the engine going full speed ahead, *St. Roch* danced like a duck on the water. We were far enough from the shore that there was no danger of drifting back and getting crushed on land, but it was impossible to keep track of our exact position all the time. Our only break was that there was not a single ice-floe in the entire Amundsen Gulf that fall, so everything turned out all right in the end. In the early morning of September 5, the wind quieted down and I headed down Franklin Bay towards our winter quarters and reached it the same night.

It was a little early to get the ship laid up for the winter, but we had completed all our assignments for the year, and it was our first wintering, so we needed all the time we could have to get ready. I was the only one on board who had wintered before in a ship, and the experience I had gained while with Klengenberg now came in very handy.

We soon found that Langton Bay was excellently suited, a well-protected harbour. During our first visit ashore we found several graves dating back to the whaling days, the nameplates giving the names of the ships the dead had served on. The next day we collected a pile of driftwood needed for cooking dog food on deck during the winter, for we had been ordered to save as much as possible of the coal we were carrying.

The dogs were tied to long lines on the shore and spaced so that they could not reach each other and start a fight. Our attempts at seal hunting failed, so we had to start cooking thousands of pounds of oatmeal and rice for the dogs and soon the poor animals started to put on weight.

In the meantime we made a frame of lumber for *St Roch*'s deck. It had to be made so that it could be taken apart in the spring and then used again. Next we stretched canvas over the wooden frame, still just trying it out, for it was too early to put it up over the deck. The ship had to be frozen in first so that there would be no danger of her breaking loose again.

This kept us really busy for a couple of weeks, and we did not have much time to familiarize ourselves with the country around us. Only on September 23 did Fred Sealey and I start inland on foot. In bright sunshine we had rowed ashore in the skiff, while Sergeant Anderton and the others remained on board.

The scenery was beautiful, a moss-covered tundra now slowly turning brown. After a while we reached some small creeks and ravines and found enormous river beds which probably had been dried out for centuries. As far as this part of the country was concerned, this was late fall, so we did not expect to see any life anywhere. Tracks of caribou could be seen here and there, but none of the animals. After a couple of hours we noticed that the air was becoming moister, a certain sign that a strong wind was coming up. We turned immediately and went back to the ship. And not a second too soon: the shore was dark when we finally got there and the weather was stormy. Our little skiff was now far up on the shore, and was too big and heavy to be moved.

The ship was fairly close by, so I signalled and asked them to come in with the motor launch to help us, but they were reluctant to do so as the sea now was swelling considerably. How could I have been so stupid as to leave the ship! I knew very well what would happen if the anchor chain broke. Sealey and I could not do anything but to spend the night on the shore. We crawled into a little earth cave, but did not get any rest, as every so often we had to get up and see how *St. Roch* was faring. The storm grew worse and in the early dawn Sealey and I had to seek shelter behind the lifeboat, shivering with cold. All of a sudden it seemed as if *St. Roch* had turned broadside against the wind. Then she stopped, but only to twist again. I realized that the anchors had lost their grip, and soon the ship started to get closer to the shore.

I could see somebody on deck, and could not understand why they did not start up the engine. I tried to call out to them, but in the howling wind it was of no use. Only when the ship was some thirty yards from the shore did I see smoke coming out of the exhaust pipe. They had started the engine, but too late. Ten yards from shore the ship ran aground, but fortunately there was only fine sand there. The fellows on board threw us a line and we climbed aboard through the ice-cold water. By then there was not much I could do. Luckily the wind came from the east and I knew from experience that the water would decline until the wind turned to the west. In the meantime *St. Roch* started to list. The storm raged for a whole day and the water declined steadily. When it was finally over, we were sitting pretty, almost on one side with a broadside facing the shore line.

A few days of clear weather followed, but it was also calm, and we just could not free ourselves. We even unloaded the thirty tons of coal by carrying it ashore across a temporary gangplank we made hastily from some lumber. This did not help either. The only thing we could do was to wait for the wind from the west. On shore our coal supply was in a big heap. If only we had taken it in bags instead of in bulk, the thought of getting it back would not have been so terrifying. What bothered me most was that it was now fairly late in the year and we could be frozen in at any moment, just as we were. But 1928 was a good year, the ice froze later that year than anyone could remember.

The wind finally turned on October 14. It came from the west, light at first, then ever stronger. In the evening it was so strong that we could notice it on the ship, which soon started to turn sufficiently that the bow came into deeper water. We were jubilant, now only the stern was aground. Together with some of the men I went below and started to shift some of the cargo while I gave orders to start up the engine. While we were down there we heard yelling and shouting on deck. Somebody shouted that we were heading for shore and another answered that was not anything new, we had been doing that for weeks now. But the situation was serious. As the ship had been floated free, she had turned around, and with the sail up and the anchor dragging behind, it looked as if she was going to run right up on the shore. The sail came down in a hurry and we threw out another anchor, and this took care of the immediate danger. Shortly after, we were properly anchored, ready to be frozen in.

19 IN THE ICE

Within a week we were solidly frozen in the ice and could cut enough ice around the ship that we could turn her around to head into the prevailing wind for the winter. A few days later, the ice was a foot thick and we knew that we were there to stay until spring.

We put the cover over the deck with the canvas and soon had a workshop there for repairing the sleds, a place for cooking food for the dogs and for getting some exercise during the blizzards we knew would be coming sooner or later. Our next job was to cut ice blocks for drinking water for the winter. We were nine men on board and needed drinking water for eight to nine months, so we cut hundreds of blocks on a lake a few miles away. It was also good practice in driving a dog team, pulling the blocks back to the ship.

After the first snowstorm a ridge of snow built up around the stern and then we cut out snow blocks and placed them all around the ship from the water line to the railings. The blocks acted as excellent insulation and helped us to keep warm.

Now that we were frozen in, Sergeant Anderton's responsibilities increased, while some of the pressure on me eased a little. Apart from keeping an eye on the ship and its equipment, I now was also given regular police duties, just like the others. It was to be a good winter, this first one I spent in the Arctic as a policeman. There were no crimes, fights, sickness or hunger among the Eskimos in our district. They often visited us, and most of these people in our area spoke good English. Measured by Eskimo standards they were well off, mainly because they were excellent hunters and fishermen. At Horton River there was also a white trapper, Patsy Wyant, married to an Eskimo. A trader by the name of Fred Matthews lived in the east near Steven's

Point and at Darnley Bay lived two French-Canadian trappers, Tom Lazare and Joe Beaupré. In addition to these, there was a Roman Catholic mission in the neighborhood of Darnley Bay; so there was no shortage of white people. They all came and visited us several times, and our hospitality was returned by Eskimos as well as whites.

One day when Joe Olsen and I dropped in on one of the Eskimo houses built of driftwood, the pot had just been put on the stove. It was late in the evening and the warmth was tempting. The stove was made out of an empty oil drum. We were grateful when we were invited to sit down with the others, who were already squatting on the floor waiting for the pot to boil. When it came, we found that it contained a white fox, cut into pieces and boiled. I was given the honour of dipping into the pot first and as I fished around I suddenly saw the head of the fox, teeth and eyes all staring at me. I could not look the fox in the eyes and pushed the head down into the pot again and fished out another piece. It did not taste bad, even if the Eskimos used neither salt nor other spices. These Eskimos, who became good friends of mine, were great caribou hunters. Although there was no restriction on the number of animals they could kill, I never saw these people kill more than they needed.

Life on board was cosy that winter. Sergeant Anderton was, among other things, an excellent cook, and once in a while he took over the galley to give Parry a welcome rest from his monotonous duties. Our cook appreciated this even more as he liked to "doctor" a bit. He was particularly happy when he could fix somebody up, whether it was a frozen finger, a toothache or some other complaint. Regardless of what the trouble was, Parry would find a medicine for it, and the Eskimos came from far away with their ailments and complaints, both real and imaginary. Parry was like a den-mother to them all and distributed cough medicine, pills and ointments, bandaged the wounded and gave stiff doses of laxatives. The Eskimos often needed a strong laxative and thought this was the best of all the medicines, regardless of what their ailment might be. The result was that in the many years I served with Parry, he came to be known as a great medicine-man. The only thing that puzzled them was that he had such a lowly job on the ship as that of a cook.

Terry Parsloe was the proud owner of a huge medical book which he used to study in his bunk. Long, learned discussions often followed between him and Parry, but unlike the cook, who was interested in medicine to help others, Parsloe firmly believed that he had all the diseases he read about himself. Once in a while we would hear a heavy sigh from his bunk and knew that he had found another disease he was "suffering" from.

Under the conditions we lived it was important to have someone who was a good story-teller. In this respect we were lucky to have both Frank Tudor and Jack Foster, who were true experts. The latter also acted as our tailor and helped to make our snowboots and socks. We used, of course, all the hides and skins we had, in addition to other material we had brought along.

20 MY FIRST SLED TRIP WITH THE RCMP

Joe Olsen and I went on several short sled trips that winter to Letty Harbour and Booth Island. We started out on one early in March. It had been impossible to make up a good team of dogs from those we had, so we only took four and a light toboggan, and had to walk most of the way ourselves.

We soon got into a raging blizzard, and as we lacked the proper clothing the first year, this was a memorable experience. Worse than the weather itself was the fact that our dogs refused to go against the wind unless we walked ahead of them and egged them on while we tried to keep their eyes free of snow and ice. This was very important, for they could freeze and the dogs would be completely blind. While doing this our hands became wet, for it was impossible to do this with mitts on. Soon our faces started to freeze too and we continuously touched our noses, which were the most exposed. The freezing itself is painless and hardly prickles the skin.

I was particularly bothered by my eyebrows and eyelids, which began to freeze so that my eyes closed. If we could only have found sufficient snow we could have camped before it became too bad, but as it was we had to continue. We knew that it would drift with high winds for several days. There was not a track to be seen anywhere, so we were taken by surprise when we suddenly saw two dog teams with Eskimos coming up from the side. They were looking for the shore line to follow it back to their camp even if this meant a long detour for them. The Eskimos were old friends of ours, Edward Jacob and Levy, both of whom had been on board *St. Roch* several times. Fortunately these Eskimos had warm hands as well as warm hearts and soon they had unfrozen our faces. We were glad to fasten our toboggan to one of their dog teams and hang on, so that we all could take turns sitting on their sled. Some two hours later we noticed the light from one of the driftwood huts and our dogs speeded up. People came running out when they heard their own dogs answering ours in a concerted howl, thinking that a polar bear was approaching. They hardly expected to see people on such a night.

Edward asked some of the people to tie down the dogs and to carry all the gear inside while he got Joe and me indoors. Even Edward's face was frozen by this time. His wife, a tall good-looking girl called Violet, stood in the middle of the floor and welcomed us.

An old woman was sitting on a bunk smoking a pipe. It was Violet's mother. Several children were playing on the floor. One of them was sitting stark naked in a big washbowl while the other children kept spinning it around like a carousel. The mother called out to them and the little one got out of the washbowl like a shot and Violet picked it up and filled it with flour and baking powder. Soon she had some kind of dough made up, and the hot bannock which she cooked up in a few minutes was delicious with hot tea, while we were waiting for the meat to cook. The storm lasted for three days and we were invited from one hut to another where we ate and ate until finally we could go on to Letty Harbour.

There were so many interesting people at Letty Harbour at that time that I could not begin to mention them all. But I particularly remember one, because of a way he symbolized how trustworthy the Eskimos were. His name was Billy Thrasher and his father had originally come from one of the Pacific islands with a whaling boat and married an Eskimo woman. Billy was a friendly fellow and a good friend of the Roman Catholic Fathers we were staying with. The night before we were to leave for Booth Island, Joe and I visited Billy and asked if his wife Mona could make a snowshirt for each of us to use on our trip. This he promised and said that they would be ready next morning. It was eleven at night when we finally left Billy and Mona and we did not notice anything out of the ordinary. The next morning when we called for the shirts, we found Mona sitting sewing on them, and Billy was full of excuses that they were not ready. It turned out that Mona had given birth to a baby shortly after we had left the night before, but if we only would care to wait for a short while, she would have the shirts all ready! We got our shirts and a glimpse of the new baby.

We were to look for a good harbour which could be of use to us in the future. On Booth Island we found two, and one near Cape Barry. Then we turned back to the *St. Roch*. Even if we had not broken any records with our three-hundred-mile trip, it had been a good beginning.

A few days after our return to the ship Sergeant Anderton and Constable Parsloe left for Baillie Island, where the latter had been transferred.

Spring was approaching now, and we received many guests on board. This is the best time of the year in the Arctic, April and May. It is daylight almost all night and the mosquitoes have not started to be bothersome yet. Because of the daylight we worked round the clock. In fact we lived like the Eskimos and soon found that it was useless to be a clock-watcher in the North.

Having visited many people during the winter, we were now visited in return, by both Eskimos and whites. It was a good thing that we had plenty of food for everybody, for the visitors seemed to have lots of time. The seals were now crawling out of their breathing-holes and were sunning themselves on the ice, and on the mainland there were birds, ground squirrels and, later, also geese and ducks. The fish were easy to catch by chopping a hole in the ice.

For the Eskimos this meant a welcome change in the daily diet, and for a while they lived on eggs only. This was contrary to game regulations, but it was difficult to be harsh with the Eskimos in this respect. I always maintained that it was of no use telling them about the game laws for the preservation of the wildlife without telling them at the same time that this was necessary if there was to be enough to eat for their children and their children's children for generations to come. When this was done, they usually co-operated.

Around the first of May we started to remove the covering over the deck and took on what was left of the coal, which we had painstakingly carried ashore the previous fall when we ran aground.

I went on some seal hunts and that helped, because even if our rations were ample, we also had to feed all our company on our supplies. The RCMP has always been very strict when it came to rations. On one of these seal hunts of mine I ran into some difficulties. I had to undress and lower myself into the breathing-hole of a seal to pull it out after I had shot its head off at close range. I had carefully followed Stefansson's directions for seal hunting and was quite happy with the result. But it was bitterly cold, particularly because I had to pull the two-hundred-pound seal for three hours back to the ship after my quick dip. The Eskimos at least seemed impressed, for they had never heard of anyone who had crawled into the seal hole to get an animal. What my friends on *St. Roch* had to say about my adventures was an entirely different story.

21 PROMOTION AND RETURN TO CIVILIZATION

On May 8, 1929, we received a wireless message to the effect that I had been promoted to corporal effective April 1. This was a great moment for me, because the promotion confirmed that I was on the right track and had taken up a profession I would want to stay with. The boys all congratulated me, and I am sure they were all glad on my behalf. Some of them had been in the Force for more than nine years without a promotion, but I also knew that I had my previous experience in the Arctic and as a navigator to thank for mine.

Shortly after I received the message, I was also ceremoniously given the following letter:

> THE ROYAL CANADIAN MOUNTED POLICE
> "G" Division
> Edmonton.
>
> Western Arctic Sub-District,
> St. Roch Detachment,
> Langton Bay,
> May 8th 1929.
>
> Memo to Const. Arry Larsen:
>
> This is to notify you that on the 1st Day of April 1929 you were promoted to the rank of Corporal in the Royal Canadian Mounted Police.

> Just to remind you that promotion has in the past been greeted by the simple method of buying drinks and cigars for all other members of the Detachment. As circumstances will not permit this at present, you are hereby advised that all members will be pleased to receive in lieu thereof a personal gift of $5.00 in cash, as a token of your good will, and personal behaviour in the future.
>
> F. Anderton, Sergeant,
> I/C Detachment.

I still have the original as a memento of my first police promotion.

In the beginning of June the summer was well under way, but the ice was still in the bay. The snow had gone on land by now and most of the lakes were free of ice. On some of them we found beautiful swans, and the wildlife on the whole increased.

Only on June 24 did we get free of the ice after having been frozen in for some seven months. At first we only moved a few yards. It paid to be alert now and watch out for the huge ice-floes drifting around loose in the bay. Farther out there was still very little open water to be seen. This period during break-up is the most difficult, as you always have to be ready to pull in the anchor and move the ship with hardly any notice at all, according to how the wind and the current turned. All went well, and some two weeks later we reached Herschel Island, where we were greatly surprised to be met by Inspector A. N. Eames. He had come up to take over from Inspector Kemp, who had gone to Aklavik with the murderer we had brought from Cambridge Bay the year before. I was glad to see Eames again. He had been in Vancouver while *St. Roch* was made ready, and was an old "Arctic fox" himself. This time he stayed in the North for four years, mostly in Aklavik and on Herschel, and often accompanied us on inspection trips.

After a two-week round trip with supplies to the various outposts, we were ordered back to Vancouver where we were to be resupplied and at the same time have certain alterations made to the wheel-house and the anchor windlass. We headed south on August 26 and had no trouble at all, as this was the best year, as far as the ice was concerned, that people could recall.

We had logged 10,300 nautical miles when we headed into Vancouver Harbour to be met by the Officer Commanding. For a few days we had our hands full with routine work, such as report writing, but I still found time to take stock of this first voyage as a policeman.

It had not been an easy trip for me. The responsibilities had been great, and even if the boys had been very helpful, they were anything but a well-drilled ship's crew as yet. The ship itself had presented many problems. She was new and untried, and the windlass, for instance, could easily have cost us dearly. But I guess this is the purpose of maiden voyages, to find out about these things.

Now we had to get Headquarters at Ottawa to approve the work that had to be done on *St. Roch*. But there was no doubt that she would be a good ship, well built as she was. In spite of all the difficulties *St. Roch* had managed well, and considering her small size, one could not ask for a stronger or better ship.

22 TO THE NORTH AGAIN

We spent the next six to eight months in Vancouver, but on June 27, 1930, we left once again for the North with 150 tons of supplies for the Arctic police outposts.

Again the newcomers succumbed to the horrors of seasickness, but after a few days they had to stand their watches like everybody else.

When, after a week or so, the sun appeared and we spotted the snow-covered peaks of Unimak Island, the crew started to revive, and one of the boys shouted that he had spotted a whale. Bill White, who came from one of the prairie provinces and had never seen the ocean before, came running up on deck, still pale, but with the look of the hunter in his eyes. His face was covered with a week-old beard, and all he had on was a "union suit" with the flap wide open. He held his shotgun at the ready and tried to keep his balance while he took aim at the big, dark shape outlined ahead. I told him that it was completely useless to try to shoot a whale with a shotgun, so he went back below somewhat dashed. But at least this did cure him of his seasickness for good.

As usual it was a race between the various ships to see which could get to Herschel Island first. We were leading when *Bay Chimo* passed us, and the skipper was not only determined to be first, but had taken a number of bets on it with his passengers. However, the last few days we all ran into thick fog and while the other ships kept safely away from the shore, we carried on as before and anchored at Herschel, the first ship of that year.

As the telegram announcing our arrival was sent off to Edmonton, it was picked up by *Bay Chimo*, still fighting the ice. Captain Sydney Cornwall was so furious that he ordered full speed ahead, rammed into the ice and broke a large piece off his propeller. "I swear you didn't even know your own position, Larsen," he yelled at me when we met later, and he was partly right in this, for the fog had been pretty thick. But Captain Cornwall was a generous old salt and as soon as he had anchored, we were all invited on board for a glass of rum of the strongest kind. Over a glass of "Nelson's Blood" I was soon forgiven. Later that night, after all Herschel's traders, trappers and policemen and other less law-abiding citizens had been treated and had left his ship, I saw him relax in his own peculiar way. Dressed only in a nightshirt which scarcely reached to the navel, he danced some kind of jig, all by himself behind the deck-house.

On Herschel we took on a number of dogs and sleds before we continued east in the beginning of August. Most of the smaller places we visited dated back to the days of the whaling ships. When a whaling ship or two had to winter, a whole community usually sprang up right on the spot. At times these places were short of drinking water, but at least as a rule the sea was abundant with herring, whitefish and seal, and in the winter one could hunt fox and bear too. When a new police post was to be built in such a place, everything was brought in from Vancouver, from lumber to fishing boats, fuel and food. The police constables who had to operate there had to put up their own quarters. In short, they had to be jacks-of-all-trades, even to making their own furniture from old packing cases. But this was not limited only to the policemen; the private trading companies expected the same from their people.

As we kept on eastward we spotted the schooner *Nigalik*. She had run aground on a shoal near Bernard Harbour and had been stuck there for ten days on her return from the winter harbour at Cambridge Bay. All told, the ship carried white fox furs to a total value of two hundred thousand dollars. We tried to pull her off with a long cable, but she did not budge, even when we put the engine full speed ahead. At the same time we had to be extremely careful not to end up on one of the many underwater shoals the lead was full of. Our own experience in 1928 was still fresh in our memories. The current was very strong and we only had a few feet of water under our keel to clear the shoals.

As we backed up to try again, our towline became entangled in our propeller and no matter how hard we tried, we just could not clear the propeller again. We were forced to anchor, and our many-sided Second Mate, Constable Dinty Moore, suggested that he dive in and cut the towline. He had learned to dive for pearls from the Maoris on New Zealand, where he had spent some time. At this point I was willing to try anything and asked him to go ahead. Shortly after, he appeared in one of the lifeboats without a stitch on and with the cook's largest butcher knife between his teeth. The weather was mild for that time of the year, and that meant that we had a storm coming up. Constable Farrar, who was quite a joker, then suggested that Dinty should go farther down and cut us some "Arctic oyster pearls" after the main job had been done. Dinty posed dramatically in the lifeboat and jumped.

This was a performance that provided a number of surprises. The Arctic Ocean is always near freezing, and the shock of the ice-cold water made our brave diver let out a scream and drop the knife, which quickly disappeared to the bottom. Before he even managed to get his hair wet, he clung to the side of the lifeboat and was pulled back in. He was frozen blue and was shivering so much that we decided that the best thing we could do was to get him back down into the cabin and the heat.

Like the other police outposts, *St. Roch* was blessed with a small stock of liquor, Hudson's Bay Demarara rum, a gift from the Government of Canada. At that time our Headquarters at Ottawa was optimistically of the opinion that all members of the Royal Canadian Mounted Police were teetotallers. Canada's Northwest Territories were completely dry and the only legal way to obtain liquor was to procure a buying permit, which was quite expensive on top of the price of the liquor itself. But members of the RCMP were not even allowed to buy permits or to store liquor itself. The wise men at Ottawa had consequently decided that each Arctic detachment should have one gallon of liquor for "medicinal purposes." On *St. Roch* we were nine, all told, and at the time when Dinty Moore made his historic dive, we had already used four bottles of our supplies, mostly to cure colds among visitors during our inspection trips.

But Moore's condition obviously called for a hot toddy. We opened the second-last bottle, while the rest of the crew stood wide-eyed watching the supply dwindle for the good of humanity.

Then Constable Jim Davies, our temporary radio operator, stepped forward and offered to cut the tow line. Cynics in the crew claimed that his courage was motivated by the prospects of getting a drink of rum before the entire supply was gone. Jim undressed and dived into the water. But before his feet had disappeared into the water, his head bobbed up again while he was gasping for air. He too was pulled on board in a hurry and taken down below where he was given a generous drink as a reward. While we had all been busy with Jim, Dinty Moore had helped himself to yet another drink, and this started to have serious effects on our liquor supply. Fired by the hot toddy, he offered to try again if he only could cover himself all over in engine grease. Unfortunately we had to decline any further offers of experiments. We were running dry! In the end we managed to free the propeller by the use of our boat hooks, and on our third try we had *Nigalik* afloat again.

Bernard Harbour consisted of a Hudson's Bay post, the police detachment and a conglomeration of Eskimo huts and tents. The huts were mostly made of rocks and earth propped up with driftwood, with grass on the roof. It was in these old huts that the Canadian Arctic Expedition of 1913-18 had lived. One of the members of the Expedition was Dr. Diamond Jenness, who later became a world-famed authority on North American natives and wrote a book called *The People of the Twilight*, in which he gives a very sympathetic description of the Eskimos and how they lived. Until Jenness arrived there, this area had been completely without contact with the white man's civilization. The Eskimos among whom the Expedition had wintered were healthy, happy and unspoiled. Jenness concludes his book by asking if the Expedition meant the beginning of a new and happier era for the Eskimos or brought forebodings of their extinction. Civilization seemed to bring merciless unhappiness for primitive natives, be it in the Pacific or in the Arctic, writes Jenness. His premonitions have long since become bitter reality. This was clearly illustrated by the picture of the harbour with all our ships full of "civilized" supplies. The white man was in the majority and had all activities under his control.

I met old Ippukkauk at Bernard Harbour. He had once been the richest and best hunter of the area, had adopted Jenness as his son and taken him around his ice-cold realm. Now he was an old man, but still the proud chieftain, dressed in traditional skin clothing. But he belonged to a dying type of Eskimos. He watched with philosophical calm and a bemused sadness the changes which took place. I met Ippukkauk often in the years to come, but in the end the police detachment was closed down, the trading posts too were closed due to lack of game, and finally even the Eskimos disappeared. Some died, others moved. A typical Arctic saga.

23 LIFE IN THE ARCTIC

Among the passengers on *Bay Chimo* was a missionary by the name of Harold Webster, bound for Coppermine where he was to take up residence. I had met him once before, when he had married Margaret Seymour and Patsy Wyant. Margaret was half Eskimo and her father had been one of the veterans from the whaling period. Both she and her father had been on Baillie Island when I visited there in 1924, but then she spent two years in Vancouver and returned a changed girl. As a lady of the outside world with lipstick, powder and the latest fashions from Vancouver she had caused quite a sensation. The old accordion she had used to play before she went South had long since been replaced by a phonograph and records of dance music. Only on the very coldest days did she change from her beach pyjamas to her elegant caribou parka. Obviously she had forgotten everything about the Eskimo way of life, and I remember that she had been very popular among the white men, mostly trappers and traders.

Patsy Wyant had been the youngest and best-looking, as well as the richest, bachelor, and within a matter of days she was engaged to him. Patsy then had lined up the missionary Harold Webster, and the wedding had taken place only hours after the engagement had been announced. All the whites and Eskimos had been invited, making quite a crowd in the little mission hut where the ceremony took place.

Old Bill Seymour sat curled up in a corner and soon was sound asleep, snoring away. But the ceremony continued without a hitch until Webster came to ask who was giving away the bride. Bill Seymour was the man, but he was fast asleep. The silence was embarrassing, while the fellow sitting next to Bill prodded him and gave him a poke in the ribs. Bill groaned madly like a polar bear, half asleep, and was known as a man who was to be feared if he was wronged. It was even said that he once had beaten Tom Sharkey, the American world heavyweight champion, during a fight in a bar in Honolulu. "What's up?" he grunted. "You have to say that it's o.k. that Margaret marries Patsy," he was told by his neighbour. "Of course it's o.k.," he declared indignantly. "What else do you think we're here for? Leave me alone!" And with that he went back to sleep.

Pastor Webster heaved a sigh of relief and declared the young couple to be married. After a short flight with one of the first passenger aircraft to find its way to the Arctic, the couple left for Patsy's trading post near Horton River. Margaret soon resumed her ancient ways and started to dress like an Eskimo woman again and became a good housekeeper. I visited the couple several times and was always given a warm welcome.

Our next stop was Coppermine, twelve hours away. As this was my first visit there, I had trouble finding my way through the pack ice. We did not have a police detachment there then, and the only houses were a trading post, the Anglican and Roman Catholic missions, a small hospital and a radio hut. We had only one man stationed temporarily at Coppermine and our main reason for stopping there was to establish a permanent detachment.

With Sergeant Anderton, I started to look for a good spot for the police. We finally found a spot between the doctor's house and the radio shack. The entire settlement was concentrated along a narrow strip of land west of the mouth of Coppermine River, and all the houses were set in a row. There were also dozens of Eskimo tents.

Rows of Arctic char were hung out to dry in the sun. Chubby Eskimo women were busy splitting the fish in two and hanging them up while their men watched. The men's job stopped with catching the fish. Children were swarming all over the place and they looked at us with great curiosity while their parents shook hands with us and gave the impression that they were anxious to establish contact with us. They knew that we were neither traders nor missionaries.

A few years earlier this place had been isolated and unpopulated, only visited by Eskimos each spring and once in a while by a white trader who came to catch char. Then the Hudson's Bay Company established a post there to get fish for their dogs. It was a good place for that, but that was about all, as it was not too well located for trade and the game was fairly scarce. With all this, Coppermine most likely would have continued its obscure existence had it not been for the hunt for minerals that started in the Arctic. The copper deposits prompted several mining companies to establish themselves there, and soon people were flown in. Whaling had turned Herschel Island into a small Arctic metropolis; the quest for minerals and the aircraft had the same influence on Coppermine. As a result, the Eskimos gathered together to admire the many fantastic things the white men brought with them. Soon the natives lost their health, their independence, and to some extent their freedom. Instead of hunting for what they needed to live, they became fur traders and trappers, and in time, slaves of their own greed and newly created need for things they previously had neither known nor desired.

It only took two years for the Coppermine Eskimos, who earlier had lived a completely free life, to become absorbed by civilization, and many died of tuberculosis, meningitis, measles and other diseases that they had never been exposed to before. I did not envy the young, able doctor who without sufficient assistance and equipment tried to stop this flood of disease and death.

One evening Inspector Eames, Sergeant Anderton and I were the guests of the doctor and enjoyed a delicious dinner of Coppermine whitefish. We also met D. W. Gillingham, one of the many young Canadians who were to make a lasting impression on the Arctic. The first time I had met him he had been a deck-hand on *Bay Chimo*, but now he worked for a large mining company. He had taken the opportunity to make a brief visit to Coppermine to renew his friendship with both whites and Eskimos. Over the years he had come to know large parts of the Arctic and had done much of the preparatory work on his excellent book *Umiak*, which in the new Eskimo spelling would be "Umiaq." In this book he displays an almost unique ability to understand and consider both sides of the picture in the Canadian Arctic, based on his own experiences among the natives and the newcomers.

One frequently hears how the advance of civilization marks the natives and at times ruins them. But it also happens that the white man who leaves the civilization he is used to behind him and goes out into the Arctic wilderness becomes marked by the world of the natives. This too can be ruinous. Our host that evening could tell us about one such case, a strange man called John Brown, who lived on a small island near by. Originally John Brown had been a trapper. One day he became lost in a snowstorm and when he was finally found by some Roman Catholic missionaries he was frozen half to death. The missionaries took him to their station where they nursed him until he regained his strength physically. But the ordeal had been too much for his mind, and he had become religious to the point of mania.

John Brown now believed that he was God, or at least that he had a heavenly mission. He ordained himself High Priest and told people that he soon was off for Rome where he was to have an audience with the Pope. With time he became wilder and wilder. Once he threatened an Eskimo woman with his gun as she came paddling near the island to set out her fishing nets. One of the whites went out to talk some sense into him. He confirmed that he had indeed threatened the Eskimo woman, but justified it by adding that there were many graves on the island and that he was going to revive the dead. The Eskimos, of course, were impressed by this, but their awe was mixed with fear. When rumours started to circulate that the Eskimos planned to kill Brown, the doctor took him to the mainland. But he escaped and sought refuge with the missionaries, who in turn wanted the police to take care of him so that it could be decided whether or not he should be committed to a mental institution.

Some constables took off to get Brown, who followed them reluctantly back to *St. Roch*. He was quite a sight. Unshaven, dirty and hungry he sat on a chair and made the sign of the cross without stop while the necessary formalities were cleared up. The doctor and one of the missionaries signed as witnesses that Brown should be committed.

Next day we continued to Cambridge Bay with Brown on board, and he behaved very calmly. One of the constables had been given the job of keeping an eye on him, and in the beginning everything went all right. But after a while we came into heavy ice and thick fog. Once in a while we ran into the edge of the ice with a crash that jarred the whole ship. This had a strange effect on Brown, who came up on deck and declared that he now was supreme commander on board. He demanded that Inspector Eames turn his sword over to him and told us that he was now going to destroy *St. Roch* and all of us. He kept on raving in this way until we reached Cambridge Bay. Brown was with us for a month before we could put him ashore on Herschel Island. From there he was shipped to Edmonton. In the meantime we had visited a number of places in the North, and our work was not made any easier by having him with us. But this was part of the work of the police in the North. At that time we had to do the work which now is divided between various federal departments concerned with the Canadian Arctic.

24 IN WINTER QUARTERS 1930-31

We arrived at Kuulugaaluk or Tree River on September 18. This, our winter quarters for the next four years, was one of the best harbours one could dream of for that purpose. It was in a well-sheltered bay with two long arms of deep water. The entrance to the bay was narrow with a little island in the middle, but ships could easily pass on either side.

The bay was surrounded by hills and a crystal-clear lake assured us of all the fresh-water supply we needed. It was also full of fish, which we could see swimming in the shallow water and could catch with our bare hands.

The scenery around us was beautiful, and during the first days of October we experienced wonderful weather with only a hint of frost, ideal for hiking. We explored the area on foot for miles in all directions. This was a welcome change from our life on board, and it was profitable as well. Arctic hares were to be found all over the place, and some of them weighed more than twelve pounds. We used our .22 calibre rifles and had the unfair advantage that the hares were white this time of the year, even before the surroundings had turned white, so we could spot them far away. There was also a wealth of ptarmigan which we hunted with rifles; shotguns would have meant sheer massacre. Each day we returned to the ship loaded down with hares and birds, and this certainly brightened up our meals. However, we were amazed that we could see no tracks of caribou. Later we learned that in earlier years this area had been full of caribou as well as muskox. But then the Eskimos had obtained rifles and shot them down like flies.

In many places we found traces of Eskimo camps, and soapstone lamps were everywhere. They were oval, hollowed-out stones, rather like deep dishes. The Eskimos filled them with blubber and used them both for light and for cooking. Now the owners perhaps were dead, because in between the rocks we also found many Eskimo skulls and faded bones which somehow had remained uneaten by dogs or foxes.

The graves were spread around without any particular plan, but mostly along the hilltops where the view was good. People who knew this area well later told me that an Eskimo as a rule picked out his burial place while he was still alive. As far as it was possible, the survivors saw to it that he was buried in the place he had picked. One thing I did notice was that all the bodies had been placed in an east-to-west direction, a remarkable thing for such a primitive people. The same custom is said to be followed in other places in the world, but always among much more developed people.

We had, of course, other things to do than to go sightseeing. One of our urgent jobs was to take care of our winter supplies. We had bought new California potatoes and eggs with our own money, and if properly taken care of, they would keep. With the changing temperatures this time of the year, these things, as well as some fresh onions and oranges, had to be stored in our cabins until the temperature dropped sufficiently so that we could deep-freeze them in the snow piles and keep them there for the rest of the winter.

When we wanted some of the deep-frozen potatoes we dropped them into boiling water so that they would not thaw too slowly. Done in this way they tasted very good, while potatoes that were allowed to thaw slowly after only having been frozen a little bit were inedible. Oranges could not be left to thaw either, but had to be dropped into a bucket of ice-cold water. Then they softened enough that they could be eaten, but once they had been thawed in this manner they could never be stored again. Thanks to this type of freezing and thawing we had fresh supplies all winter.

When the lakes had frozen we fished with nets under the ice. This was pretty cold work. To get the nets out we had to cut a row of holes in the ice and stretch a line under the ice from one hole to another, the length of the net. Then the net was fastened to the line and pulled under the ice through a hole big enough to let it pass. The net had to be set fairly deep so that the floaters did not touch the ice. If they did, the net would freeze solid and be torn to pieces when we were ready to pull it out again. We used a-yard-and-a-half-long poles to keep the nets in place, and the fish had to be removed quickly from the nets so they would not freeze to it and be ruined. All this had to be done with bare hands, and each time we had dipped our hands into the ice-cold water, we quickly put them under our shirts to warm them on our bellies. Dressed like Eskimos as we were, this was easy enough. The Eskimos had taught us this way of fishing and soon we were beating them at their own game, catching up to fifty fish each day, some of them weighing ten to twelve pounds. In the beginning of December we had more than a thousand trout or char, and this enabled us to feed the dogs and provide all our guests with plenty of food.

We put up the masts for our radio and stretched canvas over the entire ship. We also marked out a garbage dump and other conveniences at a safe distance from the ship, so that the immediate surroundings could be kept nice and white. The "other conveniences" were made of ice blocks and were promptly named the "Crystal Palace."

The winter came with intense cold and clear nights. When the ice cracked in the cold, it sounded like heavy guns and the whole ship shook. The Eskimos visited us once in a while, ate all they could and were allowed to help themselves to our tobacco.

25 DOG LIFE IN THE ARCTIC

This was the year of the Census, and I was to go to the southern coast of Victoria Island with a colleague of mine, McRae. We started our preparations right after New Year's. First we cooked several pounds of beans and mixed this with bacon, cut into small pieces, canned meat and tomatoes with an addition of onions, syrup, mustard and salt. All this was cooked up into a heavy dough. When it was all done, it was put out in the cold where it froze right away. Our next step was to cut the frozen dough into small pieces with an axe and then put them into small canvas bags, which were easy to carry. To vary the food we also cooked some rice and potatoes and other vegetables, mixed with meat. All this was put through a meat grinder, but instead of adding water to this, we used canned soup or tomatoes and then added spices. It was then made into flat pies which we again put into bags. With this we would be able to whip up a meal in a couple of minutes merely by putting it in a pot and adding water, whenever we made camp. We made hundreds of doughnuts, too, and froze them, so that they could be thawed on top of the coffee pot while the coffee itself was boiling.

Oatmeal was also easy to carry, so we usually made a big pot while on sled trips, mostly for breakfast. Sometimes we added some bacon and sugar to it and with that under our belts we could keep going all day. Frozen fish was cut into pieces an inch in length and usually eaten while we made camp and waited for the snow to melt so we could start cooking. Oddly enough, the frozen fish gives a certain feeling of well-being. The Eskimos explained this by saying that the frozen fish forces the warm blood from the inside out to the skin, and this seems to make sense.

Our supplies also included baking powder and a bag of flour. When we were forced to stay in one place during a storm, we would have time to make up some bannock. Besides, flour always came in handy when one stayed the night with Eskimos. The women love to make up a batch of bannock with lard. It tastes delicious and fills the stomach, which is what the Eskimos mainly care about.

Generally speaking, the Eskimos store very few staples, taking each day as it comes. Consequently we made it a rule to keep ourselves and our dogs with food when we were out on a trip. Like other housewives, the Eskimo women love to offer visitors some of their best food, but we always left them some of our food as a gift in return.

We never had a chance to try out the emergency rations the armed forces had developed for their people, but found that our own recipes and pre-cooked meals were more than sufficient, all through the years. All our cooking was done on Swedish Primuses, and I doubt that there has been any better invention for Arctic cooking. For the dogs we brought along dried fish, as the frozen fish would have been too heavy to carry in such large quantities. We also had seal blubber cut into suitable pieces for the dogs, as they needed a good deal of fat. The Eskimos also liked this, so we could use it for trading if necessary.

Our sleeping-bags were supposed to be made of eiderdown, but we preferred those made of caribou hides. A most important thing to take along for travels in the Arctic is a good, long knife for cutting snow blocks when building snow huts for overnight camping. Such igloos are far superior to tents, and we improved on the Eskimo igloos somewhat by covering the roof with canvas instead of snow blocks. In this way we avoided the dripping from the ceiling when we did our cooking.

A big caribou hide could also serve as roof, and the Eskimos soon adopted our idea. In the larger, more permanent igloos, however, the dripping was negligible.

Most experienced dog-drivers dressed like the Eskimos. It was most important to avoid using textiles, and use only caribou skins. On our feet we wore skin socks which reached right up under the knees. On top of these we used another pair made, whenever possible, of sealskin. The pants were made with the hairy side of the skin facing in and they reached from the ankles to well above the waist. Yet another layer of skin, this time with the hair facing out, completed that part of our clothes.

The footwear was carefully made of skins from the legs of the caribou, with the soles of moose hides. The parka, or artigie, as the Eskimos called it, also was made in two parts; one with the hair in, the outer one with the hair facing out.

As a rule the outer garments were made of heavier skins with longer hair. The mitts were also of heavy skins and reached well up over the parka sleeves. They were fastened to gaily-coloured ribbons which went around the neck so that they would not be lost in the wind or grabbed by the dogs. The rim of the parka hood was lined with wolverine fur with the hair facing out. In addition to being ornamental, this also provided protection for the nose and the rest of the face from the wind. The fur also absorbed the ice and the moisture formed by the breath and the drifting snow. The wolverine fur was particularly well suited, as the hairs do not stick together or become moist. This made it easy to wipe off the snow and the ice while driving the team. The hide of a young polar bear would do too, but the hair is a little bit rougher.

I do not think it is possible to improve the Eskimo way of dressing as we saw it in the early days in the Arctic. The synthetic fabrics and furs which are used these days may be more efficient and durable than caribou hides, but most of the things made for the armed forces and the Mounted Police these days are far too heavy and cumbersome with all the outside pockets and oversized zippers. That, at least, is my opinion: I know that they would be very impractical for the type of sled trips we went on. At times we had to keep going days on end without any other form of heating than what we had in the igloos to do our cooking and to melt ice or snow for drinking water.

With our type of clothing we had the advantage that, when the weather turned milder and the driving became especially heavy, all we had to do was to remove the outside layer and carry on in our "underwear." This was most important when driving over long distances of hard-frozen snow or frozen snow on top of a loose layer. The Arctic snow crust would carry an Eskimo, but we were generally heavier and broke through, so we had to lift our legs ten or twelve inches for each step. This meant that we quickly became heated up and unless we took off the outer clothing quickly enough and cooled off a little, the caribou skins became soaked with perspiration.

I also had the impression that Eskimos perspired less than the whites, and as a rule they only perspired on their foreheads. If we did not watch ourselves and walked until we were wet with perspiration, we had to pay for our folly by sitting up half the night scraping the ice away from the inside of our clothing. The Eskimos, incidentally, had a tool for this task. They also taught us to rub the skins, a little piece at a time, between our hands to soften them again. If we did not do this, it was rather difficult to get whatever it might be back on again the next day. Mostly this was done while we were sitting in our sleeping-bags and we must have been a sight, sitting there rubbing and rubbing.

Another innovation of ours was that extra-thick oatmeal porridge was better to smear on the sled runners than the mud that the Eskimos used. Sometimes we used up to thirty pounds of porridge and ended up with a layer of ice produced by rubbing the runners with a bear-hide rag dipped in lukewarm water. Another advantage of using porridge was that it could be eaten if need be. All we had to do was to scrape it off the runners.

I came to understand and respect the polar dogs. Before I started to lead the sled in the morning I made it a habit to give the dogs a piece of fish each. It seemed to wake them up and give them energy to start out. It also stimulated them to perform their various functions before I harnessed them. I had come to know from experience how frustrating it was to have one of the dogs sit down right after they started in the morning, and then have all the other dogs pull the poor devil away. If this sort of thing got under way, it usually took more than an hour before they all had performed and could speed up. It was as if they never could agree on doing it all at the same time. But a piece of fish did the trick. When the fish had been consumed and everything else done, we were ready to start. The first few miles were covered at top speed before the dogs switched to a steadier pace. I used a small snow anchor to tie the sled down until everything was ready, and then I jumped onto it and "weighed anchor."

In milder weather I did not bother to put up my little one-man tent, but simply stretched out on top of the sled and slept when it suited me. The dogs were staked around me. There was nothing they liked better than to be close to their master at all times and I liked their company. All the stories about the Arctic dogs being wild and dangerous are misleading. It is true that some of them at times have gone wild, but this has been due not to the character of the dogs, but rather to the poor treatment they have been given. Even today's Eskimos, who should know better, at times neglect the dogs and whip them instead of giving them encouragement. In such instances it is understandable if the starved dogs get so wild that they attack and, at times, eat small children. More than once, I have run into such starved dogs. After a couple of weeks of good treatment with lots of food and the odd pat on the head, they usually became friendly and co-operative.

There is much to be said for the theory that the character of the dog mirrors that of the master. If the driver is happy and good-natured, the dogs usually are the same. It happened, of course, that we got up somewhat grudgingly in the morning and forgot to give the dogs a smile of encouragement. On such days they would start off at a slow pace with their tails between their legs instead of their usual flying start with tails standing up straight into the air. It was also remarkable what effect a gay little song would have on the pace. When they started to become tired towards the end of a long day, I used to sing a little for them. It is hard to say whether it was my voice that scared them or not, but anyway they usually increased their pace. I believe that the most important thing was that they realized that I was in a good mood. On the other hand, it was of no use to bawl them out when they were tired.

Every time we made camp for the night, the lead dog always knew what kind of spot to look for. If I wanted to continue after he had stopped he would turn his head and look at me as if asking what was wrong with that spot, it looked good enough to him. For a while I had a lead dog who was particularly good at this. Paddy Gibson of the Hudson's Bay Company had given me this dog. He was a small dog, but had a strong, heavy neck and an exceptionally small head, enabling him to wiggle out of any collar or harness. It was almost impossible to tie Houdini up for the night. Fortunately he was a friendly dog, but it was still unpleasant to have a dog loose at night. Mostly it ended up with all dogs howling, so we were forced to get up and dress to get hold of the culprit.

When I had Houdini I had no need to look for a camping spot at all. He knew exactly what was needed, so I left it entirely to him. Houdini would continue as late as possible at night, running from one side to another to avoid the worst snow ridges which could easily upset the sled. When he was completely exhausted, he started to look for a camping spot. As he finally found one after much sniffing around he would lie down flat as a sign that this was where we should spend the night. The choice was usually perfect. An Eskimo who came with me once was really impressed by Houdini. When he searched around with his harpoon in the snow where the dog had come to rest, he always found that the snow was just right for building an igloo. All the Eskimo had to do was to move the dog a little and start the walls. Generally the Eskimos had to search for quite a while before they found snow that could be cut into blocks for an igloo.

In the summer we had more time and it happened that we turned the dogs loose and took them with us on a hike around *St. Roch*. Here they could run around freely as they pleased, chasing squirrels and birds, swim in the lakes and in short, act like pups. At times we, too, undressed and dove in with all the dogs hot on our heels in one big cluster. Two of my favourite dogs, Hunter the leader and his brother Seagull, always stuck together.

I had another pair of brothers, Mate and Coon. They were completely black Mackenzie dogs from further south and weighed about a hundred pounds each. The cold weather and the wind were hard on these two dogs, who were less endowed with fur than the Huskies. The Mackenzie dogs were used to milder weather and suffered much in the cold. Their flanks in particular were exposed, as that was where their fur was the thinnest. From time to time we had to stop and rub their flanks and bellies. This was a cold job, but it had to be done. The Huskies we could protect against frostbite by watching the teams carefully. People can tell when they are frostbitten—it feels like sharp needles in the skin—but with dogs the tell-tale sign was when the hind legs started to shiver. We used to cut strips of hides and scrape them until they became softened. These were then tied around the bellies on the exposed dogs and gave them some protection.

In the western Arctic we always drove our dogs in the Nome hitch, or tandem, with the leader up front. The dogs always knew whom they were to be harnessed with and if they had a different partner one day, it usually caused trouble. The advantage of tandem driving was that it made it unnecessary to control the dogs with a long whip the way the eastern Eskimos did when they drove their teams in fan formation. This type of driving required that each dog be fastened to a long line so that frequently they were in each other's way. But this method is no doubt the best for the geographical conditions in the eastern Arctic.

The daily rations for a sled dog consisted of four to six pounds of fish. For a skinny dog, I preferred to cook some corn or rice with tallow together with the fish. Each night I gave the dogs a big helping of this porridge, which I ladled out on top of the snow in front of each dog. It did wonders for the dogs, and my teams were always in top shape around Christmas at the latest each year. A good dog team was absolutely indispensable in the Arctic.

Mostly the policemen on *St. Roch* completed their patrols without any assistance from the Eskimos; so when McRae and I finally were ready to leave on our Census trip in February of 1930, we were on our own. We visited a number of Eskimo camps along the southern coast of Victoria Island and also met some white trappers and dropped in to say hello to the former engineer on *Maid of Orleans*, Morris, and his wife.

When we returned to *St. Roch* we were richer in experience and felt that we knew a great deal more about how to survive in the Arctic. The trip had also been a welcome change from the routine life on board the ship. Generally speaking, however, this was an uneventful summer, apart from a series of hurricanes and snowstorms, including a four-day blizzard in late August.

26 ESKIMO LOVE AND DRAMA

When we visited Bernard Harbour that year in September we attended a wedding. The groom was Paul Steen, a tall, good-looking fellow from Texas, and the bride was Bessie, the daughter of the former pilot on *St. Roch*, Jacobson. I had not seen the old man since our maiden voyage, but the Hudson's Bay man, Swoger Henriksen, told me that Bessie had had two suitors. Both were trappers who lived on the west side of Inman River, while Jacobson and his family lived on the east side. These two men used to cross the river, one after the other, to court Bessie, who was the most sought-after girl in the district. But Bessie's mother, who was an Eskimo from Herschel Island, remembered the whalers who had lived on their native island, and had a deep-rooted suspicion of the honourable intentions of white suitors. As a result she kept her shotgun ready. One day, as suitor number one, a Dane by the name of Henry Jensen, came across, the old lady chased him, shotgun in hand, all the way down to the river and forced him to swim across. Each time Henry showed his head above water, she fired, and the hapless suitor dived like a seal, surfacing only to get some air.

All told, the Jacobsons had nine children—four boys and five girls. Bessie was the eldest. The mixture of Finnish and Eskimo blood was obviously good, for the children were all healthy and good-looking. Somehow Paul Steen had managed to convince Mother Jacobson that his intentions really were honourable and was accepted, first as an official suitor and later as a son-in-law. He was twice as old as Bessie, but that did not seem to be of any importance. Bessie and Paul were blessed with one child every year for the first twelve years of their marriage, and all the children had strawberry blond or reddish hair, and freckles. As far as I know, the couple still live in the Arctic.

Fritz Shurer was another bachelor in the Arctic, but he was less fortunate than Paul Steen. He was a young German sailor who lived as a trapper near our winter quarters. His best friend was an elderly American, Peter Brandt, and the two of them lived together. Fritz had been in the Arctic only for about a year, and while he perhaps was a little bit too stubborn at times, he was what we called a regular guy. He decided to marry an Eskimo widow, and wanted, not a native wedding, but the real thing, with Pastor Webster from Coppermine to do the honours. He was fed up with white women, he said, and had no intention of ever leaving the Arctic again. It was only natural, then, that he wanted a wife who was familiar with conditions in the North.

Sergeant Anderton advised Fritz to think it over carefully before he married an Eskimo he hardly knew. Apart from that there was nothing to stop him from marrying an Eskimo, but it would be preferable for him to get to know some of the native customs and a little bit of the language. But Fritz had made up his mind. When his partner refused to have a woman in the little shack they shared, the two friends parted.

A few months later Fritz's bride-to-be, Qullilaaq, visited us together with a number of other Eskimos. She was in her thirties, big and strong, and had a daughter about ten years old. As far as we understood, Qullilaaq had been a widow for about a year. The reason that she had not remarried was simply that bachelors were scarce in that area among the Eskimos, who had been taught by the missionaries that polygamy was wrong, and that had reduced her chances as well. But at no time did she mention Fritz to us during that visit.

We were therefore quite shocked a few weeks later when Patsy Klengenberg arrived with Quillilaaq and declared that she had shot and killed Fritz.

Patsy acted as interpreter and gave us the full story. Fritz had arrived at the Eskimo camp a few days after the Eskimos had been our guests. He had asked if Qullilaaq was willing to go with him, and she had had no objections. But first Fritz went to Detention Harbour to get some supplies he and Peter Brandt had there. She had the impression that Brandt was far from happy about the marriage, but on the other hand, she had liked Pete, who was an old-timer in the North and always had been a good friend of the Eskimos. Once she had even made him a pair of mitts. Fritz did not appreciate this at all, that was obvious.

Qullilaaq and Fritz then set out to look after their traps and even if she did not understand much of what Fritz said, she noticed that he was getting more and more angry about something. She started to be frightened.

A week later they were in the neighbourhood of Detention Harbour again, and Fritz was furious for some reason or other and said that he was going to kill Brandt. According to Qullilaaq, this frightened her so much that she in turn made up her mind to kill Fritz. One morning after breakfast, she crawled out of the igloo the two of them had built, and grabbed Fritz's rifle which was standing outside. She loaded it and took aim at the entrance. Fritz, however, did not appear, so she called out to him a couple of times. Finally he too crawled out, backwards on all fours.

She shot Fritz in the back and he probably died on the spot. Qullilaaq explained that he only made a few noises and then fell still. Then she loaded all she had onto the sled and got herself ready to leave. But suddenly she came to realize what she had done. She dared not return to her own people out of fear that they might kill her. Some years previously there had been a real vendetta among the Eskimos and in the end even a Hudson's Bay official and a policeman had been killed. She also remembered that two of the Eskimos had been taken away by the police, never to return.

Qullilaaq did not like the idea of leaving the corpse where it was as she was afraid that the animals would get at it, so she pulled Fritz inside the igloo and closed the entrance with big snow blocks. Then she put the rifle back against the wall outside and decided to go to Willmot Island, some thirty miles off, to talk to Patsy Klengenberg in the hope that he could help her.

Patsy immediately decided to bring her over to us, and here they were. Sergeant Anderton had no choice but to arrest her on the spot and keep her on the ship until the following summer so she could appear before the judge in Coppermine. In the meantime Constable Arthur Jones and I took off for the igloo and the murder weapon. We were also to bring Fritz's body back with us.

This happened close to Christmas, so the days were short, but we soon found the igloo, just as Qullilaaq had described it, and there was Fritz, fully dressed for the sled trip he never went on. We wrapped him in a piece of canvas and pulled him outside as we had to spend the night in the igloo. Next day we went over to Pete Brandt's place to get a statement and found that he had no idea at all of what had happened. But he confirmed that Qullilaaq had been with Fritz and that the two of them had gone off together to check their traps. As we continued back to *St. Roch* we had to proceed very slowly, fighting our way through a blizzard. To top it off, Fritz's arms were frozen and sticking straight out on both sides, hampering us all the time.

Qullilaaq was standing on the ice when we approached the ship, and when she saw what we were bringing on the sled, she screamed and ran on board.

The rest of the story is simple enough. The next summer the judge and the jury came up from Edmonton and Qullilaaq was found "not guilty" on the grounds that she had acted in self-defence. But many of the Eskimos disagreed with the verdict. They were of the opinion that there had been far too many murders in the district and that we let the murderers get off too easily.

Fritz was buried that summer and Dad Parry, our cook, who used to serve as a medicine-man for the Eskimos, read the ritual at the graveside. It was a beautiful, sunny day, and Dad put everything he had into his rendition and closed with a prayer for the King. Afterwards he asked me if he had done a good job. As Fritz had been a sailor, he was wondering if perhaps he should not have included the ritual for burial at sea. I replied that it had been a beautiful funeral and added that the ocean had very little in common with the hard-frozen tundra where we had to work with picks for days before we managed to get a big enough hole for the grave. But Dad Parry was still unhappy, and the next day he went back, all by himself, and added the words used at sea burials.

Qullilaaq was married shortly after to an Eskimo widower, Qinnirtaaq. The two of them had many children, and for years to come they used to visit us whenever we were in the area.

The third winter we spent at Tree River we were informed of another murder drama at Sherman Inlet, seven hundred miles away. This time only Eskimos were involved; two couples, to be exact. One of the couples was brought to Cambridge Bay on Victoria Island. The husband, Aqigiq, was a quiet-looking man, getting on in years. His plump wife, Iskuuguluk, had fair skin and was in her middle thirties. This couple had lived together with another, much younger couple, as was the custom among the Eskimos. The younger of the two men had often spent the night with Iskuuguluk without any objections from her husband, but then wife-trading was quite common in those days. The younger man however, became too greedy and wanted to have both wives for himself and refused to let Aqigiq sleep with his own wife. This, of course, meant trouble, as this is the worst insult an Eskimo can be faced with. The women themselves had little or nothing to say in the matter: they simply accepted whatever the men decided to do.

Aqigiq put up with this for some time, but in the end it became intolerable and he decided to kill the younger man. He managed to get him into an ambush and shot him.

We had to take the murderer and his family with us to *St. Roch*, where he spent the winter close to the ship. Later he appeared in court in Aklavik and was sentenced to five years in prison.

Nobody was actually locked up in Aklavik, though the prisoners were under constant supervision and their movements were restricted. With time we came to appreciate Aqigiq and suggested that he should be allowed to bring his family with him to Aklavik, but this was refused. Instead we sent his wife and the rest of the family to her brother Iqalupik, or Big Fish, who was an outstanding hunter on the Adelaide Peninsula. He promised to look after them, but unfortunately, Aqigiq's fourteen-year-old son killed his uncle by accident with his gun. This meant additional hardship for the family. The police did keep an eye on things, and finally the family was transferred to Cambridge Bay, where they were equipped again. The father was released after serving two years of his sentence and was reunited with his family. During his time "in prison," he had been very well treated and was greeted with great honour when he returned to his own people. Everybody's sympathy was on his side: it was obvious that he had been the victim of a bully.

27 THE FOURTH CHRISTMAS IN THE NORTH

Late in July 1932 we took *St. Roch* farther west. On Herschel Island we found that Inspector Eames had been replaced by Inspector Rivett-Carnac. We also met a new sergeant, George Makinson, who had recently been promoted and was to take Anderton's place on *St. Roch.* Many of the other men also returned to the South with Sergeant Anderton, who left for a well-deserved leave. Naturally I was sorry to see Anderton leave us. I was not to see him again for many years.

The summer passed quickly and soon the ice returned. We went through all the usual preparations for wintering for the fourth time; by then much of it had become routine.

Our fourth and last Christmas in the ice on that voyage was a lively one. I had obtained some 16-mm. films and invited all the Eskimos to attend the first show they had ever seen. In the beginning they were a little apprehensive, but soon they screamed with merriment over the films from New York, the Pacific Islands and scenes from the war at sea during World War I. The climax was reached when we showed them some short films we had made of them earlier. These we had to run again and again. When the missionary announced that they all had to go to Mass, they were very disappointed. Fortunately the missionary was an understanding man who realized that Mass was something they could go to every Christmas, while they most likely would never have another chance to see movies. The result was that we continued to show films, and I became a big and famous man in the eyes of the Eskimos because of these simple performances.

Today, more than thirty years later, the Eskimos are more used to movies. But heaven only knows what influence they have had on the natives, for as a rule the films are of the worst kind, with murder and drinking, just the very things both the missionaries and the police had taught them not to indulge in. There is no doubt that they consider what they see in the movies as the true face of the white man.

On one of my sled trips I also met the Dane Rudolf Johnson again. He was an Arctic old-timer who had come up there long before I was born, and had worked both for the Hudson's Bay Company and on his own. I had met him several times when sailing with Klengenberg. The Eskimos loved Rudolf. Many years later Commissioner Wood of the Royal Canadian Mounted Police got him a job in the Force as Second Engineer with me from 1943 to 1949. He was with us on the voyage through the Northwest Passage together with another old-timer, Ole Andreassen. Commissioner Wood was also responsible for his employment with us. Ole died in Vancouver in 1946 and was buried with full Mounted Police honours. When I last saw Rudolf in Vancouver in 1963, he was almost ninety years old.

On our long sled trips I often had the opportunity to explain our principles of law to the Eskimos in a language they could understand. When they had resorted to violence, and at times to murder, I had to tell them that as a representative of the King it was my duty to arrest the guilty person, regardless of how good a hunter he might be. The King, or the Big Chief, would then let his court, made up of white men, pass judgment on the offenders, who would be either killed or locked up in a small room which they could never leave. They would never see their own people again and never again go hunting or travelling. I explained that the police had orders always to find such wrong-doers, never to shoot them or harm them in any way, but to bring them back to the white man's court. I went on to say that for this reason, they should never try to settle their arguments and disagreements by killing each other. On the other hand, if both parties came to the police, we would help them in every way possible.

Those who stood around me while I talked seemed to be appropriately impressed. I explained it in this way because they themselves did not really understand that they would be doing anything wrong. I also took the opportunity to impress the game preservation regulations on them, and once we took the trouble to explain these things to them in detail, they did their best to adhere to those new and strange rules.

28 DAILY LIFE IN THE IGLOO

When the trapping season was over, a whole igloo village grew up around *St. Roch*, and most of the Eskimos stayed there until it became so mild that their igloos melted. Much of what has been written about life in the igloo is romanticized, giving the impression of an idyllic existence in which all Eskimos were very happy. I cannot think of any type of dwelling less suited for human habitation than such a snow house, particularly in the fall and spring when the weather changed between thaw and frost, with rain and sleet. Everything became soaked —clothing, furs, utensils and all kinds of equipment—and it was practically impossible to use the primus stoves or the oil lamps because the heat could bring down the entire igloo. The larger, more permanent igloos could be quite comfortable in the winter when the cold arrived for good, provided that the people had enough seal oil on hand to allow the lamps to burn around the clock. Such huts could be four to six yards in diameter and up to four yards high in the middle, where a pipe usually ran through the ceiling from the stove which heated the house. Some of the more well-to-do Eskimos also covered the inside walls of their igloos with hides.

During the spring, the Eskimos loved to travel and to attend parties. That was the season to get married and even to practise a little bit of wife-trading. They were all good friends, so they did not seem to mind. Frequently a couple would get along much better after such a trade, perhaps because they had found that the grass is not always greener on the other side of the fence.

We too went on long trips that time of the year and often spent the night with Eskimo families. Such a stay usually was pretty hard on our food supply, as we could not avoid treating the whole family. The wife and children used to sit around and watch us while we cooked our food, not necessarily because they were hungry, but mainly to see if they would be able to try some of the strange food we used.

On a trip to the bottom of Bathurst Inlet, Farrar and I stayed overnight with two good friends of ours who had visited us on *St. Roch* several times. One of them was an old man with a big mouth, thick lips and a roguish smile. This was Kuugukuuk, who had two wives, both in their thirties. The other Eskimo was Ijlik, a big man around forty years of age who had lost an eye in his youth and resembled a pirate. His wife was unusually small even for an Eskimo woman and looked like an ermine as she darted in and out of the igloo with quick movements. They all insisted that we should spend the night with them: I let Farrar go to Kuugukuuk and his two wives while I stayed with Ijlik in his big, comfortable igloo. When I took in our supplies from the sled, both families gathered in Ijlik's igloo for supper; there was no point in wasting oil in both places at the same time just to prepare food. Both the men, incidentally, were excellent hunters and good providers of the old school and had ample supplies of dried char, caribou meat and frozen seal.

No sooner had I pulled out a big container that I used for food than Ijlik's wife grabbed it and started to empty the contents for a closer inspection. I did not even have a chance to get close to it myself, but let her help herself. Her husband, however, was of a different opinion and shouted to her to leave it alone. I understood from his tone of voice that he was annoyed with her inquisitiveness. She immediately put everything back in order, while Ijlik explained to the rest of his people that the two of us would need all our supplies ourselves for the long trip. Perhaps, he added, we would even meet some Eskimos who did not have enough to eat and then we could help them. He, Ijlik, the great hunter, had enough food, he said, so the women had better start to prepare a meal for all of us of what he had to offer.

It was not too often we encountered men like Ijlik; most of the Eskimos felt that the white men's supplies were inexhaustible. On this occasion, nobody daring to oppose the lord of the household, we pulled out only our own cutlery, plates and mugs. Sugar and tea, which we had lots of, was also brought out, and not even our host refused that.

The three women now started to cut up caribou meat for cooking and while we waited for it to be ready we ate heaps of frozen and dried fish, which was so fat that we could see the oil gleam in the light. The char, which had been dried in the sun, was not salted and we washed it down with gallons of tea. It took two hours for the meat to cook while we four men sat comfortably with our legs stretched out on the sleeping-platform, slightly elevated above the floor. The women and children stayed close to the oil lamps used for cooking. Because of the cooking the ceiling was dripping all the time, and once in a while they would make a snowball, put it on a long stick and push it up into the ceiling where it was dripping. As soon as the ball had fastened the dripping stopped for a while, but it also happened that the snowballs came tumbling down again and hit one of the women on the head, which was great fun for the children.

Finally the meat was ready. The women pressed the water out of it with their fingers and quickly licked off the rest of the moisture so that we would not get too much on our hands. Then the pieces were passed around. We held a piece of meat with one hand while we cut it into smaller pieces with a knife. A dog and half a dozen pups who had stayed on the sleeping-platform now appeared and received their share, mostly pieces that were too tough for us to eat.

It was well past midnight before the party was over, and Farrar left with Kuugukuuk and his two wives. In our igloo there was enough room for all of us on the sleeping-platform. This was a big igloo: when I stood up on the platform, which was two feet above the ground, I still could not reach the ceiling. The platform itself was made of snow and had a layer of small rocks and pebbles. On top of these were mats of woven branches and then a double layer of caribou hides, the first with the hairs facing down to insulate the snow completely. In this way we avoided having the platform melt from our body temperature. This happened often in smaller igloos with the result that uncomfortable hollows were formed. At the foot of the platform was a large snow-free area where all the clothing was placed, as this was the driest spot in the igloo. Everyone slept with the feet towards the wall and the head towards the centre of the igloo, packed together like sardines.

As the guest of the house I slept next to Ijlik in the best spot on the platform, with the rest of the family in a row next to the mother. I used my sleeping-bag, but the others had a wedge-shaped bag with a big opening on one side so that it could be turned down like a blanket and cover everybody, who slept naked.

Ijlik and I went to bed first, while the children took turns using a one-gallon gas can for a chamber pot. Ijlik's wife flattened the wick on the oil lamp so it gave less light during the night, and after she had used the gas can herself, she placed it, contents and all, right under the noses of Ijlik and myself. He was already asleep and snored away, but I gasped for air from the sudden ammonia smell from the can. My eyes watered, while the entire room was filled with an aroma which reminded me of anything but perfume. But thanks to the reduced wick the air soon grew colder and that helped. Still, I could not go to sleep. Everything was quiet except for Ijlik's snoring. Then the dog and her pups started to sniff around in the dark, searching for remnants of the meal. Every so often the big dog pushed the can a little, and I was in constant fear that she would upset it.

Ijlik's wife hissed at them like a furious cat and the pups disappeared in the dark. Then it was quiet for a short while, but as soon as the dogs realized that the hissing was not going to do them any harm, they started the racket all over again. In desperation the woman threw everything she could lay her hands on after them. The pups yelped so that one would think they were being beaten to death, and then resumed their nocturnal activities.

This kept on all night. Tin mugs, plates and utensils flew through the air, while Ijlik happily snored away next to me completely unaware of the disturbances. I do not think he missed a beat of his snoring except that once in a while he turned over, gasped for air, and grunted. I managed, more or less by accident, to place my knee in his back a couple of times, but that did not do much to stop the snoring; he only wheezed and groaned through his moustache. And it was difficult enough for me to move my leg inside the sleeping-bag to get my knee into position. Towards morning I finally managed to doze off for a while, but awoke shortly after to find Ijlik's wife putting a huge piece of frozen, raw seal liver in my hand. The children too were awake and sat upright on the sleeping-platform, naked from the waist up, gnawing away at something.

The wife was fully dressed and was picking up the various items she had thrown at the dogs during the night. The dog and the pups were sleeping innocently in their niche in the wall.

The frozen liver I started to munch tasted good, a little bit like nuts. I was then served a big mug of tea with a liberal sprinkling of caribou hairs floating around. The mug was not my own and I had a few misgivings about it as I had watched Eskimo children on many previous occasions helping themselves to any container handy, relieving themselves and pouring the contents into the larger family can which was still sitting right under my nose. But I drank the tea, hair and all, while I promised myself that from then on I would carry my own mug whenever I spent the night in an igloo with children.

The piece of liver was not the only solid food we had for breakfast; it was meant only as an appetizer. The woman had bannock sizzling in hot fat in a pan, and even if it did taste a little bit flat without any salt, it was hot and really hit the spot together with more tea. To top it off we had cold meat left over from the previous day. All told we had a solid breakfast before we even got dressed.

Farrar, it turned out, had slept well all night, as there were neither children nor pups to disturb the peace in that igloo.

29 OLD AND NEW MEDICINE MEN

I am full of admiration for all the missionaries I met in the Arctic throughout the years, be they Anglican or Roman Catholic. Without exception, they were all good, hard-working people, able dog drivers, hunters and fishermen. The Eskimos of the old school had little use for white men who could not look after themselves. In fact, I met very few whites who were unable to do so, whether they were trappers or traders, policemen or missionaries. Some even exceeded the Eskimos in their own skills.

The missionaries also learned how to navigate in Arctic waters. During a visit to Herschel Island with *St. Roch* we anchored next to the Oblate Fathers' mission ship, *Our Lady of Lourdes*. Captain Pedersen had bought her in San Francisco and brought her in on the deck of *Patterson* a few years earlier. How Pedersen had managed to unload the boat at Herschel was beyond my comprehension, but then he was an old whaling skipper and was used to handling this sort of thing.

These Fathers were handy men. None of them had ever worked on a ship before, but they soon caught on. They hired the half-blood Eskimo Billy Thrasher as captain. His father had come from one of the Pacific Islands, and he was a born sailor—obviously an inheritance from the father he had never seen. He was also a great leader. The engineer was a German, Father Kraut, and the deck crew consisted of two other

Fathers, the Belgian Biname and an American from Texas, Griffin. Bishop Falaize acted as cook and extra deck hand.

When we met *Our Lady of Lourdes* everybody was busy carrying bags of coal on board, while the Eskimos directed the storing of the bags so that there would be room for as many as possible. The Eskimos on the island were still well off after the catch that winter and not the least bit interested in working, a least not on such a dirty job as loading coal. The result was that Father Kraut and two of the others were carrying the heavy bags while old Bishop Falaize followed hard on their heels in his worn cassock, also lugging a coal bag. He had just been consecrated Bishop and I suggested to him that perhaps he could take life a little bit easier now with his new rank and with age catching up with him. "It makes no difference whether I'm a Bishop or not," he answered, "I want to be a good example to the Eskimos and that means hard work without any consideration for one's own self."

Father Griffin, a husky young fellow, had been in the Arctic only a year. As an American and a Texan he stood out from the European Fathers and could easily have been taken for a policeman or a trapper. He was open and friendly and liked to talk. I asked him why he had entered the priesthood. To me he looked more like a heavyweight boxer. His answer was that he had, in fact, given some thought to becoming a boxer rather than a priest. But there had been eight brothers in his family and one of them, it was decided, was to become a priest. "So I ended up living in the Arctic carrying coal and living like the Eskimos," he said with a smile. In addition to being strong, he was also a smart fellow, and I would have been very happy to have had him as a member of my crew on *St. Roch*.

In the beginning I think the Eskimos were a little bit confused by all the different missionaries. It was far from clear to them what the missionaries had to offer or what they represented. I believe that the natives at first regarded the missionaries as a new kind of white medicine-men. They were used to their own medicine-men practising certain rituals on special occasions, so that was not at all new to them. But the different denominations had no meaning to the Eskimos, who in the beginning moved freely from one mission post to another and participated in the services everywhere. They sat fascinated by the music and full of awe as they watched the Roman Catholic priests conduct Mass with all its rituals. They were probably somewhat less impressed by the Anglican service, which seemed less mysterious. Sociable as the Eskimos are, they love to get together and sing, and the various mission posts offered wonderful opportunities for just that. But the missionaries could not expect the Eskimos to understand everything that was said and done or to be converted right away. That was to take years.

There is scarcely any doubt that the few remaining medicine-men, or angakkuqs, hated the missionaries and all they stood for. But with the invasion of the white men and all their technical wonders, the angakkuqs quickly lost their influence. However, there is a general belief that neither the Eskimos nor other primitive people could have survived without their medicine-men. The Eskimos, in particular, had no common leader and consequently the medicine-men assumed even more importance in their lives.

When the first white men arrived, they tried to make fun of the medicine-men and their role. No doubt the purpose of this was to further their own aims by securing the power and influence the medicine-men had held. This was simply done with the technical aids the white men had at their disposal and the old angakkuqs found it hard, if not impossible, to compete.

The old Alaska Eskimo Ikey Bolt, and Patsy Klengenberg and his brothers, told us that practically all the medicine-men they had known had been brilliant, able men and great leaders of their people. Often the angakkuq was also the best hunter of the group. With time they established many taboos and rules to live by for the good of the tribe, which regulated their way of life. Take, for instance, the question of game preservation. They made it taboo for the Eskimos to hunt caribou in the wintertime. Nor was it permissible to eat caribou meat when the tribe was camped on the ice. This was the right time of the year to hunt seals in their breathing-holes. At that time the Eskimos had only bows and arrows, so they were unable to hunt seal anywhere else but on the ice. The Coronation Gulf, or Coppermine, Eskimos were unfamiliar with the big kayaks or skin boats their kin in Alaska and the eastern Arctic used. The caribou became skinny and poorly in the winter and did not offer much food anyway, but the seal was practically swimming in his own fat just then. It was therefore only natural that it was the seal that should provide the Eskimos with fuel, light and food, as well as footwear and summer tents and clothing. Patsy Klengenberg often stressed that the taboos and rules made by the medicine-men served the same purpose as our game regulations and other restrictions which govern our daily lives. The natural instincts of the angakkuqs when it came to game preservation and the taboos they had enforced for generations were more effective than the best modern legislation for the Arctic. Today the game has almost disappeared as the result of the introduction of fire-arms and the fact that the taboos no longer are respected.

Patsy told us that when the first whites came to Victoria Island the Eskimos had not bothered to hunt for the white fox. The fur could not be used for clothing and the meat was eaten only occasionally. When the first trading post was established on the island it was possible to shoot caribou in the wintertime right from the door of a cabin. But the Eskimos wanted none of this, not until the white people managed to convince them that the taboos of the medicine-men had no meaning at all. To prove their point, the whites shot the caribou in front of the eyes of the Eskimo and left the carcasses out as bait for the white fox, which they then could catch at will in full daylight. All they had to do was to set out their traps.

The Eskimos became anxious to obtain things such as knives, saws, files, matches, tea and food. In the beginning this was all they required and they paid no attention to the rifles. This all changed when the whites systematically started to buy up all their bows and arrows and offered them guns and ammunition in exchange for furs. Once the white man had succeeded in breaking down the taboos, the wholesale slaughter of the game started in earnest.

Many of the older Eskimos who attended the services at the missions continued their ancient rituals during the seal hunt. After they had killed a seal they offered their thanks to the Goddess of the Ocean, Nuliujuq. The killed seal was pulled away from the hole a little bit and the fortunate hunter cut a slit in its stomach and pulled out the liver. All the hunters near by then assembled around the seal, and each was given a piece of the liver, which he swallowed with great awe while he gave thanks to Nuliujuq for the gift. In a way I believe that this ritual, which is found among many people, has much the same meaning as Communion has for Christians.

This all took place in the 1930's, which represented the very last round for the medicine-men of the old school. One of the last of the old breed, Komayak, then lived at Coppermine. It was known that perhaps he had not been one of the greatest of angakkuqs, but still, he had at one time held an exalted and important position among his own people. But the missionaries, the doctor, the weather-station people and the many white trappers who came to the district quickly undermined his influence. One day Komayak came to visit us on *St. Roch*. He was all by himself and a sad sight, badly dressed and with only a few skinny dogs. There were rumours that he had killed his wife, but this was never proved and I do not believe it. He had little contact with the missionaries and Doctor Margin, who had been there for two years. In a way, I suppose, they were old Komayak's competitors and much stronger than he was with all the resources they had behind them. We treated him with the respect that we accorded all Eskimos who visited us. We fed his dogs all they could eat and he himself ate with us and smoked our tobacco whenever he felt like it. Our own "medicine-man," old Dad Parry, fussed over Komayak just as he did with all our other visitors. No matter what they said in Coppermine, the old man was very honest with us. He went all the way to our winter quarters at Tree River to return a thermos bottle I had lost from my sled a few miles outside Coppermine. He showed up with it several weeks after he had found it and this proved, at least to me, that he could not be so bad after all. He was only an old Eskimo from an age gone by, not quite willing to admit that a new era had come—an old, lonely man, often laughed at and bullied, even by his own people.

The fate of old Mannirakkssak, the last medicine-man at Cambridge Bay, is perhaps the best illustration of how the new era finished the angakkuqs. The various diseases of the white man proved to be too much for the medicine-men. Most feared was measles. When Cambridge Bay was hit by an epidemic, many Eskimos hovered between life and death. Thanks to a tremendous job by a former nurse, who was married to the Hudson's Bay man, Frank Milne, only one Eskimo died: the old medicine-man Mannirakkssak.

In his later years he had been forced to abandon hunting, and when his former prestige was gone, he and his wife were reduced to cleaning skins for the Canalaska Company. Before he died, he mentioned the spot where he wanted to be laid to rest. It was on top of a hill, and from there he would be able to look round and watch the changing of the seasons —the last sundown before the dark of the winter descended, the first ray of sunshine on the horizon with message of spring after its long absence. The sun had much meaning to the older Eskimos.

We made up a rough coffin of some lumber we had, and the trading post supplied some canvas to line it with. Then we carried old Mannirakkssak to his last resting place on the hill with a view of the fiord. Many Eskimos participated in the burial, and a few of his most precious possessions were placed on top of the coffin, the way he would have wanted it. Though we would call him a heathen, at least he had been a good heathen, the last from an era now almost forgotten.

30 SOUTHERN INTERLUDE AND MARRIAGE

Break-up came exceptionally late in 1934, and we were unable to get under way before July 20. After brief stops at Baillie and Herschel islands we headed south and docked in Vancouver on October 12 after more than four years in the Arctic.

It seemed strange to be back in a city again and to be faced with a civilized environment. I must admit that I found it rather difficult to adjust to traffic in the streets and, having used only mukluks for four years, I found regular shoes or boots awkward.

That winter turned out to be quite different from those we had spent in the North. Only the engineer, Kells, and I remained on board at Esquimalt, and even though we had more than enough to do, life was almost a continuous holiday in comparison with the harsh conditions we were used to. We were often invited to dances, and for the first time in my life I developed a liking for that type of recreation. Dad Parry, who had gone home to Wales on leave, decided to get married while he was there, and I think it was that staid bachelor's decision that got the ball rolling. One after another of the crew members from the *St. Roch* took the same step. At the time the regulations said that a Mounted Policeman had to have at least seven years of service and be able to prove that he was free of debt before he could get married. I still feel this was a good regulation. Its main purpose was not to keep the young constables from getting married, but to retain the mobility of the force. Later the required length of service was reduced to five years, and now it is two.

It turned out that even I was vulnerable. Shortly before we went north in 1930, I met a young girl by the name of Mary Hargreaves, and we kept up a fairly regular correspondence. When I returned south I proposed and, to my great amazement, the answer was yes. The great day was set for February 7, 1935. I was then a sergeant with many friends in the Force and it was decided that it would be a military wedding. An old friend of mine, Sergeant-Major Watson, was to be best man and look after all the arrangements. Having been in the Mounted Police for years, he was quite familiar with the necessary protocol and knew exactly how things should be done.

Watson assured me that all was well in hand and that I should stop fretting: he would get me to the church on time. That was my greatest worry, I remember. Naturally, I had also given a great deal of thought to whether I was doing the right thing. I was used to a free, independent life and knew that, married or not, I had to return to the North. My fiancée and I, of course, had discussed this in detail and she knew that the Arctic had no facilities for white women at the time. At best I would be able to visit her in the South for brief periods. But this didn't seem to scare her off and I, at least, have never had reason to regret that I married this fine person.

While Sergeant-Major Watson faithfully got everything in order, I remained at Esquimalt until the day of the wedding. When the big day came around and I tried on the new uniform I had ordered I found that the trousers didn't fit, being much too long. I was very upset, for the tailor shop was closed, but fortunately the tailor told us to bring the pants around to his house and promised to have them ready in time. The pants were sent off, but when the time came for me to pick them up the wedding day nearly ended in disaster. Unfamiliar as I was with the residential part of Vancouver, I couldn't find the tailor's house. Constable Scott Alexander, a young fellow who was stationed in Victoria and was going to join the *St. Roch*, acted as my guide as we set out in my newly-acquired automobile. Scott's knowledge of Vancouver turned out to be as scanty as my own, however, and we were able to retrieve the missing pants barely in time for the ceremony.

When we finally got to the First Baptist Church, the bride, Watson and the usher had already arrived. Finally, to my great relief, the ceremony was over, and as we came out of the church we were met by a Guard of Honour composed of my colleagues, in full dress uniform, forming an arch with their lances. We then repaired to the Hotel Georgia for the reception, where Mary and I cut an enormous wedding cake prepared by Mary and decorated by the police baker. Sergeant-Major Watson had again come to the rescue and provided the sword required by tradition.

A few days after the wedding I received orders to proceed to Ottawa to discuss the future northern operations of the *St. Roch.* This was perfect, as I had some six weeks of leave coming to me, and I decided to bring Mary along and make a honeymoon out of it. Neither of us had ever been east before.

In Ottawa we were met by my old friend Anderton, who was then a sergeant-major at the Rockcliffe Training Station. There I also met Inspector Vernon Kemp, whom I had met on Herschel Island on my first voyage to the North.

For several days I was involved in a series of talks on the North and our future duties there. Most of these discussions were with the then Commissioner of the Royal Canadian Mounted Police, Sir James MacBrien, and the Officer Commanding "G" Division, Superintendent Pete Irving. Little did I dream then that some years later I would become O.C. of that Division and remain in that post longer than any of my predecessors.

Mary and I stayed with Anderton and his wife Edna and enjoyed hearing all about life in the Force in the nation's capital. Anderton, as usual, ran a good show and took us around to see all the horses and the many sled dogs used for training the policemen in travelling by dog team. Mary, who had never seen sled dogs, was anxious to get a ride, so Anderton obliged by having a young constable, Gifford Moore, take her out on a little trip.

It was a crisp, cold day with lots of snow and the trails around Rockcliffe were in perfect shape. The sled they used was a small thing, rather like a racing sled, with handlebars for the driver to hang on to as he stood on the back of the runners. My new bride was decked out in a police buffalo coat and was in high spirits as the frisky team of eleven dogs took off with Anderton's admonitions to the constable to look out for trucks and cars.

Anderton and I decided to try two of the horses and after some twenty minutes or so we were surprised to see the dogs racing towards us in a cloud of snow, trailing an empty sled. Like a flash of lightning they disappeared in the general direction of the barracks while Anderton muttered all kinds of curses as we galloped in the opposite direction. In a few minutes we met a truck, and who should be riding up front with the driver but Mary. The unfortunate constable got the dressing-down of his life for losing his team when he finally returned, on foot, to the barracks. He was full of apologies as he explained how he had lost his grip on the handlebars during a sudden burst of speed with the result that he fell off the runners. As soon as the dogs realized that the sled was considerably lighter they increased speed; Mary, of course, screamed at them to stop, which only made them run even faster. Eventually the sled bumped into a snowbank, in which Constable Moore found Mary. He had in the meantime stopped a truck and come back looking for the runaway team. It could have been serious, although luckily everything turned out all right in the end, but poor Constable Moore was in for a good deal of ribbing from his fellow policemen.

Another lasting memory from our Ottawa visit was the Annual Headquarters Ball. It was a glittering affair with government officials and senior officers of the armed forces in full-dress uniforms. Not having my uniform with me, I had to go out and rent the necessary formal wear; and for the first time in my life found myself in tails and hard-boiled shirt. To say that I was uncomfortable is an understatement as I hopped around the dance floor very self-conscious about my poor footwork. I would greatly have preferred to have been on a pair of snowshoes instead, hunting somewhere with my Eskimo friends.

We had a table with Anderton and his wife and a couple of other friends, when the Commissioner, Sir James, came over and asked to be introduced to the newest "recruit," Mary. Having led her in a dance, he wished her good luck as a member of the Force, as he put it.

When Mary and I finally headed back west we both had some wonderful memories, and for me the discussions had been very fruitful. We were equally impressed by our return trip across this vast country, the seemingly endless prairies and then the mountains before we reached Victoria where the roses and daffodils were in full bloom. It was still early March and the rest of the country was covered in snow. Victoria, without doubt, must be the most beautiful city in Canada and we were indeed happy to make it our home for many years, even if I myself spent the larger part of that time in the North.

Mary and I took a small apartment when we arrived and I became a shore-dweller for the first time in many years, with the exception of a few months I had spent in the police barracks in Vancouver when I first joined the Force.

31 FOURTH VOYAGE TO THE NORTH

I soon got used to married life and settled into a routine. Every day I went down to the dockyard to see how the work progressed on the *St. Roch*. In order to make it easier to navigate in the ice I had an extension fitted from the steering-wheel side in the pilot-house to a steering wheel on top of it. We also installed a compass and an engine-room telegraph, which was to mean a great deal. Until then all signals to the engine room had been given by means of bells only, and this could easily lead to confusion in critical situations.

Our new, open wheel-house was used extensively in the years to come on all our voyages and in all kinds of weather. Some other improvements also turned out to be of great use.

While the work went on through the winter I got to know Constable Scott Alexander better. He had been the helpful guide when I was searching for my trousers on my wedding day, and I soon learned that he was utterly fed up with his monotonous guard duty at the naval dockyards. Here, I felt, was the right type of man for our crew. Alexander had been born on one of the islands close to Vancouver and was an excellent sailor, having spent almost his entire boyhood in small boats. He was also an expert handler of canoes and had distinguished himself in a canoe race across the Juan de Fuca Strait from Victoria to Port Angeles, Washington.

As soon as I suggested that he should apply for a transfer to our detachment, he was all for it. Early that spring his application was approved and Scott Alexander joined Kells and me as replacement for our Second Engineer Jack Foster, who had decided not to come with us on our next trip. Alexander was then around twenty-three years old.

Another fellow I also had my eyes on was Constable Frank Willan, who had served briefly on an oil tanker before he joined the Force. After a couple of years as policeman he had transferred to the newly-formed Marine Section and had been posted aboard the *Adversus*, the RCMP cruiser. In due course he also joined our crew which, strangely enough, was a regular land force operation, a floating Arctic detachment with the same rules and regulations and uniforms as other members on shore duty. All crew members had to be regular policemen —a fact that seemed to amuse the Navy people we met. Even the *Adversus* crew, who wore navy uniforms, laughed at us and called us "horse-sailors." And yet we went to sea for far longer periods than they ever did, as their duties consisted primarily of Customs prevention.

The *St. Roch* sailed to Vancouver on June 5 to take on supplies for us and for the Arctic detachments we were to visit. We also were to take on coal and fuel oil to last us for two years. However, when we arrived, we found that the entire Vancouver waterfront was deeply involved in the worst strike of its history. All the longshoremen were on strike, and other dock workers soon followed in sympathy. The piers were full of ships waiting for cargoes of lumber and grain. There were police patrols everywhere, and some of the strikers had even taken over some public buildings such as the post office and the railroad station. In the beginning the sit-down strike, as it was called, went off in an orderly fashion, and I felt that the strikers had the sympathy of a good many people. But then the whole atmosphere changed. Trouble-makers started to arrive from out of town, and soon there were serious disturbances and vandalism all over the place. The Mounted Police, which of course is a federal force, was called finally to assist the city and provincial police forces, and RCMP *Adversus* was patrolling the harbour.

We were moored at our usual berth for loading, the Evans, Colman and Evans Wharf, right in the heart of the city with no longshoremen available, so we did our own loading with some help from the younger recruits from the Fairmont Barracks. Fortunately our load of coal came in sacks and it was good exercise for the crew to carry the sixty tons of coal. The policemen went to it cheerfully, and the many longshoremen who were loitering on the wharf watched us intently, some of them even complimenting us on our efficiency. We knew many of these men who had helped us load before, and were very pleased that some of them even presented us with their cargo hooks as a token of goodwill and friendship. This happened at the very time when other strikers in other locations were engaged in bloody battles with our own colleagues. When we finally were ready to leave, some strikers came up to us to shake hands and wish us a safe journey, quite in contrast to the many newspaper stories of waterfront battles and police brutality.

It was early in the morning of June 25 that we said good-bye to our friends and relatives. I found it very strange to have someone close to say good-bye to. I had been a bachelor and wanderer for so long that I had become used to taking off at any time, regardless of where I was heading for. As a newly-wed I was, of course, a bit sorry to take off on a voyage that would last at least two years, but I knew that my duties were in the North for the time being.

As usual it was quite a race to see who would get to Herschel Island first in the season, but this time we met the *Patterson* at Point Barrow, and realized that we had no chance of beating her. She was twice as big as the *St. Roch* and could do twice the speed. Until we reached Point Barrow we hadn't seen any sign of ice, but as the two ships rounded the point together we were faced with so much ice ahead of us, that we could almost believe that it was a floating continent drifting with the wind and the current. We managed to get into very shallow water, although neither ship had any business being there. In such close-packed ice both the ships and their crews could easily be endangered, but the temptation was too great, particularly as we were now two ships together. But it was not long before the *Patterson* became stuck between two ice-floes, which began to press against her sides so that she shook and trembled. With her heavy load and straight sides and a conventional bottom, the *Patterson* was unable to lift with the pressure. We, however, were still afloat in a small pool of open water right behind the *Patterson*, so we were able to back up a couple of hundred yards and then charge ahead, hitting the ice only a few yards away from the other ship's starboard side. We kept this up for about half an hour, chipping off a few chunks of ice at a time, while the *Patterson* at the same time went full ahead, working her rudder hard over from one side to another. With joint efforts, we finally managed to get our friend freed, but shortly after it was our turn, and Captain Pedersen repaid the courtesy. In this way, we helped each other alternately, but then our old clutch equipment became overheated and we had to shut down for a while to let it cool off while the *Patterson*, which had a direct reversible engine, was able to continue and soon was out of sight.

It turned out that it was an unusually bad year for ice, so we managed to advance only a few ship's-lengths at a time. Quite often we were forced to use small charges of black powder to relieve the

The St. Roch *stopped in Franklin Strait, Northwest Passage. August, 1942.*

The St. Roch *in drydock.*

Larsen on the St. Roch *1948.*

The General Gordon.

Larsen at 21 in the Royal Norwegian Navy.

The St. Roch *on her trial voyage, 1928.*

The St. Roch *nearing Vancouver on her last triumphal voyage, October, 1954.*

The St. Roch *and the icebreaker* Labrador, *the ship which followed her.*

The St. Roch's *crew, 1930. Standing (*l. *to* r.*): Foster, Anderton, Farrar, Larsen, Parry. Sitting (*l. *to* r.*): Jones and two Eskimos.*

Tree River, 1931. From l. *to* r.*: Duke, Peter, Brandt, Fritz, Jack Lickert, Larsen.*

The St. Roch's *first Spring in the North.*

Taking on fresh water.

From l. to r.: Bob Kells, Larsen, Jack Foster.

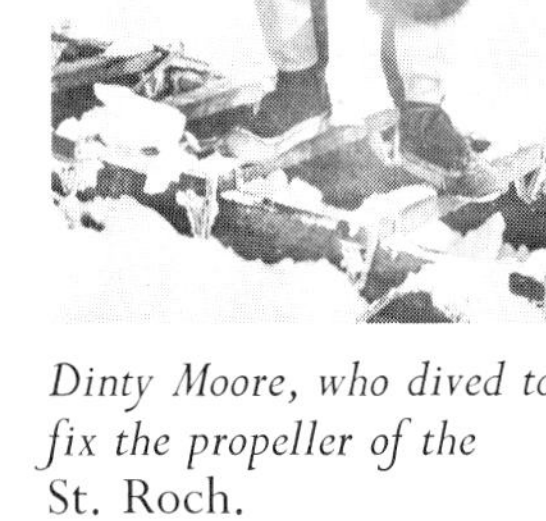

Dinty Moore, who dived to fix the propeller of the St. Roch.

Arreak, the boy who did soapstone sculpture of Larsen, and Kudloo look for a clear stretch of snow travel. (Clyde-Pond Inlet patrol.)

Anguyok, the old hunter from Perry River.

"Scotty" McClelland with Chartrand.

*Larsen and Klengenberg,
Vancouver, 1928.*

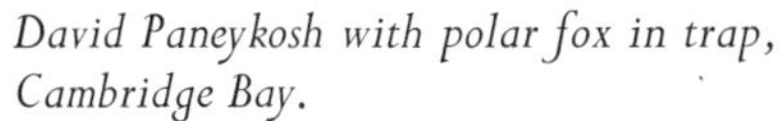

*David Paneykosh with polar fox in trap,
Cambridge Bay.*

*Eskimos in old-style clothing.
Victoria Island, 1924.*

Overnight igloo, made on the patrol from Clyde to Pond Inlet 1952. Photo taken in moonlight. Light from candles inside shows through cracks in the igloo.

On the right, Neokak's wife, who cleaned the tea cup in her own way.

Ready to take off.

Fritz Shurer's funeral, Tree River.

Walrus on the St. Roch.

Eskimo with walrus.

Larsen, in early Arctic garb.

Midnight sun at Coppermine.

Herschel Island detachment. The St. Roch *in winter quarters, 1948.*

Princess Royal Island, as seen from Prince of Wales Strait. (Believed to be the first picture taken of this island.)

Stone house built by Father Henry, Pelly Bay.

Cairn built by Larsen at Walker Bay in 1941. Here Commander Collinson wintered with HMS Enterprise, 1851-52, while searching for Franklin.

Franklin monument on Beechey Island. From l. to r. Cpl. Peters, Stan McKenzie and Ole Andreassen.

Kellet's Cache, Daly Island. Built in 1852.

Larsen and Cpl. Burton at Franklin's Cairn, Victory Point. August 17, 1949.

The Old Maid *drifting in icepack at 72° N. Photo by Larsen, 1926.*

The Maud, *sinking. Carl's Bay 1932.*

The St. James *goes down, August 1937.*

Stefansson and Larsen in Hanover, N.H., 1962, while making National Film Board movie, shortly before Stefansson's death.

A soapstone carving of Larsen, done by 16-year old Arreak in 1944.

Larsen and young admirer, Erik Sheer, Ottawa 1963.

pressure on the ship. Scott Alexander and I acted as bombardiers. The charges were made up of about five pounds of black powder in a bottle, made watertight with Sunlight soap. We then inserted a fuse in the top and tied the bottle to a long pole. At the Naval Dockyards I had obtained a dozen or so long rods used for cleaning the large naval guns and, being fifteen to twenty feet long, they were ideal for our purpose. Before we lit the fuse, we had to find a suitable opening between the ice-floes so the charge could be shoved down in such a way that it would explode a few feet below the ice. The sudden heave of the water then would lift the ice and crack it. It was imperative that the fuse be only a few inches long because the current often moved the charge or the ice out of position and there was a danger that the charge could be carried under the ship and explode there. Once the pole came rushing back up through the hole where I had pushed it down. By our count it was almost ready to explode next to where Scott and I were standing. There was nothing else for me to do but to grab the pole and push it back down as far as I could and keep it down until it exploded. I was showered with water and small chunks of ice, and it gave me an uncomfortable feeling to see the red flame through the ice under me.

The ice was extremely dirty that year—almost black, and covered with heavy layers of silt and mud which probably had been blown out from land during the winter. The ice-floes, which seemed very old and rotten at first, turned out to be completely blue and hard as rock. The dark colour of the ice made it difficult to distinguish between leads of open water and ice. What looked like water often turned out to be huge areas of black ice. All this, combined with wet drizzle and fog, made 1935-36 perhaps the worst navigational season I ever experienced in the North. At times we merely drifted along helplessly without any water in sight.

The Arctic pack ice along the coast in this area never really breaks up completely. Around the perimeter of the pack there is an endless breaking away of huge ice-floes, which then break into many smaller ones that are pushed back on top of the pack. In this way floe is piled on floe so that finally there are ridges up to one hundred feet in thickness. When these ridges run aground in shallow water and are exposed to a constant pressure from the ice pack, they are pushed closer and closer to the shore. They helped us a great deal, providing protection against the pack ice as it came floating in. But it was important to get inside these ridges at the right time and in the right places to have sufficient water for sailing.

As there are no glaciers in the western Arctic Islands one never sees there anything like the tremendously awe-inspiring icebergs produced by the eastern Arctic glaciers. On the other hand, the east has no ice pack which could even remotely compare with that in the west. As a rule the ice is a dirty white on top and a vivid blue-white or green below the water line. These colours are unforgettable, particularly against a background of the crystal-clear, blue depths of the Arctic Ocean, which changes constantly, depending on the light conditions. The countless facets of ice colours glow like diamonds in the purest blue-white. Nine-tenths of the ice is below water level; the ice is therefore the greatest obstacle in the summer. It became almost indispensable during the winter, when we made long sled trips on it. The Eskimos have made their homes on the winter ice and have found their food, fuel, clothing and other necessities there for countless generations.

Blue ice, floating for miles around on a calm sea during a sunny summer day is perhaps the most beautiful sight Nature has to offer. But on a stormy day this same blue ice is an entirely different thing, overpowering as it thunders and crashes down on the ship, with the larger and stronger ice-floes crushing the smaller ones. At times the ice formations take the oddest shapes: towering cathedrals with magnificent spires, battleships, bears or dancing girls. I never tired of watching the ice in the Arctic twilight, whether I was fighting it or not. Through my many years in the North the ice became both an enemy and a friend and companion. During the countless long hours I spent in the crow's-nest, I got the feeling that I had constantly to match wits with the moving pack ice. Many a time did I head for an opening in the ice only to watch it crash together just ahead of me, as if it were a living thing deliberately trying to keep me from reaching open water. On other occasions the ice would snap shut behind me, as if it held me in a trap. But it also happened that when things looked hopeless and I was almost resigned to giving up, the ice would suddenly open up as if by some magical force, and as the bell rang for full speed ahead the leads would gradually get wider and wider and allow us to slide through the cracks for mile after mile.

It was the captain's job practically to live in the crow's-nest in those days, for we had neither ice reconnaissance nor other reports, and the binoculars were in constant use. As a result of this and the glare from the ice, captains ended up with a permanent squint after a few years. Our crow's-nest, by the way, was a narrow cylindrical one with barely room for a man to stand upright. Not being able to sit down, however, had its advantages. In this way, one was sure to remain standing even if one fell asleep from sheer exhaustion.

When we finally arrived at Herschel Island, having used almost fifty pounds of powder to blast our way there, we learned that Captain Pedersen and the *Patterson* had arrived only a few days ahead of us. We also learned that Inspector Rivett-Carnac had arrived to turn over the command of the detachment to Inspector George Curleigh.

As the police post on Baillie Island was in danger of being washed away by the sea, we headed east to Maitland Island to pick a suitable location for a new post. In addition to Inspector Curleigh and his young bride, we also had another passenger with us, a trapper famous throughout the Arctic, old Jaky. One of the many stories about Jaky was that during his first year in the Arctic he had suffered from hemorrhoids, a common enough affliction in the North. Baillie Island being the nearest community, that was where he went to get some help. He approached the local Hudson's Bay man Swoger Hendriksen, who was known for his practical jokes. Poor Jaky had a very painful trip to Baillie Island, but was gratified to hear that Swoger had "just the thing" for his problem. He poured a pint of colourless liquid into a bottle and gave it to Jaky with instructions to go back to his own camp and pour the entire content into a wash basin and then to sit in this as long as possible. He guaranteed the treatment, but failed to add a warning that the "medicine" was pure turpentine. Jaky followed the instructions to the letter and old-timers claim that he spent the next week sitting in a snowdrift trying to cool off his posterior, armed with a shotgun ready to shoot the first person on sight.

Almost a month to the day after our arrival at Herschel we went to Bernard Harbour for a brief rest, having transferred from Herschel to Maitland Point all the equipment that was required for the new post. Our next stop was Coppermine, where we had a great reunion with Constable "Frenchy" Chartrand, the Roman Catholic missionaries Delalande, Buliard Tesniere and Boschaffer, and not the least with the Anglican canon, Harold Webster. The weather was beautiful and warm while we took on fresh water and Scott Alexander, dressed only in a pair of long-johns and with his chestful of red hair, put on a demonstration of the Australian crawl. No wonder he made quite an impression on the Eskimos, who had never seen such a sight in the water before. Scott, who could swim like a fish, was the hero of the day, partly, I suppose, because very few if any Eskimos know how to swim. When he finally came back out of the water, he had goose-pimples all over and this, of course, was an added attraction. He also had a glass eye with him which he pretended to remove and put back in. The Eskimos had seen white men with dentures, but never had they seen a removable eye. It was a good thing that the days of the medicine-men were over, or Scott would have been a dangerous competitor.

We then left a cache of dog food on Wilmot Island together with other supplies we planned to use later in the winter on patrols. These patrols were often quite lengthy and didn't always deal strictly with police business. As a matter of fact, our police duties were the least of our problems. If we met sick or needy Eskimos we had to look after them, and when their children were off to one of the two mission schools at Aklavik, it was our job to get them there and make all the necessary arrangements. We also had to keep track of the animals killed, including caribou, Arctic hares, foxes, bears and wolves. The wolf hides had to be marked and the bounty paid. A clear sign that civilization had started to make its mark was that we received the odd hide of a dog from an Eskimo in the hope that we would pay wolf bounty for it. At times it is difficult to tell dog's hide from a wolf's, and I am sure that the Eskimos picked up that trick from their more enlightened white brethren who were trapping in the area.

32 MARITAL COMPLICATIONS AMONG THE ESKIMOS

Early in the morning of September 13, 1935, we saw the Hudson's Bay flag at Cambridge Bay. It was flying from an old flagstaff which once had served as foremast on the explorer Amundsen's ship *Maud*. The rest of the ship lay on her side near the shore, looking like a stranded whale.

The first visitors on board the *St. Roch* were Constable Alec MacKenzie and Special Constable Malik, a fine-looking Eskimo. I suppose MacKenzie was anything but happy to see us, as it meant that he now had to move in with us and live in our cramped quarters instead of on land. It had been decided to close down the land-based post for the duration of *St. Roch's* two-year stay there. All told, the white population numbered eight, including the Hudson's Bay manager Frank Milne and his wife Alice. With our arrival this number was doubled.

Cambridge Bay, one of the best fur areas in the Arctic, had a large Eskimo population. About two hundred Eskimos were trading in furs at Cambridge Bay, and as they were good trappers and hunters, the competition between the two trading posts was sharp. Frank Milne and the Canalaska Fur Company's man Ernest Pasley had the best Eskimos pretty evenly divided. As policemen we were naturally neutral and were always welcomed by both.

Shortly after our arrival we were informed that an Eskimo was suspected of murder and that his wife was being kept in custody by the local detachment. Constable MacKenzie gave us all the details of a report the detachment had received about a man being shot and killed during the summer of 1934. The constable had then set out the following spring for Sherman Inlet in order to investigate this further.

The suspect was a young Eskimo called Kujuluu, who had openly confessed that he had killed Quppa, an elderly Eskimo with whom the young man had been staying. Quppa's wife, Sivuraq, and her mother, Ilveak, made up the rest of the household. This arrangement had lasted for a number of years. Kujuluu assured Constable MacKenzie that although he liked Quppa and had had no intention of killing him or of taking over his wife, he finally had given in after Sivuraq had kept after him constantly. She was much younger than her husband, and was a lazy foul-mouthed woman, which was rather rare among the Eskimo women. Quppa therefore frequently had to give her a beating and Sivuraq had started to make eyes at young Kujuluu. In the beginning, he had ignored the woman's pleas that he should shoot her husband, and finally had packed up and left. But being on his own like that he had been unable to find a family he could join, so in the end he had returned to Quppa's family, and then in the spring they had all left for the interior to hunt caribou and fish in the inland lakes.

On the fateful day Quppa, Sivuraq and Kujuluu had left their little camp to look for caribou. Quppa had finally managed to get within firing distance of an animal, but the shot only wounded the caribou and it jumped into a lake. The second shot finished off the animal and Quppa then removed his footwear, pants and parka and waded out into the water, dressed only in his shirt. When the water reached his armpits, Sivuraq started to dare Kujuluu. "Shoot him now," she insisted. "You can't miss him now, and he can't hurt you. Hurry, shoot!"

Kujuluu became utterly confused and finally took aim and fired, with out really knowing what he was doing. He left both Quppa and the caribou in the water and returned to the camp with Sivuraq, without even getting close to his victim.

Kujuluu insisted that he hadn't shot Quppa to get his wife. I must say that she wasn't too inviting—a big, unkempt woman, downright ugly. The Eskimos at Cambridge Bay wanted no part of this couple while they were in custody. Part of the reason for this was perhaps jealousy, because they felt it was unfair that these two now would get all the food, fuel and free quarters from the police only because they had killed a man. The couple had a young baby, a little girl, but nobody knew who the father was. The child was in poor health and for some reason or other couldn't be breast-fed. Sivuraq didn't bother with the child, and if it hadn't been for Alice Milne, who looked after the girl, she surely would have died.

Special Constable Malik was a young Eskimo who had worked for the police for years. He had visited us a number of times while we were at Tree River and had been an excellent guide on many of our trips. We also appreciated his skills as an igloo-builder. He was short and squarely built with strong, white teeth, a good-looking fellow. His wife, Shorty, was heavily built even for an Eskimo woman and was considerably older than Malik. She had been married before. They lived in a little wooden hut near the police detachment. We now learned that Malik no longer seemed too keen on going out on long trips. The reason was another Eskimo, Sam, who had come from the western Arctic, and now was a steady visitor to Shorty when Malik was away. This didn't go over too well with Malik, who was far from being as generous as Eskimos are supposed to be in this respect. Sam had many points in his favour. He had had several years' schooling, spoke fluent English and associated freely with all the whites. His features indicated a fair amount of Indian blood, and this too proved irresistible to Shorty.

Finally Malik came up with an ultimatum. Shorty either stayed with him, or left for Sam's place. If, however, she picked Sam, Malik would commit suicide, he said. The choice was a difficult one for Shorty. With Malik, she knew she had a nice little home, plenty of fuel and food rations from the police. The future certainly would be more of a gamble with Sam, but then Shorty wasn't altogether convinced that Malik's threat was a serious one. So in the end, she indicated to Malik that if that was the way he felt about things, why didn't he go and shoot himself, if he was man enough to carry out his threat.

Malik marched straight into his little hut, and shortly after a shot rang out. Shorty, Sam and a policeman ran in and found Malik on his back with a big hole in his parka. He was obviously dead. Shorty threw herself on the body with a scream and kept repeating again and again the few English words she knew: "Malik why you do? Malik why you do?"

In the meantime the two others rolled the "body" over on its side. When they couldn't see any blood they became suspicious, and on closer examination Malik was found to be very much alive. He had removed his parka, fired a shot through it and pulled it on again. The policeman heaved a sigh of relief, but Sam left immediately in search of better "hunting grounds," since Shorty had become convinced that it was Malik she loved. Later on, by the way, Sam did find himself a beautiful Eskimo girl and they were married in an official ceremony by Pastor Rockeby-Thomas. We all attended the wedding and the Eskimos who were present were so impressed by the ritual that both young and old alike, among them even some grandparents, decided to get a Christian wedding at the same time. Among the bridal couples were Shorty and Malik.

Until then marriages had been pre-arranged by the families when the children were small. It even happened that a family with a son would adopt a little girl, so that there would be a wife for him when he grew up. If it was difficult to get girls, a good hunter could perhaps buy one. As we have seen, it also happened that men killed to get a wife, and a great hunter frequently had two wives. Sometimes a woman would have two husbands and all three would live happily together. The Eskimo way of marriage also had the advantage that if a couple fell out with each other, the husband could simply trade the wife and get himself another without any loss of prestige or social status. At times such a trade was for only a short period of time, but it could also be a more permanent arrangement.

Now all this belongs to the past. As the various churches became entrenched in the North, wife-trading disappeared. The women, admittedly, became more independent as a result of this change, but they also became more quarrelsome. Now a wife knew that her husband couldn't get rid of her as easily and get another one, at least not officially. Wife-trading did not disappear altogether, of course, but continued in secret. I, for one, feel that this contributed directly to the increasingly loose morals among Eskimo women, including the unmarried ones.

When an Eskimo couple wants to dissolve their marriage now, they must go through the entire procedure with judge and jury, often to their own great consternation. Some of my old Eskimo friends have been through this ordeal, and I often wonder for what good. Had they maintained their old marriage customs, perhaps it would have been possible to patch things up again. Through the years I have met many Eskimo couples who lived together with loyalty and devotion, sharing days of plenty and starvation with a friendship and a love that I doubt any marriage rituals could have improved upon.

During my years in the Arctic I often felt that it really was a crime that these children of Nature couldn't have been left alone to live their lives according to the customs and rules their forefathers had followed through generations. When the white man arrived with his ideas of right and wrong he changed, by force, in a way, the lives of these innocent and gullible people, who always did their utmost to please the white man and follow his rules, even to the point where they were the losers.

33 AN EVENTFUL WINTER

Marital complications apart, this became a busy winter for us. We were new to Cambridge Bay and had to get enough fish for ourselves and the dogs. Fortunately there were plenty of fish around and we went to it. In the meantime our radio operator, Tommy Welsh, rigged up his equipment and soon established contact with other police detachments.

About this time, we noticed the first indications of the measles among the Eskimos. Earlier, during the summer, there had been a few cases elsewhere. As a rule measles was fatal to the Eskimos, particularly if there was no medical assistance to be had.

Little June, the daughter of Canalaska's man Ernest Pasley, was the first to come down with the measles at Cambridge Bay. In late October it was Pastor Rockeby-Thomas's turn, followed by his Eskimo helper.

Fortunately for the little group Mrs. Frank Milne was an experienced nurse. She mothered the sick day and night. Oddly enough, even the strongest among the Eskimos had little or no resistance to the diseases they were unfamiliar with. Somehow they gave up easily and died. When Eskimos started to run a high temperature, they often stripped to the skin and sat outside their igloos to cool off. Mothers took their perspiring children out in the raw, cold air, and pneumonia and death followed quickly. It was difficult for us to make them understand how dangerous this practice was.

On an inspection trip to Warrender Bay we found that a well-off Eskimo, Ambrose, his wife and three children had succumbed to the measles. The only survivor was a thirteen-year-old daughter, Lena, who had managed to stay alive for two weeks, surrounded by her dead family. Scott Alexander and I also examined a little Eskimo baby who had died from intestinal worms. In the little igloo were a dog with five pups, two babies and their mother and an older dying child who cried all the time. There were also six grown-ups, who stood around the child, unable to do anything. She coughed and spat without pause, and was indeed a pathetic sight.

The little girl died the next day and we buried her in a small wooden coffin. In those days there was no medical service in the western Arctic, and only the most severe cases of tuberculosis were taken on the *St. Roch* to a small hospital at Aklavik.

The white people did not, in the beginning, interfere with Eskimo burials. There were no cemeteries as we know them, because the Eskimos themselves used to pick the site where they wanted to be buried and friends and relatives usually did their best to meet the last wishes of the departed. Following tradition, they often left arrows and bows beside a dead hunter, and perhaps his knife or the spear he had used on the seal hunt. Women usually were buried with a soapstone lamp, or a small replica of one, and needle and thread. Before the arrival of the whites, it was quite common for the Eskimos simply to put out their dead in a skin, with a few stones piled up around the body. Only rarely were the bodies buried. Consequently, one frequently ran into skulls and bones, wild animals having done away with the rest.

Early in the morning of November 6, I was busy hitching up my dogs in preparation for a day of fishing out on a near-by lake. Suddenly Tommy Welsh came running up to us, waving his arms and calling out something or other. When he reached us, completely out of breath, he handed me a piece of paper. It was a telegram that just had arrived and had been scribbled down in a hurry. I was a father! Our first-born, Karen Doreen, had been born two days before in Vancouver. For a moment I was speechless, but then I realized how happy I was and thanked Tommy for the wonderful news. For once, I wished I could have been in the South; I knew that Doreen would be almost two before I would be able to see her since we didn't expect to be back in Vancouver before the fall of 1937.

In December the temperature fell to –40° and the snow felt like sand under our feet, while the northern lights lit the sky in fabulous colours. The moon was more beautiful than ever and the stars seemed like giant lanterns in the sky with a bright shine that can only be seen in the Arctic. With a little bit of imagination one could pretend that all one had to do to reach one was to step up on a pile of snow and stretch a little bit.

December 23 was Makinson's birthday and signalled the beginning of our Christmas celebrations. The Eskimos at Cambridge Bay had only recently started to celebrate this holiday and were looking forward to the days ahead. We, on our side, decided to make the most of it together with the two white traders. The Eskimos had never seen or heard of Santa Claus, and the men decided that with my great, red beard, this would be a perfect part for me. Mrs. Pasley made up an enormous red coat and cap for me, while Frank Willan supplied an addition to my beard in the form of some rope. The traders supplied gifts, and so did we togther with Rockeby-Thomas. They were mostly sweets for the children and useful things such as files and sewing kits for the grown-ups.

All told, there were almost three hundred Eskimos gathered on Christmas Eve and at least twice as many dogs. The entire shore outside the two trading posts had been transformed into a small village of snow houses, and the Eskimos were dressed in their Sunday best. They had been told that Santa would descend from the sky around nine o'clock at night and were eagerly awaiting the great event.

It was a clear night at some –23° and completely calm. Even the dogs gave the impression that they knew something was in the air. When the policemen had said that Santa was coming, there could be no doubt about it: The Mounted Police never lied, the Eskimos knew, and sure enough, all of a sudden there was a big bang high up in the sky. Before either Eskimos or dogs realized what was going on they heard yet another explosion, and then the entire bay was bathed in a bright, white light which dissolved into thousands of small stars. We must have used at least six of our big Very lights, and almost impressed ourselves. Every single Eskimo and dog remained rigid. Some were far from brave at that particular moment. Others seemed happy that Santa finally had arrived, for what else could this mean!

When the red-coated figure started to move towards them across the ice, escorted by policemen with blue and red signal lights fastened to long poles, the odd mother picked up her children in a hurry and headed for her igloo. At the Hudson's Bay house Santa was received by Frank and Alice Milne, who assured the Eskimos that Santa was a generous and gentle person. Then Santa started to unpack the mailbag he used for the gifts. The children seemed most impressed by Santa's size, but then he was well padded front and back. If the children had been frightened by Santa, all their fears disappeared when he started to distribute the gifts. Some of the older Eskimos looked me curiously in the face, and perhaps the odd one recognized my eyes. Old Kitapo put his hand on my big belly to see if it was real and everybody agreed that it was a tremendous success and that Santa would have to come back next year too. I had the job as Santa again the next year and in 1938 and in 1945. By that time they all knew Santa's real identity, but that didn't seem to matter much.

The Christmas service was conducted by Rockeby-Thomas. The crew of the *St. Roch* was split into two groups, which had Christmas dinner at the two trading posts. On Boxing Day the Eskimos were given a free dinner, and that was quite an experience. Not a word was uttered as long as there was any food left. The only sound heard was the smacking of tongues and the licking of fingers. The menu consisted of boiling-hot stew, biscuits, loads of tea and all the sugar they desired. On top of that there were tobacco and cigarette paper for all. Again they were all dressed in their best, but Malik's wife Shorty took the prize. She showed up in high-heeled shoes and silk stockings to impress the others and let them know that she, who was married to a Special Constable, was better than the rest. The result, of course, was frozen toes and feet, but not badly, fortunately. I think that not even our own representatives of the fair sex with their long experience of suffering in nylons in the cold winter could have survived -26^0 below. Their Eskimo sister, who was used to wearing skin pants and mukluks, certainly didn't stand a chance.

The last week of the year is important to the Eskimos. Almost all of them were busy trapping fur, so we found we had a little time on our hands. We continued our celebrations of the season and received many guests aboard the ship, where the Eskimos ate to their heart's content and watched movies. New Year's Eve our youngest crew member, the six-foot-tall Constable Johnny Cheetham, played the role of the New Year, dressed only in diapers, while Tommy Welsh had the part of the Old Year, to the great delight of the Eskimos.

Our two "guests," Kujuluu and Sivuraq, had by now become part of our little group on the *St. Roch*. Sivuraq had been given some material so she could make up some clothes for herself, because she hadn't been any too well equipped when she arrived. We also introduced her to the mysteries of cleanliness and got her to wash and comb her hair, so she would be more presentable. Kujuluu helped us with our fish nets and other odd jobs, and it was hard to imagine that he perhaps was a murderer, and that this woman had been the reason for that tragedy. Both were free to move around freely on the ship, and were treated just like any other Eskimo couples who visited us. They lived in their own igloo right next to the ship, and had they wanted to escape, it would have been easy for them. But they could not have left without dogs, and you don't hitch up dogs without the animals making it known loudly and clearly. I also found that Kujuluu was getting quite devoted to me and followed me no matter where I went, and I just couldn't help liking him.

With the festive season behind us it was time to start to think about work again. I had planned a patrol together with Malik to Coppermine, while Makinson was to take Kujuluu and Sivuraq to King William Island and Sherman Inlet to question the Eskimos there in connection with the murder.

To our surprise, however, Malik still doubted Shorty's faithfulness, in spite of the church wedding, and simply refused to leave with us at this time of the year when there were so many Eskimos visiting Cambridge Bay. Although he was a special constable, experience had taught us that it was no use forcing an Eskimo to do anything he didn't want to do, since he would always find some kind of excuse for not doing it. I was not looking forward to going to Coppermine alone in January. Kujuluu volunteered, however, and this left me in quite a spot. Police regulations said that we always should have an Eskimo with us on patrols as guide and interpreter. But on the other hand, Kujuluu's qualifications couldn't be said to be the best. He had never been west of Cambridge Bay and didn't talk English. To top it all, he was under arrest on suspicion of murder. Makinson reeled off all the various police regulations and rules and added that Headquarters would have a fit if they found out what I had in mind. My argument, on the other hand, was simply that if Malik refused to go, we had to find somebody else. At this time of the year, the Eskimos could make good money hunting, and it seemed unfair to take any one of them away from that. The result was that I left with Kujuluu. Admittedly, I was reprimanded by Headquarters later for my decision, but everything worked out just fine. We left on January 8, 1936. I am sure that my guide was the happiest man in the Arctic, dressed in brand-new clothes that I had bought for him out of my own money at the trading post. Part of his happiness seemed to stem from the fact that he would be away from Sivuraq for a while.

We met our first Eskimos on Wilmot Island, where we spent a day and stayed over night with Patsy Klengenberg. On January 24 we reached Coppermine and had a great reunion with Constables Chartrand and Parkes. Both Kujuluu and I had frozen cheeks and chins, but fortunately Reverend Webster, who also acted as an unofficial doctor, had some ointment which worked wonders within days.

The mail plane from the South had been delayed and there were people from all over gathered at Coppermine waiting for news. Inevitably there was some poker-playing, and where else was there a big round table besides in the living-room at the police detachment! The policemen had no objections. In this way it was possible to keep an eye on the players and make sure that none of the Eskimos played for money. Not a few of them had quickly picked up the secrets of the game, and were more than willing to try their luck, but it was strictly prohibited for any white man to play for money with an Eskimo. In our district, at least, I think this was respected, but that didn't, of course, prevent the Eskimos from playing with each other in their igloos.

When the plane finally got there, we had to sort the mail. This too was one of our duties, and all told we had about two hundred pounds of mail to distribute between Coppermine and Gjoa Haven. Among other items, I remember a registered letter to a trapper, containing two thousand dollars!

By the time Kujuluu and I returned to the *St. Roch* after more than a month's absence, we had covered some seven hundred nautical miles. Our total expenses for the patrol were $4.88 for a new primus stove we had bought from the Hudson's Bay trading post at Coppermine.

We were doubly welcome because of the mail. When all the letters had been distributed, quiet reigned on the ship. Everyone was deep in thought or reading. I myself, had read my letters at Coppermine and had seen the first photographs of my first baby girl.

Next Makinson left for King William Island with Kujuluu and Sivuraq, among other things, to look for the body of Quppa. Makinson took along a nineteen-year-old boy, Luke, as interpreter. He had attended the Anglican mission school and spoke very good English. However, he was totally inexperienced as a hunter, so Malik also went along. The group left in early March with two dog teams.

When they reached Perry River, about 150 miles from Cambridge Bay, they stopped in with Angulalik, who was one of the most outstanding Eskimos of his day and owned a little trading post and a fifty-five-foot boat with a diesel engine. A local Eskimo, Piruwanna, joined Makinson's little group, and both Kujuluu and Sivuraq were very helpful in pointing out the spot where Quppa had gone into the water to retrieve the caribou. They also helped in the search, but the body could not be found. After some days they continued to Gjoa Haven, where many Eskimos confirmed that Quppa had been killed, just as Kujuluu and Sivuraq had told us. But none of them had witnessed the shooting. This left us in a difficult position. Even if Kujuluu had confessed to the murder, he couldn't be arrested or put on trial without the main evidence, the corpse. In the end the couple was freed with a strong admonition to go straight from now on. In fact, they received a punishment, perhaps worse than being put in jail at Aklavik for a couple of years, as none of the Eskimos, not even their own relatives, wanted to have anything to do with them. They had a hard time surviving on their own.

34 GUEST OF HONOUR IN THE IGLOO

When Makinson returned in May he had covered more than nine hundred nautical miles. In the meantime Frank Willan and I had left on a trip to the east along the coast of Victoria Island to look for new potential harbours. Not far from the channel that separates Victoria Island from Lind Island, we ran into a large Eskimo camp near some huge pressure ridges. From here they could see around for quite a distance and keep an eye on the seal, which now had started to appear on top of the ice. These Eskimos came from Perry River on the mainland and were seal hunters. We could see several dark spots spread out on the ice, where the Eskimos were patiently waiting with their spears poised over the seal holes, ready for any animal coming up for air. Their dogs were tied up a good distance from each hunter. The dogs were not in teams, but single dogs on long leashes and were used for locating the seal holes, which had yet to be opened by the seals themselves. This was the whelping season, and the little white-coated baby seals don't take to the water for several days after they are born, but remain hidden under a cover of snow scooped out by the seal during the winter. Only the dogs could trace them, completely covered as they were. These were the permanent Arctic seals, not the species caught by professional seal hunters on the drifting ice-floes during spring.

When they spotted us, nearly all the Eskimos left their seal holes and we all went together to their little snow village. It was a fine group of people, happy and well fed with lots of seal meat and blubber. The women and children had just finished a meal of boiled seal meat when we arrived, and the faces of the small children were smeared all over with blood from the seal ribs they held in their grubby little fists. Seeing that we were white, and knowing that we were policemen, the women immediately got busy cleaning off their children with whatever was at hand, using pieces of rags, flour sacks or what have you. The older women, however, scorned these new-fangled ideas and very efficiently used their tongues, licking their children's faces and hands completely clean of blood and fat in a few seconds.

It was still early in the afternoon, but a huge pot of seal meat was hung over the lamp right away. We had been quartered in Niaquq's house. He was the most important man in the camp, a short, stocky fellow with a big head and a face to match, and this perhaps was the reason for his name. (Niaquq means "head" in Eskimo.) His wife was a large, motherly, middle-aged woman, and like many of the older people in the camp she had a very light skin. First of all, of course, we were to be served tea. I got out our primus stove and she produced her largest kettle, which held three gallons or so of water. This was an occasion for a celebration, the visit of the police; and the entire camp, grown-ups and children, soon crowded the little snow house, each with a mug or empty tin can for the tea party. While we waited for the water to boil, our hostess searched around among some of her belongings in a box and finally came up with a china tea cup with large red roses on it. No doubt it was one of her most cherished possessions and used only for VIP's. She held the cup up to the light with an appraising look. Even from where I was sitting I could see that it was a bit dirty, to put it mildly. She started to clean it, first on the inside, by spitting on her forefinger and rubbing it vigorously all around. Then she spat on the outside and began to polish it with her thumb, particularly a stubborn spot around the handle. Once finished she gave the cup a second critical look, and apparently wasn't happy with what she saw, as she then pulled up her long parka well above her knees and began to rub the cup against her thigh. It was a good thing that she wore a pair of fairly respectable-looking men's heavy long-johns instead of the regular skin pants. It turned out that the highest portion of the underwear was the cleanest.

By then I had put a couple of handfuls of tea in the pot, and the lady of the house handed me the cup with a charming smile of the perfect hostess. As the honoured guest I was supposed to take the first dip in the pot, and I must confess that I didn't relish the idea too much. On the other hand it would never do to insult so gracious a lady after the trouble she had taken to clean my cup. So I thanked her and accepted the cup. In a flash I decided on a little gesture. I declared that the men had been hard at work hunting all day and that I would like to serve them all first before the tea got cold. I then had them all hold out their mugs, which I filled by dipping the china cup into the kettle of tea a couple of dozen times, nearly burning my fingers on the little handle. Everybody was satisfied and well pleased that the Kabloona had been so kind to fill all their mugs first, keeping the last cup to himself, and by that time I didn't worry about drinking from the cup, which had been licked and scalded. It was clean.

35 VISIT FROM THE SOUTH

In late July of that year we received a distinguished visitor, none other than Commissioner Sir James MacBrien, our top boss. He arrived on one of the Air Force's small float planes, and I was immediately impressed by his personal concern for us when he congratulated me on the birth of my daughter. He also showed great understanding for our problems. He was interested in everything he saw aboard, although his visit was a short one, for he wanted to take the opportunity while the weather was good to visit as many detachments as possible. We served tea, and I had the opportunity to mention that I would like one day to proceed right through the Northwest Passage with the *St. Roch.* I pointed out that since it had been decided that we should spend the winter of 1936-37 in the King William Island area, the logical thing to do would be to go on east from there instead of trying to get back west through the ice-filled channels, and perhaps get to Point Barrow too late to head south that year. However, I was told that our role was not to be explorers, but to carry out the various duties connected with the administration of the North on behalf of the federal government. But the Commissioner added that he also hoped that the opportunity to navigate from one side of the Arctic to the other would present itself some day.

It was the first time the senior ranking officer of the Force had travelled so far north, but then Commissioner MacBrien was able to take advantage of air travel, something that had not been available to his predecessors.

Sergeant Makinson, who had asked for a transfer and was going to Fort Smith, NWT, was told that his wife was waiting for him at Aklavik, and couldn't get there fast enough. Reverend Rockeby-Thomas was another who also was eagerly awaiting our departure. He was coming with us to Coppermine where he was to meet his bride, coming up from the South. They were to be married by Rev. Harold Webster. Alec MacKenzie was also due for a transfer, having served three years at Cambridge Bay. Sergeant J. U. Eddy, who was to take Makinson's place, and Peter Cranney, who had been with me at Tree River, were on their way to the *St. Roch.*

That year, 1936, produced a lot of ice in the summer right at Coppermine, which we finally reached in August. We had to move the ship constantly while we waited for the Hudson's Bay ship the *Margaret A.*, which was bringing us new supplies. It turned out that she had run into trouble with the ice and therefore we went out to meet her, making contact at Pierce Point in late August. Makinson boarded the *Margaret A.* and Eddy came over to us, and the transfer was complete.

Our next winter quarters were to be on King William Island, perhaps at Gjoa Haven, and that appealed to me. This was a part of the Arctic that always had held a certain fascination for me, but I had never been there before.

On our attempt to reach King William Island, I sailed the Queen Maud Gulf for the first time heading for Nordenskiold Island. The Eskimos call it Putulik, meaning "the island with the hole in it." It is a good landmark and the course for King William Island lies just south of it. When we were a few miles from the island a northwest gale sprang up right on our tail and soon there was a heavy swell that made the vessel roll violently. In time we also had a full snowstorm with hardly any visibility at all.

When the storm was over we realized it was too late in the year to try getting farther east, and we returned to winter at Cambridge Bay.

36 ABOUT QUARLILAAK, MUKKAANI AND ANGULALIK

That year not many of the local Eskimos were in need of any assistance from us. One who did need us, however, was old Quarlilaak, who originally had come from Bathurst Inlet. He was also known as Hullalark and was tall and rangy. His claim to fame, if you like, was that he was one of the Eskimos who had murdered two American explorers and prospectors, Radford and Street, in 1910. At that time the case had been investigated by an Inspector French and the then Sergeant-Major Caulkin, who had gone all the way from Churchill in Manitoba to Chesterfield Inlet and Baker Lake and then set out across the Barren Lands. Together with an Eskimo and his wife, they spent two winters and a summer on this journey, living off the land like the Eskimos, before they found the camp of the suspected killers. When they made inquiries from some Eskimos they were staying with, they found to their surprise that their hosts were the men they were looking for. They were the two most outstanding Eskimos in the camp. Soon the two men were giving the policemen all the details. Neither of the two Eskimos had known any English when they met the two Americans, who didn't speak their language. In the beginning things had worked out to everybody's satisfaction. The Eskimos acted as guides and looked after the Americans, but then apparently the white men wanted the Eskimos to guide them out of their own country to where they could find Indian guides and reach civilization. When the Eskimos tried to explain that they could not leave because of their families and added that they would get two single Eskimos instead who had no objection to the long haul, this was misunderstood and one of the Americans hit out with his dog whip. The Eskimos, who had never met a white man before, retaliated by sticking his sealing spear through the man, and the other prospector then had run for the sled to get his rifle. Quarlilaak, however, beat him to it and killed him with his spear or harpoon. Both Eskimos assured the police that they had no intention of killing the white men, and had only defended themselves, frightened as they were of the white men's guns. With the details, the police also reached the conclusion that it had been self-defence, but explained to the Eskimos that they should not kill any strangers who might come to their camp in the future, and explained the white man's law regarding murder.

Now poor Quarlilaak was a very old man, blind in one eye, with the fingers on both hands crippled by arthritis, so it was difficult for him to do any work at all. As he did not have a wife he was totally dependent on others for clothing and most of his food. When we saw him he looked awful, walking around skinny and worn in ragged old deerskin clothes. But he still had one precious asset, a very pretty ten-year-old daughter. She was just as ragged and filthy as he was, but otherwise she was healthy-looking with red, rosy cheeks and gleaming white teeth. Quite tall for an Eskimo girl of her age, she was her father's constant companion, and also his insurance against old age, because if she made a good marriage to a great hunter or the son of such a man, her old father would also be taken care of. The couple soon became regular visitors to our ship at mealtime and they were never turned away, all through the winter.

Mukkaani was another Eskimo I remember from those days. He lived at Cambridge Bay and was one of the best Eskimo hunters I've ever met. He worked for Frank Milne. Even though Mukkaani lived in a nice log cabin he had built from his profits as a hunter, all was not well with this handsome man in his late thirties, in spite of his fame as a great hunter. He had no children, and his wife was at least twenty-five years older than he.

As I heard the story, Mukkaani had lost both parents when he was a small boy and had been adopted by an Eskimo couple who had a couple of sons about his age. After a few years his foster father died and the three boys set out hunting to support their mother until the two brothers married and got families of their own. Now only Mukkaani remained to look after his stepmother, and as he now was a full-grown man, she became his wife. I never found out if there had been any eligible bachelor in that area at the time, or whether this arrangement had been Mukkaani's or his wife's idea. To ask them seemed too personal, and besides it was anything but unusual for an Eskimo to marry his stepmother when she became a widow. Her age really didn't have anything to do with it.

In this case things worked out quite well. Mukkaani got along fine with his two stepbrothers and his wife looked after him. But it was only reasonable that Mukkaani would want another wife, a younger one who could bear a child. As mentioned in connection with old Quarlilaak's story, children were in fact life insurance.

As it happened, there were no eligible young maidens near Cambridge Bay, where Mukkaani lived. Furthermore he knew that the white people, and the missionaries in particular, frowned on the practice of having two wives. By chance he heard that one of the great Eskimo hunters on the Adelaide Peninsula had been shot by accident by his nephew during a rabbit hunt. The dead hunter, Iqualuppik or "Big Fish," had had two wives. One was rather old, but the other was young and beautiful and was called Pamiuq. As soon as the news spread, many Eskimos in the district between Cambridge Bay and Perry River started to make preparations for a race of over three hundred miles to reach the widow first. Mukkaani was determined to be the winner and made a quick trip to the trading post to get some supplies for the trip and announced his intentions. The Reverend Rockeby-Thomas too got wind of this, and told Mukkaani that this just wasn't right, and he even asked me to see Mukkaani and try to talk him out of it. My reply had to be that the Police did not wish to interfere with native customs, and at that time there was no law prohibiting an Eskimo from having more than one wife. I also felt that the old Mrs. Mukkaani probably would be very pleased if her husband managed to get a younger wife. This would give her, as the senior wife, a great deal of prestige, to be married to a great hunter who could afford to have two wives. Consequently I declared that I hoped that Mukkaani would win the race, seeing he was such a great hunter. The missionary, however, was more concerned with the fact that Mukkaani could not be married to a second wife according to the rites of the Church. Later, when schools and education became more widespread in the North, the Eskimos eventually were forced to have weddings performed by clergymen, but that was still some years off.

Poor Mukkaani, however, didn't win the race. He had the greatest distance to cover, and by the time he reached his goal, both widows had been claimed by two men who lived closer than he. In those days a widow did not have to stay single very long, and in a way this was not a bad system at all. Long before the days of all the various welfare agencies, a woman could hardly expect to be able to support herself and would soon have starved to death if she couldn't have remarried.

One of the best providers I ever met in the North was Angulalik, the Eskimo trader at Perry River. He had two wives, of whom the elder was the mother of his children. The younger one, whom he had taken for his wife in his later years, mostly for the sake of the prestige of having a second wife, had, to his great sorrow, not blessed the union with a child. After a long, frustrated wait for a child of their own, they adopted twin girls, daughters of a blind Eskimo woman. Angulalik and his two wives adored these two girls. Among the Eskimos it is really of little importance whether or not the child they raise is their own, as long as they have children in the igloo.

One day the young missionary came up to Perry River on one of his many visits in the area. Here he baptized both young and old and performed a great many marriages. At least superficially these people had become good Christians and members of the Anglican faith—that is, all of them but their most influential and outstanding man Angulalik. No one was more puzzled than he was when the missionary would not baptize him. Angulalik saw no reason for being left out, he sang as loudly as any of the others during the services, and insisted that he too should be baptized and married. The preacher, however, explained to Angulalik that as long as he was living with two women, there was nothing the Church could do for him. He had to give up one of them, then he could be married to the other. But Angulalik happened to be a gentleman as well as a heathen and felt that he could not let either of his two wives suffer the indignities of being discarded after so many years, this being the worst that could happen to an Eskimo woman. And yet he wanted to be treated like the other Eskimos, as a good convert, and therefore offered the missionary a compromise. He had many rooms in his house, he said, and the two wives could take turns sleeping in his bed, perhaps a week or a month at a time. This, in his opinion, certainly would solve the problem, as he then would have only one wife sleeping with him at a time. But this solution didn't satisfy the Church, and so Angulalik remained a heathen for a few years longer until both wives died in a measles epidemic. The great hunter had no trouble at all in getting himself a third wife, a young girl who was the daughter of another great hunter. And this time, he was baptized and received a church wedding before he raised a good-sized family, all with the blessings of the missionary.

During an inspection trip in the spring of 1937 I again visited

Angulalik. This time I had with me a young Eskimo boy called Mark Luke, and we were both invited to stay with the hospitable hunter. He still had his two wives at that time, and they kept his little house in perfect order. We had been spotted long before we reached Angulalik's place, and by the time we got there, a big pot full of caribou meat was over the fire. Within a few minutes the little room was thronged with people, while others were gathering on a large, roomy snow porch outside. When the meat was cooked to the satisfaction of the senior Mrs. Angulalik, she got a few of the people moved out of the way so she could put down a small table, which had been hidden under a bed. The legs of the table were only six inches high, but it was placed in the middle of the room and plates were set out for Mark Luke and myself. We all squatted down, in Japanese fashion, round the table while the older lady of the house picked out the choice pieces of meat for the two visitors. It was quite a feast. Our host had associated with white people and knew how to entertain guests. In addition to the boiled meat, we were also given a tray of frozen raw meat and another one with frozen fish, all nicely cut up into fist-sized chunks, just the right size to hold in one hand for carving away at with a hunting knife. The meal was topped with a can of California peaches and, of course, gallons of tea. The visit from the Police was an annual event and Angulalik never failed to make the most of it. We, in turn, tried to show our thanks in any way we could.

All through the meal I had noticed that Angulalik was squirming from time to time as if in great pain. Somehow I felt sure that it was neither the meal nor the visitors which made him feel ill at ease, and it turned out that I was right. When the other guests finally had left, he took me aside into another room and pulled down his pants while he bent over. He had two large, ugly-looking boils right on his behind. He explained that they were probably caused by the rubbing of a pair of caribou-skin underpants he had worn on a hunting trip, when he had gotten wet. Judging by their colour, I realized that the boils had been painted with something and when I asked him, he turned to one of his wives and whispered to her. After a minute she returned with a small bottle, which she offered to me. The label read "Nitro Powder Solvent"—used for cleaning gun barrels. When I explained this to him he first seemed stunned, but then he burst out laughing with that unique sense of humour and ability to laugh at themselves that the Eskimos possess. The tears rolled down his cheeks as he stood there laughing, still with his pants down around his ankles, and his two wives, who had treated him, also felt it appropriate to join in the amusement. The many Eskimos hanging around outside heard the laughter too and soon joined in, not knowing what they were laughing at. When they were told that the mighty Angulalik had boils on his behind painted with gun cleaner, there seemed no end to the merriment. I then asked one of his wives to bring me some hot water and washed his buttocks as clean as I could with some cotton. All around, the other Eskimos watched and rolled on the floor with laughter at the sight of Angulalik having his behind washed by the white man. This was indeed a good story.

In all fairness I should add that Angulalik also had some small bottles of iodine, and had gotten the labels mixed up, as he was unable to read, and figured that one bottle was as good as the next one. I explained to him that he had to be careful with such things, and I also left his wives instructions how to treat his boils. When I returned later that summer, he was as good as new and the boils were gone.

37 HANORIE UMIARJUAQ

On the same trip Mark Luke and I continued eastward past Gjoa Haven and ran into a camp out on the ice. Whom did we meet there but our old "guests" Kujuluu and Sivuraq! He still wore the same clothes I had bought for him the year before at Cambridge Bay, and Sivuraq was even uglier than I had remembered. She was also very obviously pregnant and was quite a sight as she introduced me to her friends in a shrieking voice. "This," she said, "is Hanorie Umiarjuaq" (Henry with the Big Ship).

Their camp, situated some ten miles north of Hovgaard Island, was a sad sight. I think it was the dirtiest camp I ever saw, and it was quite clear that the people there had had a hard winter. The dogs were in miserable shape, only skin and bones, and many had been killed for want of food. Mark Luke and I went from snow house to snow house. The women stayed in as much as possible, poorly dressed as they were against the bitter cold, and their footwear was so worn that one could see the bare skin. But they all smiled when they saw the Kabloona. It must have been difficult to keep smiling when even the children were half-naked in the cold and so hungry that they were chewing away at old rags of skin in the hope that they still held some bits of fat. The men were slightly better dressed as they had to stay outdoors hunting, but their equipment was very poor. The seal had failed them that year, and on top of that they were short of clothing. Had they only been more warmly dressed, they could have gone off on longer hunting trips and brought back food, but half-naked as they were they had to stay fairly close to the camp until the weather turned milder.

When I saw the conditions these people lived under I couldn't help thinking of Amundsen's book, in which he told about his two winters among these people during his trip through the Northwest Passage. The book also had many photographs showing well-fed and well-dressed happy people. Amundsen wrote that his highest hope for his friends among the Nassilimmiut Eskimos was that civilization would never reach them. Little did he know that he himself was the forerunner of this very civilization. Even if these people were left in peace for some years to come following the visit of the *Gjoa*, the progress of civilization could not be halted. More and more people followed in the footsteps of the early Arctic explorers and the lives of the Eskimos underwent a complete change. Some say that these children of Nature are better off today than in the olden days, others claim that civilization has brought them only misery. The Eskimos themselves make no comment. Fatalistic as they are, I suppose they say "Ajurnarmat" (it can't be helped, that's life).

38 NIVIASSIAQ'S CURSE

While I was visiting this camp I also had to investigate the death of an old man, Niviassiaq, who was supposed to have committed suicide.

After Kujuluu and some of his friends had built an igloo for me, I settled down to talk to Niviassiaq's widow, Aklak, or Brown Bear, and her fifteen-year-old daughter Magook. The widow's story was that Niviassiaq had been ailing for some time with a sore back, and at times had been almost doubled over, unable to straighten himself up. Yet he carried on his seal hunting for quite some time by having some of the other men pull him on a little sled and place him near a seal hole, where he would sit for hours, harpoon or spear in hand, with his eyes glued to the little indicator sticking up through the snow covering the hole. If a seal emerged underneath, the indicator would be pushed upwards by the water. Niviassiaq had lots of patience, and his widow said he had been a good hunter. At other times he had been placed near the rocky shore of some small bay where he would jig for Arctic cod, or Ogak, as the Eskimos called it.

All through the winter, Niviassiaq had carried on in this way, continually getting worse until he had become so crippled that he no longer could sit at the seal holes, and had to be left helpless lying on his old skins. He could barely manage to get up on his knees, but could not get on his feet. He was not a man who could be content with being a burden to others without being able to contribute to the common good and, as had been the custom among his people for generations during hard times, he felt the time had come for him to leave by his own hand, as it appeared that he was not going to die naturally. One day he informed the men that he wanted his rifle, and told them why. He did not want to use a knife, his widow said, out of fear that he would lack the strength to carry it through. The men, however, refused to give him the rifle. Not that they were against what he intended to do. That was his decision, but by now they knew the white people's views of murder, and they wanted no part in it.

They carefully hid all the rifles so none of the women or children could get at them and give Niviassiaq a weapon. But the old man kept on begging them for a rifle. One day, the widow told us, when all the men had left for the hunt, Niviassiaq ordered his wife to fasten the braided sinew line from his spear through the top of the snow house. He had decided that hanging was the only way out. Niviassiaq's wife said her older sister and her own daughter were the only people there, besides the old man. All of them refused to go out and cut the hole in the top of the igloo, where the line was to be fastened. Niviassiaq then got very angry, and they had all cried, she said. Finally the daughter, Magook, went out and fastened the line, using a set of caribou horns as toggle. After she had dropped the line down into the igloo, she left and didn't return. The old man then got up on his knees and adjusted the line just so and made a loop in it and put it around his head. When this was all done, he wanted one of the women with him, but they refused. Again he worked himself into a fit and demanded that they fetch Magook. This they did, and when she at last entered, they all stood around crying. Niviassiaq looked at them, then he leaned forward, still on his knees, and in a little while he was dead.

After a while they cut the line and rolled the old man up in his old deerskin, which had served as his bed for so long. They wrapped it tightly around him, finally tied him up with the line and dragged the body outside the igloo. When the men returned, they dragged the body to a little rocky inlet close to shore and laid him there, overlooking the sealing grounds. Around the body they placed a few rocks, but couldn't find too many then in the winter. His only possession, his seal spear, was stuck upright in the snow next to the body.

All this had taken place only a couple of weeks before my arrival. After having laid the good man to rest, they had broken camp and moved it, as they were afraid that the dead man's spirit would haunt them. No doubt this was a sincere belief, because it must have been quite a hardship for these badly-dressed people to move their camp ten miles.

I proceeded with my interrogation and questioned Niviassiaq's daughter at length, but all the people I spoke to gave me the same story. While I fully believed this story and understood the circumstances, our laws nevertheless said that nobody could assist another in committing suicide. On this point the Criminal Code was quite clear. But I had no intention of letting this get any further or to have any of these people appear in a court, at least not if it was up to me. I did, however, impress upon them that in the future they should not assist anyone in committing suicide, in spite of the fact that they only considered it "helping people to die." This, I explained, would be misunderstood by the white people, and there would be trouble. The Eskimos assured me that they understood what this meant.

Anyway, I had to go out and have a look at Niviassiaq's body, so that I could report to my superiors. One of the younger Eskimos offered to take me to the dead man, but the older men kept reluctantly in the background. They had no wish to disturb the dead. After I had viewed the body and satisfied myself that Niviassiaq had died the way it had been told to me, I considered the case closed.

Strangely enough, an odd sequence to this tragedy was to follow years later, in January of 1949. The constable then stationed at Cambridge Bay one day received a message from the Hudson's Bay man Learmonth to the effect that nine out of a group of sixteen people who were hunting and fishing in the vicinity of Union River had died during the past summer and fall, apparently suffering from some type of flu. The message went on to state that the remainder of the party was in desperate straits and that more surely would die unless they were removed to a hospital without further delay. One young man had lost the flesh from both feet and ankles, and only the bones remained. Although Learmonth was doing what he could for these people, immediate evacuation by air was urged. The message had been sent in mid-November and had been relayed by dog teams for over four hundred miles. Another message, accompanying the first, mentioned that what appeared to be a very sordid murder had been committed at a place on the east coast of Boothia, about half-way between Thom Bay and Fort Ross. A young man by the name of Eerkiyoot was supposed to have strangled his mother, Nakasuk, and had been assisted in the deed by his cousin, Itigak.

Constable Dick Mead immediately got in touch with Ottawa and recommended that an RCAF Dakota fly in supplies and a doctor. As always, the Air Force responded quickly, and soon a ski-equipped aircraft was under way from Edmonton with Doctor Harvey of the Department of Health and Welfare on board. The plane stopped off at Cambridge Bay where it picked up Constables Mead and Wikert, but due to weather conditions, they were unable to land at Fort Ross. Only ten days later were they finally able to land with a good deal of supplies.

After assisting the doctor in helping these unfortunate people, Constable Mead hired a Labrador-born Hudson's Bay Company interpreter, Ernie Lyall, to go with him as guide down the coast of Boothia to look into the alleged murder case. When they arrived at the Eskimo camp it was found that the murder suspect, Eerkiyoot, was visiting at Thom Bay and that Itigak was at Gjoa Haven. Both Eskimos were located after a good deal of travelling around, and placed under arrest. Then the investigation started. Eerkiyoot's wife, Annie Piitikkuut, told Constable Mead that she had moved to a camp at Illaunakkiq, where she and her husband had lived together with Eerkiyoot's mother, Nakasuk. The old woman had abused her daughter-in-law without stop, to the point where she tried to keep away as much as possible. Early in the spring, however, Nakasuk became sick and started to cough up blood from her lungs. It became increasingly worse and the old woman kept repeating that she wanted to die.

One summer evening, Annie said, she was told that her mother-in-law had asked to be hanged, and that her husband and his cousin had done it.

The body was duly disinterred and witnesses collected. One of these happened to be old Kikiak, a man I had interviewed twelve years earlier in connection with Niviassiaq's death. Then the body, the accused and witnesses were flown to Cambridge Bay for the trial.

An autopsy was performed to establish the cause of death, which was confirmed to have been strangulation. The dead woman's son gave a heart-rending testimony of how his mother had begged him to kill her, and how he had refused, telling her that he feared what the white people would do to him if he gave in to her wish. But in the end he had done his duty toward his parent, just as Niviassiaq's daughter had twelve years before. But the times had changed. Now there was a judge and a jury and Eerkiyoot was found guilty, although the jury entered a plea for leniency. Itigak, who appeared before a different jury, was found not guilty after two hours' deliberations, but Eerkiyoot was sentenced to one year in prison at Cambridge Bay, with parole to be applied after four or five months, if there were then an opportunity to have him returned to Spence Bay and his own camp.

I wasn't in the Arctic that year, but I followed the case with great interest, not the least because Nakasuk was none other than Niviassiaq's widow, who earlier had been known as Aklak. It was she who had explained to me the circumstances surrounding her husband's death during the winter of starvation of 1937. Her son, Eerkiyoot, was the very same little boy who had been with her then. Now he had done for his mother what his sister once had done for their father. But there was a difference brought on with the march of time. In 1937, I had taken it on myself to investigate the circumstances without a trial and a court of justice and had decided to let the case rest. I couldn't help thinking that perhaps all the money spent on convening the court and flying in coroner and judge would have been better used to help the poor Eskimos who were still alive, though only barely so.

But let us return to that winter of 1937. Shortly after I had been up to Niviassiaq's grave and viewed the body, which I had respectfully put back in place, a terrible storm broke. Our local guide, Ikualaaq, was convinced that it was Niviassiaq who had sent this storm because we had disturbed his sleep. All the way back to Gjoa Haven the storm raged without let-up, for three full days and nights, while the temperature dropped to –40°. This in itself was most unusual for the month of April.

When we reached the camp, the people there were all highly surprised that we had made it back at all, for the snowfall had been quite heavy. When Ikualaaq told the others what I had done, they too were certain that this was the work of the dead man. Strangely enough, none of them seemed to hold this against me, and again I was the object of their hospitality.

For the next two days I stayed with the Hudson's Bay's man, Jack Learmonth, and was greatly impressed by this man's profound understanding of the Eskimo way of life. Many years later, in 1946, he wrote an article in Hudson's Bay's magazine, *The Beaver*, and told the whole story of Niviassiaq's curse. It started: "If there is any place in the Far North that is haunted by ghosts, it is certainly King William Land." He then went on to tell how the Franklin Expedition had been lost near by a century ago, and how old Eskimos had told of entire groups of their people who had died from starvation in the area, the last as late as 1922, before the Hudson's Bay Company had established its trading post at Gjoa Haven. The Company had also lost one of its men there, a young apprentice by the name of Harold Luca, who had disappeared during a storm. One of the Company's interpreters, Siberia Mike, had committed suicide there and the two men mainly responsible for the establishment of the trading post, Paddy Gibson and Peter Norberg, both had come to a violent and untimely death in that neighbourhood.

Learmonth also tells of the old Eskimo, Aluki, who had lived in this hard country all his life. One day as he travelled along the shore near Starvation Cove, where several of Franklin's men had succumbed, he found a large piece of much-weathered spar, which had drifted in from some shipwreck of long ago, possibly from Franklin's *Erebus* or *Terror*. Old Aluki could hardly believe his own eyes. This was enough wood to make himself a fine new sled like those that some of his more fortunate brothers had been able to buy with fox furs.

The sled that he built, with a great deal of work, became Aluki's pride. Shortly after it was finished, however, he took sick and when he knew that his days were numbered, he asked his family and his closest friend, who was no one else but Niviassiaq, to bury the sled with him. His last wish was fulfilled, and the sled remained in Aluki's grave, until one day Niviassiaq gave in to the temptation and removed it. He then left with his own and two other families for the mainland, where they were going to hunt caribou. But they ran into persistent bad luck and were forced back to the coast, where they lived under very difficult conditions. It was then that Niviassiaq became sick and depressed. Scared, he replaced the sled in his friend's grave, but to no avail. He felt that he had ruined his own life and decided to commit suicide.

Learmonth went on to claim that the Eskimos were convinced that I had been placed under a double curse by Niviassiaq after I in turn had disturbed his grave. And it is true that on my way from Gjoa Haven to Cambridge Bay that year, Niviassiaq, (or whatever) punished me with a tremendous fall of black snow. A year later, when I passed the grave on another patrol, almost all of my dogs took sick and many of them died. This, perhaps, was merely a reminder that the curse was still in force. Some years later, in 1941, when I sailed the *St. Roch* through the Northwest Passage, the entire crew was met by the curse in Queen Maud Gulf. Never have I seen such a storm! The ship froze and got stuck so we had to spend the entire winter at Pasley Bay, near the Magnetic North Pole. While we were there, I sent Constable Chartrand out on a patrol to King William Island. There he visited Learmonth, but died shortly after. Later that same winter Constable Hunt and I too spent some time with Learmonth, waiting for the mail plane. Once again Niviassiaq made his presence felt—the plane crashed somewhere between Eldorado and Coppermine with all the mail and our friend Paddy Gibson on board. "Perhaps, then, it isn't really so strange that the Eskimos firmly believe in the curse, even if Larsen later had some luck with his travels," comments Learmonth in his article.

The black snow that Learmonth describes, incidentally, was not such a rare phenomenon in this area. It wasn't quite black anyway, even if it was rather dark in colour for snow. We took samples of it in a washbasin, melted the snow and then boiled it dry. All we were left with was a spoonful of fine dust, which the meteorologists at Toronto afterwards told me probably came from the Dust Bowl in the United States.

39 SUPERSTITION, INFANTICIDE AND SHIPWRECK

Many times on the return trip to Cambridge Bay, we thought our last hour had come. Near Lind Island we met some of the Perry River Eskimos, who told us that the old Eskimos had been saying that there was supposed to be a big island near by. It was called Umimalik or Muskox Island, but we were unsuccessful in locating anybody who actually had been there. Patsy Klengenberg also knew about this island, but had never seen it himself. For some reason or other the Eskimos were afraid of travelling eastward along the coast of Victoria Island. They said that area was taboo because the "little people" lived there and they could send storms and other misery if they were disturbed. Such stories about little people were quite common among the Eskimos, who claimed that these small neighbours of theirs lived in houses under the snow. I have even met Eskimos who claimed they had seen small footprints along the southern shores of Victoria Island. These footprints always disappeared in some mysterious fashion when they were heading north or further inland on the island. The Eskimos also told of some giants, now dead since many years, and consequently no cause for fear any more.

In the area around Cambridge Bay we heard of cases of infanticide. According to our informant an Eskimo woman had killed her newborn baby girl. Infanticide as such wasn't too uncommon in that part of the world, even at that time, but what really shocked us was that we knew this woman Qujaakjuk. Usually such murders were done by the mother placing herself on top of the baby until it suffocated. Such overlying, could, of course, also happen by accident while the mother was asleep, as the Eskimos always sleep in a long row one next to another.

It is not really fair to condemn the Eskimos too harshly for this practice of infanticide. I have talked to many old women who admitted having been forced to kill their own babies, much against their will. When this had happened, the reason was usually that it was the only way the other children in the family would get a chance to grow up. Never did I hear of anything like this done out of cruelty or lack of love for the children. An important reason was that the balance between the number of boys and girls had to be maintained. The death rate for boys and men was far higher than that of women, simply because so many half-grown boys were killed in hunting accidents or drowned. There were also families who had only girls.

The Eskimos truly love their children, but the harsh country they live in often forced them to do things we now consider horrible. I heard it said that infanticide mostly was practised during the starvation winters when it was impossible to maintain any more children than a family already had. Such killings were decided upon in advance, before the baby was born. Had the baby first been breast-fed by the mother, however, no attempts were spared to save the child.

When we questioned Qujaakjuk and her husband Iisipana we reached the conclusion that their child had died by accident. The Eskimos were warned and told to look after their newborn babies in the future, and we added for good measure a little reminder that it was our duty as policemen to investigate all suspicious deaths.

The summer of 1937 again was a very difficult one as far as the ice was concerned in the western Arctic. After we had left our winter quarters in late July, we had to cope with a tremendous amount of ice and had to fight our way westward. This was not merely the usual winter ice from Coronation Gulf and Amundsen Gulf, but also a heavy bluish polar ice which a steady northwesterly wind had brought down straight from the Arctic Ocean. Some of the floes must have been five to seven feet thick, judging by the water level where they ran aground.

It got steadily worse as we passed Wilmot Island, Tree River and Coppermine, and particularly around Cape Krusenstern. At Cockburn Point we were completely stopped by heavy incoming ice as a strong gale came up from the northwest, forcing the ice back into the narrow channel we just had passed through. About ten miles to the northwest we had spotted the masts of the Hudson's Bay schooner *Fort James*, which had spent the winter at the company trading post on Read Island. It seemed that she had left her winter quarters a short time before, judging by her position. Soon the masts were out of sight as the visibility deteriorated and we were pushed backward, now helpless in the grip of the ice. We were unable to use our engine as the ice was jammed solidly against our propeller and rudder. The ice pressure increased with every projection of the land we passed. We were squeezed like a nut in a nutcracker, and at times our little ship was forced over on her side, up to thirty degrees or more.

Early in the morning of July 30 the situation seemed extremely critical and I ordered all hands to dress and stand by. Two French priests who were travelling with us, however, calmly walked up and down on the cramped and now slanting deck in their morning meditation as if nothing unusual were happening. Somehow we managed to keep afloat, and later the same day we established radio contact with the *Fort James*. We found that she had been forced back and then was near Bernard Harbour, facing the same conditions as we were. In the meantime we were still being pushed backward, and reached the harbour at Cape Krusenstern after having covered some forty miles in this manner. The pressure kept up, to our great disappointment, and we therefore had to continue until we found a little spot free of ice some five miles farther south-southwest.

The next day the wind finally died down a little and we started to work our way north-northeast of Hope Point. We had by then heard that the *Fort James* was some fifteen miles north of the point and was trying to reach land. Some days later we managed to catch up with the other ship and we both moored to a huge ice-floe. It must have been at least seventy feet thick and, to our great joy, had a fair-sized pool of sweet water close to the edge. In short order we had taken on one thousand gallons of fresh water. As the *Fort James* by now was very short of oil, we pumped some of our spare diesel fuel aboard her. The next day both ships started to drift eastward at a rate of about one mile and a half per hour, while the ice was tightening up all the time. Finally the ice-floe we had been moored to broke up, and for a while we had a hard time sticking together until we could reach another floe to tie up to.

The gale showed no sign of relenting, but we were partially protected from the grinding ice by a projection jutting out on the heavy ice-floe we were moored to. The *Fort James* was only seventy-five feet away from us and we kept a watchful eye on each other. At times it looked as if the other ship got the worst of it, at others we must have been in the tightest spot. The *Fort James* was a bit bigger than the *St. Roch*, but of a different construction, more like a Nova Scotia fishing schooner, although it was heavier built and reinforced for the ice. However, she didn't have the round-bilged hull of the *St. Roch*, and took quite a beating all the time, not the least when the grinding ice had worn away the projecting point which had sheltered us. At times the ice pressure lifted us several feet and forced us over on the side. The woodwork creaked around the stern, and when we examined it closely we found that our heavy rudder-stock was split nearly its full length. I was now concerned about the propeller and we tried to move or turn it over by hand. It was stuck solid, pushed up by the ice, but luckily we later found that it was undamaged in spite of the fact that the blades were bent.

Our round shape proved to be a blessing. A good-sized ice-floe which was being pushed against the sides of our ship suddenly up-ended and the continued pressure pushed it right under our keel until part of the floe appeared on the other side of the ship. The *St. Roch* was now lifted at least three to four feet and there she lay, more or less rocking on the floe, which in turn took the brunt of the pressure from the ice. This certainly saved us from being crushed. The *Fort James*, with her conventional bottom and keel, was less fortunate. The ice did not slide under her, but kept pushing against her sides, almost turning her over on her beam ends.

Late in the evening of August 6 we saw the *Fort James* make a tremendous heave and with a mighty shiver, as if in pain, her keel was shorn right off, leaving the bottom wide open. She filled almost instantly. For a moment it looked as if the top of her masts were going to hit us, but then the ship returned to an upright position. In a flash, we rushed over the ice, took off an Eskimo woman and five children and brought them back to our own ship. The captain and crew of the *Fort James* had no time to save any of their belongings. Even Captain Summer's dentures had to be left behind in a glass of water in his little cabin below. In her hold, the ship also carried some thirty thousand dollars' worth of fur, but none floated up so it could be saved. The ship, however, stayed up for several hours with her decks level with the ice or the water, due to the pressure of the ice. Then she started to go down, head first, until only the top of the mainmast was shown at a forward tilt before even that disappeared.

Fortunately all hands were rescued unhurt, but the thirteen dogs that had been aboard the *Fort James* had to be shot, cramped as we were for space. We were by no means certain of our own fate yet either, so both the lifeboat and the launch were swung out in their davits and provisioned, in the hope that they at least might stay on top of the ice if the ship went under. In time we reached Coppermine without any further complications, having drifted some seventy miles with the ice.

The people at Coppermine were surprised to see us, because we had been unable to get through to them on the radio, so they had no idea of what had happened to the *Fort James*.

A couple of hours later a large aircraft belonging to the Eldorado Mining Company arrived, carrying the viceregal party of Lord Tweedsmuir, the Governor General. With him was the Hudson's Bay Fur Trade Commissioner Ralph Parsons as well as the District Commissioner for the Company, my friend Dick Bonnycastle. There were also various aides.

When Dick Bonnycastle, unaware of what had happened, asked the Chief Engineer of the *Fort James* where that ship was, the sturdy Newfoundlander answered: "Out there in eighteen fathoms, sir." We were then introduced to His Excellency and Mr. Parsons and told them the story of the *Fort James*. This, naturally, was a hard blow to the Hudson's Bay Company, not the least as it already was short of water transport in the Arctic.

All the Eskimos were dressed in their best to meet the Isumataq, the Chief of the White Men, who had come to visit. No doubt, they were a little bit disappointed when they saw a very small man, dressed in an old tweed jacket, a slouch hat and a pair of breeches. This, reasoned the Eskimos, could not be the great chief of all the white men. The Air Force Aide, Flight-Lieutenant Dave Harding, in full uniform, was over six feet tall, and looked more the part they decided.

I was invited to lunch at the trading post with the visiting party, and after a while the Governor General expressed his wish to visit the *St. Roch*. We all had the impression that he thoroughly enjoyed his brief stop on board, chatting with everybody, including the crew of the *Fort James* who were still with us, as we were to take them to Tuttujartuuq. His Excellency was surprised to see how small the *St. Roch* was as he crawled under the big boat we had lashed to the deck and made his way among some twenty dogs tied here and there. His aides scrambled high and low after him, and a young Navy lieutenant constantly looked at his watch and reminded the Governor General that he had a busy schedule and many calls to make. Lord Tweedsmuir, however, wanted to see and hear as much as possible about our work and about the Arctic and even visited our little galley and the engine room before he finally left.

40 REUNION WITH MY WIFE AND FIRST MEETING WITH AN UNKNOWN DAUGHTER

On our way from Tuttujartuuq to Coppermine something else happened that could have meant the end for the *St. Roch* and all of us. It was shortly after lunch and Frank Willan had just taken over the deck watch for me so I could turn in for a while, as I was pretty tired by then. I was only dozing fully dressed, on top of my bunk, when I smelled smoke coming up from the engine room right below me. I grabbed the little Pyrene fire extinguisher from the wall and dashed down the companionway that led to a door to the engine room. The door had been slammed shut by Scott Alexander who had had to get out in a hurry, and when I opened it was nearly knocked down by a puff of smoke that threatened to choke me. I gave a few squirts of the extinguisher, which had no effect at all. By now my lungs were nearly bursting, so up the ladder I went and found all hands on deck.

The main engine was going full speed ahead at our regular six knots and it was impossible to get into the engine room to stop it or to get at it so we could use it for our pumps. The fire was burning around a two-hundred-gallon tank of gasoline, which had just been filled and which had caused this fire. Scott, who had just taken over the watch from Bob Kells, had been cleaning out the sump strainer in this tank, and had let the gas sediment run into a can from the cock in the bottom. Then, according to Scott, some of it had spilt on the electric wiring leading up along the wall and beam near the tank. A flash had ignited some oily waste rags in a pail and that was that. Scott had immediately grabbed a fire extinguisher hanging by the door but all he could do was to turn on the valve and throw the whole thing into the fire before rushing up on deck.

Then I remembered that we had another Pyrene extinguisher in a locker forward, and also that we had twelve one-gallon cans. I shouted for Frank Willan, the Mate, to get these up on deck quickly and ordered the ship to head right into the wind and for those of the crew who were not of any immediate help to get forward and get all the blankets they could put their hands on and wet them in sea water. Scott and I put wet towels over our faces and took turns rushing down with a can of extinguisher foam, tossing can and all into the roaring fire. At the same time, we beat away at the flames with the wet blankets the others were preparing for us. The worst of all was that behind the engine room and at the same level as the tank, was a little locker where we had stored three hundred pounds of blasting powder. The engine-room side of the locker was an inch thick and was now on fire. If the gunpowder and the gas exploded, it would blow the after deck and the deck-house as well as all of us to Kingdom Come any minute.

Time seemed to stand still, but finally the fumes created by several gallons of foam tossed into the flames smothered the fire between the gas tank and the powder locker, and we got busy again with the blankets. It was several minutes before the air cleared sufficiently for the engineer to get down below to survey the damage done. Some guardian angel must have watched over us, for all we found was some badly-burned woodwork and burnt paint on the engine clutch and the gas tank as well as on the door to the locker. Looking back at this, I think it was an even worse experience than seeing the *Fort James* go down next to us.

The fire was our last dramatic experience in the Arctic that year. The rest of our trip eastward and then to the South went off without a hitch until we docked at Evans Colman Wharf in Vancouver on October 5.

There was a crowd to greet us on the wharf, and there I saw my wife—with a blonde little girl, almost two years old, who was jumping up and down, shouting "Daddy, Daddy" as she waved at me. Surprisingly enough she seemed to know me when I got ashore, and talked away with the chatter of a two-year-old as if we were old friends. By the time I headed north again in 1938, Doreen and I had established a warm relationship which was to last through the years.

41 AMONG THE INLAND ESKIMOS

On the next trip I was sorry to have to make out without Bob Kells, who had decided that he had had enough of the Arctic and obtained a posting ashore in Victoria. Bob had been a good shipmate for eight years, steady and reliable. But I was happy to learn, to my surprise, that Jack Foster had volunteered to serve aboard again as engineer. Frank Willan left us too, and was replaced by Farrar, who since I had last seen him had tried his luck as a trader on the west coast, but had lost his ship. Now he was back in the RCMP. Constable Derek Parkes, whom I had known at Herschel Island, joined us as assistant to the engineer.

In Coppermine, Constable "Frenchy" Chartrand joined us to stay on board while we were in winter quarters at Cambridge Bay, where we arrived on September 19. The ice came late in 1938, but by the beginning of October we were in complete winter quarters. Word soon spread that umiarpak, the ship, was back again, and the visitors started to arrive, among them many old friends.

Cambridge Bay then had two mission posts and the newcomer, the Roman Catholic Father Delalande, was quite effective competition for the Anglicans. In the beginning the Eskimos were somewhat mystified and intrigued by the Mass. Besides, the priest had a beard, just like the Apostles they had seen in pictures. Some of them probably thought he was Christ himself, for his services were quite different, of course, from the Anglican ones they were used to. Both impressed and bewildered, they decided to play it safe, and attended services at both mission posts.

Shortly after New Year's many of the Eskimos went hunting again and soon the place was almost deserted. Among the last to leave were crippled old Qingakutaaq and his family. Once he had been a great hunter, but his pride in life at that time was his son, David, who had come back with us from school in Aklavik. There he had learned to read and write and could now talk to the white men in their own language. When their sled passed the *St. Roch*, Qingakutaaq's wife, old Taipana, was walking in front of the five or six skinny dogs together with a daughter of about ten or twelve. Qingakutaaq was limping away, leaning on a stick and holding on to the sled with his free hand. On top of the load David was sitting majestically, plunking on a guitar and humming a sentimental cowboy tune he just had picked up at Aklavik.

On one of my patrols I met Angulalik, who had then been "properly" married in church to his youngest wife, Taipana, after the older ones had died. But not even the blessings of the Church had made any difference, he confided to me. This new wife hadn't presented him with a child either, so he had his doubts about the effectiveness of baptism and church weddings. With the consent of his wife, the couple had practised a bit of wife-trading with another couple, but still with no results for Taipana, although it had fruitful results for the other man's wife.

I was told that there was a seal-hunt camp out on the ice, some twenty-five miles from shore in the direction of Nordenskiold Island, in the Queen Maud Gulf. The Eskimos there had been busy all winter and some of the Inland Eskimos from Perry River had been out visiting the others to do some trading. The seal hunters came from the area around Garry Lake and knew very little about seal hunting, as some of them had hardly seen a seal before. These people, who were completely ignorant of the coastal district, had spent their entire lives far inland, hunting caribou and sometimes fishing the rivers and lakes. There had been some contact between the Inland people and those on the coast for many, many years, but hardly any friendship. My friends on the coast clearly let it be known that they looked down on the others. Angulalik described the Inland Eskimos in terms that could best be described as applicable to "underdeveloped" people. They owned few dogs, had scarcely any possessions, and their sleds were long and narrow and in such a poor shape that nobody could ride on them.

My first meeting with the Inland Eskimos took place at Ogden Bay. They were two families. Their womenfolk must have been the dirtiest I ever saw anywhere. Their hair was hanging in greasy tufts down over their eyes and was used as towels when they wiped fat and dirt off their fingers. The women on the coast, in contrast, as a rule were quite particular about their appearance.

The snow houses were poorly built and were littered with all kinds of meat from killed animals. At least eight caribou carcasses were lying around on the dirty snow floor, some skinned and some frozen. The people helped themselves from these carcasses, just as the dogs did whenever they felt like having a bit of meat. Although these people lacked stone lamps and blubber for cooking, they seemed healthy and well fed and had plenty of food. Having seen the indescribable filth and dirt the Inland Eskimos lived in, I could well understand why the coastal people stayed clear of them and refused to mix or intermarry with their inland brethren. It is difficult to understand how people could live, raise children and thrive under these conditions. I also kept in mind that this happened to be a winter with plenty of food, and shuddered at the thought of what it would be like in a poor winter.

Usually I wasn't too particular about how and what I ate, but this time I built my own separate igloo and refused to eat with the Eskimos. Furthermore they spoke a dialect that my interpreter, David Paniujakak, understood only with great difficulty. In all fairness, however, it must be said that these people were very friendly and hospitable in spite of all their failings, but we made our stop as brief as possible and headed back to the coast.

42 BIRTH IN THE IGLOO

The seal hunters' camp out on the ice consisted of some thirty people who lived in seven snow houses. They came from Sherman Inlet and around Perry River and we were well received, as many of them knew my guides from Perry River. Mannik, who had been a witness at the Aqigiq trial at Tree River in 1934 and had spent some time with us then, introduced me to his old father, or perhaps it was his grandfather. He was an old man with a small white beard and a home-made peg leg. The foot of the leg was made of heavy muskox-horn. When he noticed how interested I was in the leg, the old man invited me to his igloo where he took off his pants and showed me how his own leg had been severed a few inches below the knee. It was a good healthy stump with lots of flesh over the bone. The wooden leg was made of a piece of driftwood, which had been cut to the required length and thickness and made in such a way that a part of it had been cut out and padded with caribou skin. That was where the stump fitted in neatly, without chafing, while the wooden leg extended up along the thigh. This portion, too, was covered with a tightly-fitted caribou skin to prevent chafing. With the solid base, the old man was able to move nimbly around, and demonstrated his agility by kicking a piece of ice that went flying.

The old man told me that the leg had been amputated long before the arrival of the white men, and the operation had been performed by an angakkuq or medicine man, whose only instrument had been a crude knife. As far as the old man could remember, his foot had been frozen and gangrene had set in. First the amputee had been tied up with rawhide lines so he was unable to move. Then the knife. When the angakkuq had cut off sufficient bone, he had folded flesh of the healthy part over the stump and fastened it by stitching with caribou sinews. This part of the operation over, the entire stump had been held in a fire to sear and cauterize it. Needless to say, there had been no anaesthetics available and the poor man had been conscious all through, but tightly bound! As the stump and the result proved, it had been an expert piece of surgery and I doubt that any doctor in our hospitals could have done a better job.

This was not the only Eskimo with a wooden leg. There were two more in the King William Island area, but this was the only time I ever got all the details of the operation and the method used.

The weather had been very poor when we reached the camp. It had started to get dark and I didn't really feel like starting to build an igloo. But I had no reason to fear; I was invited to live wherever I wanted and picked a large, new house. My choice was instantly approved by all, not the least the young hunter and his wife who lived there.

Once I had installed myself, I started to cook a meal, enough for all of us. We were just getting ready to go to bed when David, the interpreter, mentioned that the wife of the house was just about to have a baby. With the big caribou parkas the women wore it was impossible to tell what shape they were underneath, so I replied with confidence that it surely wouldn't happen that night. "Oh yes," said David, "tonight, very soon!" They must have noticed my consternation when I said that I wanted to get out of there. I had no intention of getting stuck in an igloo where there was going to be a birth. If anything went wrong I would likely be blamed for bringing bad luck.

They all laughed, and not the least the woman herself, at how shy I was. In the meantime some of the men were busy building some kind of lean-to of snow. It was built into the wall of the big igloo, and David and I shoved all our gear through a hole in the wall into this small separate bedroom and crawled in ourselves. Small was perhaps not the word for it. The men had made sure that it was big enough to hold quite a few of them too so they could visit with us. So out came the teapot again while we settled down for the long wait for the baby.

When our little anteroom was filled up, a latecomer had to lie down flat on his stomach with his head and shoulder inside, while the rest of him was out in the big igloo, which now was full of women and a number of half-grown boys and girls. They were all there to watch and celebrate the coming event. Nothing was kept secret from Eskimo children, neither the birth nor the conception of children, living as they did all together in very cramped quarters.

A lively conversation was flowing back and forth between our little room and the big igloo as I handed out plates of porridge, liberally sprinkled with sugar and lumps of butter and mugs of tea, to the man on the floor, who would pull back a little and pass them on to those on the inside. After all the people in the igloo had been fed, I passed the tea mugs around to my guests, and nobody seemed to care that there were some bits of porridge floating in the tea. That was no worse than all the caribou hairs that always covered all the food.

Around ten o'clock I was wondering how the expectant mother was doing, and was assured that everything was in order. Then all of a sudden the laughter and chatter stopped: the time had come. The man on the floor who could pull his head out of the door into my room and look around in the igloo began to give us a running account of the developments. Yes, now the woman was getting ready to have the baby. She was getting up on her knees, which was their favourite position in such situations. Now some of the other women were assisting her; the mother-to-be was inexperienced and needed help. I heard some murmuring and all of the menfolk listened in anticipation when our master of ceremonies on the floor announced with a smile on his face that the baby's head now was coming out, then shortly after we were told of the arrival of the arms and finally he announced with a triumphant shout that the *whole* baby had been born and that it was a boy! A son! I was warmly congratulated, for it was I who had brought them luck, a boy. This, of course, called for further celebrations, and I participated with gusto. Had anything gone wrong, particularly with a male baby, I could easily have been blamed. There was little sleep that night.

43 THE GREAT ASSIGNMENT

When we returned south that year I met my one-year-old son, Gordon, for the first time, but there was little time for family life. The Second World War had broken out while we were in the North and although we had been too busy up there to think about the world-shaking events, we quickly got the feeling of the changes that had taken place. Almost everything that could float had been requisitioned for war duty, but the *St. Roch* was unwanted. She was too slow. I also found that I was unable to join the military forces as the RCMP would not release me. Many of our people had already joined the recruitment had been halted. Our service during the war years was to be confined strictly to the North.

Some time after New Year's Day 1940 I was sent to Ottawa to attend an advanced police course at the Canadian Police College. I was a sergeant at that time and during the years in the Arctic had been unable to keep abreast of the latest developments in police administration and law enforcement as it was practised in the more settled parts of Canada. This, therefore, was a welcome assignment. We were stationed in the new RCMP Rockcliffe Barracks and while I attended the course I was to meet many of the men I later would have a great deal to do with as the Officer Commanding of "G" Division. At that time, of course, I had no idea that I would end up at Headquarters in Ottawa myself.

The course included lecture upon lecture on the Criminal Code, all aspects of counterfeiting, fingerprinting and so on, with drill, revolver shooting and physical training thrown in for good measure.

One morning I was sent for by Assistant Commissioner T. B. Caulkin who had been my friend at Herschel Island in 1926. As Officer Commanding of "G" Division, which took in the entire Arctic, he was my commanding officer. I was glad to see him again and to be able to give him a first-hand account of his many friends in the North, both Eskimos and whites. After the preliminaries were done with, he told me that Commissioner S. T. Wood wanted to see me and personally discuss the next voyage of the *St. Roch* with me. I had never met Commissioner Wood, who later succeeded Sir James MacBrien as Senior Officer of the Force when the latter died in 1938. But Wood had been the man responsible for the building of the *St. Roch* and he had always taken a personal interest in the ship and its activities.

When Caulkin and I arrived in the Commissioner's office I was completely taken aback when I learned that I was to take the *St. Roch* into the western Arctic with a full load of supplies for all the detachments there and retain eighteen months' supplies for ourselves, so that I could take the ship into the eastern Arctic in an attempt to reach Halifax. If this turned out to be impossible, we were to winter somewhere in the eastern Arctic waters, near Lancaster Sound. In short, we were assigned the task of sailing from the west to the east; if successful, ours would be the first ship to conquer the Northwest Passage in that direction. After having outlined his plans, the Commissioner added that we were to leave as soon as the season permitted and asked if I thought this voyage could be successfully completed. I replied that I couldn't foresee any great difficulties if the season was anything near normal as far as ice and weather conditions were concerned. The past season had been perfect with regard to the ice, but on the other hand we might run into conditions like those of the 1935-36 season, and then we would have to winter somewhere and complete the voyage in two seasons. We agreed that in such an eventuality Banks Island would be ideal for wintering, as we could go out on long sled trips from there to cover a large area which previously had never been patrolled by the police, being too far from the nearest detachment at Coppermine.

So here it was. My great moment. Canada was at war and the government had realized the need to demonstrate the country's sovereignty over the Arctic islands. To me it seemed only natural that it would entrust this responsibility to the Royal Canadian Mounted Police, who had carried the responsibility in the North ever since the first detachment was established at Cape Fullerton on the west side of Hudson's Bay in 1903. When the government had sent an expedition into the Arctic for the purpose of patrolling, exploring and establishing authority on the northwest coast of Hudson Bay and the islands to the north, it was understood that all these islands were being looked after by Canada. They had been discovered by British explorers in the early 1800's, but our trip would be the first time in twenty-three years that a Canadian ship had visited many parts of the Arctic Archipelago. The Norwegian Otto Sverdrup had also discovered and drawn attention to a great deal of new land in the very middle of the Archipelago Canada was supposed to control.

When he sailed northward into Baffin Bay, Sverdrup met nobody but a party of Americans who had seized a great chunk of land in that area. This was Admiral Peary and his party, who were interested mostly in reaching the North Pole. Something had to be done quickly and in May of 1903 Prime Minister Sir Wilfrid Laurier decided that the Canadian government had to assume full responsibility for the Far North. With that followed the opening of the North West Mounted Police post on Herschel Island where for years American whaling ships had been trading with whites and Eskimos, without any questions being asked. Canadian rights were now to be enforced.

In the eastern Arctic the old sealing ship *Neptune* left Halifax that same year, 1903, on an expedition under the command of a government geologist, A. P. Low. Major J. D. Moodie of the then North West Mounted Police was appointed Acting Commissioner of the still-unorganized Northeastern Territories. Under his command were one non-commissioned officer and four constables, the nucleus of the force that later would man several posts throughout the area.

The *Neptune* went as far north as Smith Sound and west to Beechey Island, and on Ellesmere Island Major Low conducted a brief ceremony formally taking possession of it for Canada. While the *Neptune* was still in the North, another government expedition was actually being planned under Sea Captain Joseph Bernier who for more than a decade had advocated an expedition into the Arctic. The Canadian government bought the German Antarctic ship the *Gauss*, which was of a similar construction to Nansen's *Fram*. It was only natural that the able Captain Bernier was put in command and with this ship he patrolled the eastern Arctic waters until 1926. He wintered at Melville Island in 1908-9 and, under a commission granted by the British Crown, took formal possession of all the Arctic islands lying to the north of Canada. During the 1930's three of the police detachments that had been established in this area were closed down owing to difficulties in supplying them. By then the Hudson's Bay Company had taken over the transportation of supplies to the North, and in the east the company had the Eastern Arctic Patrol, which included government officials concerned with the administration of the area. By 1940 there were only two police detachments left, at Craig Harbour and near Lancaster Sound at Pond Inlet. Since we were at war, however, it was imperative that Canadian sovereignty be exercised in this huge area. Our policemen, who had operated in the Arctic for years, no doubt were the best choice for this task.

Ever since I had joined the *St. Roch*, and even before, when I had talked to Inspector Kemp at Herschel Island in 1928, I had been looking forward to the time when we could get away from the beaten track along the western Arctic coast and carry out some of the work that had been on the program when the vessel was built. I had also spoken to Sir James MacBrien about it when he visited the ship at Cambridge Bay in 1937, but at that time I had been somewhat rebuffed when he reminded me that we were policemen and not explorers. But he had added that he hoped that I some day would get my wish granted. It took the war to bring this about.

The government realized that the area had to be patrolled to avoid any enemy intrusions in the empty spaces and it had no intention of losing sovereignty over its Arctic Islands, a territory of half a million square miles.

Being Norwegian-born, I was familiar with the controversy over sovereignty which had taken place between the Canadian government and Otto Sverdrup, the Norwegian explorer. For the entire period between 1907 and 1930 this had been going on. Sverdrup, who had discovered the islands in 1898-1902, had claimed them in the name of King Oscar II of the United Kingdoms of Norway and Sweden. The explorer had assumed that the Foreign Ministry in Stockholm had taken the necessary steps to legalize this claim, but it turned out that the Swedish part of the Union had a tendency to regard this as being of lesser importance. However, even if a formal claim had been made through diplomatic channels at the time, it now seems doubtful that it would have remained valid for long, because such men as Peary, Frederick Cook and MacMillan had crossed Sverdrup's island and territory numerous times, without the question of ownership ever being raised. On the other hand, Stefansson had made a wide sweep of all the Sverdrup Islands, discovering and mapping those Sverdrup himself had missed and thereby no doubt had strengthened Canada's position as far as the sovereignty was concerned.

In 1919 the Dane Knud Rasmussen had gone on a rampage of muskox killing on Ellesmere Island and the Greenland Eskimos soon followed his example. When the Canadian government protested and complained that Rasmussen had not obtained permission to hunt in Canada, he answered that he considered the territory no-man's-land. The Danish government seemed to back up this contention. In the meantime, Sverdrup, now back in Oslo, renewed his efforts to get something done about proclaiming Norwegian sovereignty over the area, which he felt should be occupied by the Norwegians. This, finally, did raise some eyebrows in Canada and when a dispute broke out between Norway and Denmark over some fishing rights on the north-east coast of Greenland, Ottawa decided that the time had come to dispatch the old *Arctic*, which was recommissioned and hastily placed under Captain Bernier's command. The old salt was now almost seventy years of age, but set out on the first annual summer patrol to maintain Canada's jurisdiction in the Archipelago. Police posts were set up on Baffin, Devon and Ellesmere Islands, and thus for the first time Canada had effective control over the region. Sverdrup, however, still did not give in, even though the Norwegian authorities never really supported him. A few weeks before his death in 1930, he had the satisfaction of receiving a cheque in the amount of $67,000 from the Canadian government.

In my opinion Otto Sverdrup was the most competent and practical of all the Norwegian explorers of that area. Being both shy and humble, he was satisfied with taking a back seat and was, of course, greatly overshadowed by other Norwegians like Nansen and Amundsen. However, from my own personal experience in the Arctic I consider that Sverdrup was the greatest of the three men.

These details of explorations and rival territorial claims may help underline the importance of the mission we had been given by Commissioner Wood. The Northwest Passage, moreover, had always held a very special fascination for me and I had read the whole interesting story about it in John Cabot's son Sebastian's account of his travels to Hudson Bay in 1504. As a former Norwegian I had also been particularly interested in the explorer Roald Amundsen's voyage with the *Gjoa* in 1903, when he sailed through the Passage from the east in search of the Magnetic North Pole, which he located. The Magnetic Pole then had moved considerably since James Ross first had found it in 1831.

The next great expedition was that of Stefansson, and his observations and discoveries are still of the greatest importance today. In many ways Stefansson was unique: it was typical of him that he maintained himself in the Arctic by fishing and hunting like the Eskimos. His many books on the Arctic are today considered textbooks on the polar regions.

For many years after these great explorations, the Canadian Arctic was thought of in terms of two separate regions. The eastern Arctic remained largely unknown to those who lived in the west, and not until the 1930's, when two ship crews met, one from each part of the vast area, was all of this territory thought of as really one entity. Although the Police had carried out some history-making sled patrols in the North, it was the aircraft that brought about the final "unification" of the North. At the time when we sailed through the Northwest Passage, however, planes were still rare in the North.

44 TOWARD THE GREAT ADVENTURE

When I returned to the *St. Roch* after the completion of my course in late March, I was full of enthusiasm over what was ahead of us. Our destination was to be kept a secret until we reached the North, as no undue publicity was wanted. Only two crew members—the engineer, Corporal Jack Foster, and the Mate, Constable Farrar—were informed of the project, but I was under orders not to tell even them until we had reached Arctic waters several weeks later.

It was imperative that we get under way no later than June if we were to complete our assignment, and I was quite upset on my return to the ship to find that nothing had been done to her in my absence. The Naval Dockyard at Esquimalt was working to capacity with other commitments for the Navy in connection with the war, and I had to pull quite a few strings to get the work done. Actually all that really had to be done was to install another little auxiliary engine to charge the bank of batteries we needed for electric light, which previously we had been able to use only when the main generator was running. We also removed the old iron sheathing around the stem and replaced it with a completely new shoeing, bent all around the stem and extending several feet back, where it was fastened with heavy bolts. Our new bow became very sharp instead of almost a foot across, as it had been. With the almost knife-sharp bow we would be able to split even fairly heavy ice-floes, and this was something I had wished for ever since I had joined the ship. All told, I would say that by the time the *St. Roch* was ready to sail, she was in much better shape then she ever had been.

We headed north on June 21, 1940. In addition to Foster and Farrar we had on board such old hands as Dad Parry, the cook, and Albert "Frenchy" Chartrand. The newcomers were constables Jimmy Friederick, who was assigned to assist Jack Foster in the engine room, Johnnie Monette, another young Westerner, Patrick Hunt, who was only going as far as the Coppermine detachment with us, and finally our youngest crew member, twenty-one-year-old Edward Hadley our wireless operator. Not too impressive a crew in comparison with other Arctic ships, but they were all good fellows and what they perhaps lacked in experience, they amply made up for by enthusiasm. Only Fred Farrar and I could steer or understand the compass fully, although Frenchy Chartrand had picked up quite a bit of the necessary knowledge on our previous trip.

Two changes in the crew were made later as Constable Friederick went ashore at Herschel Island and was replaced by Constable Bill Peters, and Constable Monette joined the Coppermine detachment instead of Patrick Hunt, who stayed with us and ended up being one of the best sailors I had with me over the years.

We managed to get as far as Cambridge Bay, which we reached in early September without a hitch, but then found that it was too late in the season to get through the Northwest Passage. Reluctantly we headed back with the intention of wintering on Banks Island. Here we ran into some difficulties, and ended up wintering at Walker Bay on the east coast of Victoria Island late that month. We were locked in by the ice.

It was here that Captain Collinson had wintered with H.M.S. *Enterprise* ninety years earlier during the search for Sir John Franklin. We were, of course, disappointed that we had been unable to sail through the Northwest Passage in one season, but knew that we had a busy winter ahead of us, patrolling the surrounding area as well as Banks Island.

We were pleasantly surprised to meet Klengenberg's widow and the rest of his family, with the exception of Patsy, near our winter quarters at Minto Inlet. Mrs. Klengenberg was a wonderful person who led a full life with her children and grandchildren. It was obvious that the children had inherited the best of both parents. Although none of the Klengenberg boys had received any formal education, they could all read and write and were great hunters and fishermen. They lived entirely as Eskimos, surpassing the full-blooded Eskimos in their own skills.

When Christmas came we celebrated alone. A terrific storm prevented all our invited and uninvited guests from reaching us. The Christmas dinner consisted of ookpiks, small Arctic owls which taste quite a bit like turkey, and the climax of our holiday celebrations was radio greetings from the Commissioner of the Mounted Police and others, not the least from our own families. The messages were loud and clear, and I was thrilled to hear the voices of my wife and daughter.

The longest sled patrol we made that winter was to Banks Island, where we had many police tasks to perform. It was particularly important to find out how the Eskimos there viewed the new hunting and trapping regulations. These were not just ordinary Eskimos, but highly skilled hunters and trappers who had been trained by white experts on Herschel Island and in the Mackenzie District. Some of these Eskimos were very wealthy. In a good year a man could make up to ten or fifteen thousand dollars if the fur prices were right. Banks Island, incidentally, was closed to white trappers as it was a game preserve.

Accompanied by Constable Bill Peters and the interpreter George Porter, I left Walker Bay on March 17, 1941. We had two teams and a good load of provisions. Dog food had already been cached at Berkely Point where it was looked after by Qaaunnak, and as promised he came with us as far as De Salis Bay to help us with our loads across Prince of Wales Strait, where it was very difficult to travel over the broken ice. We found that there was so much open water that we had to proceed quite a distance to the north before we even dared set across.

When at last we reached Banks Island the going got even rougher and it was almost impossible to advance with our heavy sleds, which were badly suited for that type of travelling and made it very hard on the dogs. The weather turned bad too, with heavy snowstorms, and only after almost two weeks did we reach Sachs Harbour, where there was a great Eskimo camp. On the way we had seen foxes and large groups of rabbits who scarcely moved out of our way, and we shot quite a few to feed our dogs.

All told, there were seven families at Sachs Harbour, and I was happy to find that the stories I had heard of illegal trapping were false. I had known most of these people for years and considered them friends. They had no idea that we were coming; as a matter of fact, they did not even know that we were wintering at Walker Bay. The trapping season closed on the day of our arrival, and all the traps had already been picked up for the season. The Eskimos were busy skinning and drying fox pelts and there were heaps of frozen carcasses piled up, out of reach of the dogs. We then continued further north to Storkerson Bay, where there were five additional families, and then returned to Sachs Harbour, where we spent Easter.

Among the people I met were old Adam and his wife. When I first met Adam in 1924 I had considered him very old and I remembered him specifically because of his dentures. At one time the area around Herschel Island and the Mackenzie had been a Mecca for itinerant dentists. They visited Eskimos who were rich from trapping and filled cavities, extracted teeth and made dentures. On Herschel Island I had even seen Eskimos who had had healthy teeth extracted and replaced by gold teeth which they proudly showed with big grins. Both Adam and his wife had dentures, but unhappily they kept on falling out. This annoyed Adam no end, as he had paid quite a bit for the plates, but in the end he decided to make his own. Using the dentist's plates as models, he carved himself a durable set of teeth from muskox horn and he claimed that these worked much better than the set of plates he had bought. His wife confided to me that she thought the dentist's plates were nice to have in her mouth and to smile with, but that she couldn't bite with them.

I later heard that old Adam froze to death the next year. He had been out hunting with a grandson when they were caught by a blinding snowstorm which lasted several days. They ran out of food and fuel and the old man was too weak to build an igloo. The two of them therefore sought shelter in a hollow they dug out of the snow. Adam put most of his own clothes on the boy so that he shouldn't freeze to death and placed himself on top of the boy to keep him warm. In this position they were found, but too late for the old man. He had, however, saved the life of his grandson by sheltering him.

Our last sled patrol before we left Walker Bay started on May 17. On this trip Chartrand came with me and we headed for Prince of Wales Strait looking for possible anchorages we might find useful when we were to sail the channel. We found the Princess Royal Islands particularly interesting, as it was here that Sir Robert McClure had wintered with the *Investigator* in 1850-51. How he had managed to hang on there in the strong current without an engine was a mystery to me, but then McClure was one of the greatest Arctic navigators. He had come in from the western Arctic and the Bering Strait and then gone into the channel he named Prince of Wales Strait. After wintering, he went around Banks Island and explored it on foot. From a vantage point on the northern tip of the island he could look across to the mountains on Melville Island over the short stretch of water separating the two islands. This strait was blocked by heavy polar ice when he reached it. It is this small body of water which practically constitutes the real key to the Northwest Passage, or at least one of the routes. It was later named McClure Strait, and the *St. Roch* was the first ship to sail through it, later in 1944.

A few hours after Chartrand and I had gone to sleep on the Princess Royal Island, which we had reached in heavy fog, I woke in brilliant sunshine. Still on my knees in the sleeping-bag and peering through the tent flap I spotted an enormous ujjuk asleep on the ice a few hundred yards away. We could do with some meat, so I dressed in a hurry and woke Chartrand to tell him what I was up to. Carefully I stalked the ujjuk and managed to get within less than a hundred yards of him, protected by small drifts of snow and pieces of broken ice. The animal looked up once in a while only to drop his head again. I aimed and when he lifted his head again, I fired and killed him instantly with a shot through the brain. All set to run up to the dead animal I suddenly realized that there was blue water rushing past under the snow and that I was standing only on a hard crust of snow honeycombed by the water. I felt my way carefully around and realized that it would be impossible to reach the ujjuk without a line for safety in case I fell through. Chartrand came running up to see if he could help me, but I shouted to him to keep back. Now we understood why the snow had been so bad when we had set up our tent in the dark, and in a hurry we broke camp and started to move our things to safety. The ujjuk, however, was still waiting for me. With the dogs hitched to an empty sled I moved as close to the seal as I dared, and then unhitched them and turned them around, facing away from the animal. I then tied a long line to the dogs, with myself to the other end of it, so that they could drag me out if I fell through. Slowly I crawled forward on my stomach and in the excitement I didn't even notice that I was soaked to the skin. Fortunately the seal was on a solid piece of ice or the gallon or so of blood pouring out of him would have melted the snow long since. But the line was a few feet too short even after Chartrand had let it out to the very last inch. Quickly I took off my heavy leather belt and fastened it to my end of the line, then cut a few slits in the heavy lips of the seal and fastened the belt in them. With a jump I straddled the ujjuk and shouted to Chartrand to pull away. With a sharp flick of his whip and a mighty shout of "Mush, you brutes" to the dogs, off they went in a streak with the heavy ujjuk, weighing more than a thousand pounds, sliding along very easily across the ice. The meat was most welcome and the liver was delicious. Perhaps the meal tasted even better for knowing that the two of us had been so close to losing our lives on the weak ice.

45 THE SUMMER OF BROKEN EXPECTATIONS

When Chartrand and I reached the *St. Roch* again, the season for sled patrols was over and spring was near, so we started to get the ship ready for the summer operations.

Close as we were to the key to the Northwest Passage we were then ordered to return to Tuttujartuuq to assist in moving incoming supplies to various detachments and posts. With the war there was an acute shortage of other transportation along the coast and we were, of course, disappointed. Here we were with a summer full of daylight ahead of us, ordered back to start handling cargo.

When we left Walker Bay on July 31 it was to be the last time I saw Mrs. Klengenberg. I later heard from her daughter Edna that she kept strong for another two or three years, but then began to get weak and was anything but her old self. Yet she continued to hunt and trap until one day she went out never to return. First they started to search for her, and then they realized that she had left dressed in her oldest clothes. A storm came up, making it impossible to search any further. Her son-in-law, Ikey Bolt, understood that the old woman had deliberately walked out into the storm to die alone at a spot she had probably picked in advance so as not to be a burden to her family. She was never found.

Tuk-Tuk, with very shallow water and a strong current, is a very difficult place to moor a ship. The only way to do it was to get an anchor out and then swing the ship around in the desired direction and quickly get out a line from the stern and fasten it to the beach. Chartrand and a couple of the other men were put ashore to catch the line and fasten it to some heavy chains that had been dug into the ground. Chartrand, strong as a bull, often did two men's work. He ran into the water and grabbed the heavy stern line, and before anybody could give him a hand with it, ran up the beach dragging it behind him. He had just fastened it to a loop in the chain when he collapsed, with perspiration pouring from his face and hands. He recovered just as quickly, but sat up visibly shaken. As soon as we had the ship securely moored I got him aboard and asked how he felt and suggested that perhaps he should take the opportunity to see the doctor who was expected very shortly. But no. Chartrand wanted no part of that. One never knew what a doctor would say, he answered. A doctor might even send an otherwise healthy man back Outside, he added. After a couple of days the incident was completely forgotten and Chartrand was his old self again.

When we reached Coppermine on our return trip we realized that the ice was again too heavy and that we had small chance of making the Northwest Passage that summer either. During the almost completely calm months of June and July the ice had remained instead of breaking up and drifting away with the wind and the current. I had noticed that if we had good breezes of easterly and southeasterly winds during these months there would be plenty of open water for navigation. But we got the winds too late and, what was worse, they came from the wrong direction. I therefore decided to continue eastward through Queen Maud Gulf, now certain that it would be impossible to get through McClure Strait. I was not too keen on wintering at Walker Bay again, no matter how beautiful the place was, and I also knew that we would have our hands full with the Census in the east. That in itself would be quite a job, for the Eskimos often changed their names. Missionaries, traders and policemen could have different names for the same people.

I was back in a familiar area and when we reached Gjoa Haven, I felt sure that we would get to Halifax that year, in spite of our previous pessimism. But again the ice barred us. In the middle of Rae Strait, between Cape Colville and Mount Matheson, it looked as if old Niviassiaq's curse was in force. Again we were met by snow and hail, but this was no place to get stuck; so we headed for the southeasterly point on Mount Matheson and dropped anchor as close to the shore as possible. When the weather let up a little we continued, with one man constantly sounding and with myself at the wheel. Another man was in the lookout trying to peer ahead.

46 A VERY CLOSE SHAVE

When we approached the area between Spence Bay and Matty Island we ran into some large shoals which came up abruptly from ten to two and a half fathoms. We had to be very careful and constantly turn around to look for deeper water.

When the weather finally cleared, we proceeded cautiously eastward, but in the narrowest point between Matty Island and Boothia we were completely stopped by a solid pack of ice which extended right across our course from shore to shore. Much of the ice was aground and the current was very strong there. This was close to where Amundsen had grounded with the *Gjoa* and nearly lost her, and I had no wish to go through that kind of ordeal. As the ice started to surround us, I back-tracked a bit and proceeded to the Boothia shore, as close as I dared, and then anchored by a small rocky islet, not much longer than the ship. We had barely settled down when a strong snowstorm came up from the northeast. Both anchors were let out and we prayed that they would hold. We had the engine going most of the night, with huge ice-floes crashing down on us. With the engine we managed to turn some of the floes aside, but we were in constant danger, and all of us spent the whole night on the fo'c'sle peering into the darkness and the blinding snowstorm. This was, without doubt, one of the most difficult nights I, or any of the others, had experienced. The next morning the wind changed to south and began driving the ice northward and us with it. We had another hard night, and some were all for returning to winter at Gjoa Haven, as it was obvious that we wouldn't be able to make it further east that year. This did not appeal to me, the weather being what it was, and besides, I did not particularly want to give up any of the hard-earned miles we had behind us, only to try again next summer and perhaps be forced to give up and return west.

Heavy blue polar ice-floes being pressed down the McClintock Channel were now surrounding us and I decided to head for Pasley Bay, halfway up the east coast of Boothia Peninsula. The old British Admiralty charts made in 1855 showed an inlet in the bay which should give us the necessary protection. As we headed into it, I knew that this was it. Had we not found the inlet, we would have been pushed by the ice right up on shore.

It was not long before we were completely locked in and drifting with the ice, dragging our anchors along. The ice slackened slightly, enough for us to heave in the anchors and head for a little patch of open water in the basin, but then the wind came up stronger again, driving all the ice ahead of it. Starting the engine, we tried to hold ground, but again got carried along helplessly by the tight-packed ice which now was held together by thick slush and snow. It was almost impossible to see or even to keep one's eyes open. It looked as if the elements were bent on our destruction.

Around four o'clock in the morning of September 6 the ice had carried us toward one of the big shoals we had spotted previously. The ship struck, pivoted twice and then remained on the shoal for a few minutes before she started to list to port. It looked as if she was going to topple completely when the ice started to climb right over the starboard side, now high out of the water. Our port rail was already buried under the ice. This was a most uncomfortable situation, and we were all on deck trying to hang on to anything we could get hold of. All the time, the deck seemed to be in instant danger of being completely buried.

I wondered if we had come this far only to be crushed like a nut on a shoal and then buried by the ice. Then suddenly a larger ice-floe came crashing through the darkness and hit the side of the ship, making it list even more. She was practically on her beam ends and it was our luck that the pressure did not let up just then, but kept on as if by a miracle until the ship was pushed over and a few moments later floated on an even keel in deep water. We were still being pushed along with the ice, dragging both anchors with ninety fathoms of chain on each. Incredible as it sounds, the *St. Roch* was still in good shape, both the rudder and the engine undamaged in spite of the terrifying bombardment by the ice and the slide across the shoal. Once more the little ship had proved that she could take it and had come through with flying colours.

Our troubles, however, were still not over. The ice started to push us over to the east again, but as we neared the other shore I spotted a huge boulder or rock on the shore we were pushed alongside. On the fo'c'sle head we had a reel with several hundred feet of wire cable and this was an opportunity to use it. By now we were only some one hundred feet from the shore, lying parallel with it. The only thing that kept us from being pushed right up on land was the ice between the ship and the shore line. Our starboard anchor was out to the last chain-link when I shouted to Chartrand, Hunt and Hadley to get down on the ice in a hurry and grab the end of our wire cable and head for the rock. By fastening the cable to the rock I hoped to hold fast. The boys realized the importance of what they were doing and soon had the wire fastened, while Farrar and I managed to snub it and make it fast to our heavy bollards with a couple of hundred feet out now. The wire tightened up with a jerk and the ship was hanging as though in a bridle between the anchor and the wire. Our calculations were correct. This prevented us from drifting backward and the great ice-floes across our bow now swung off and drifted by.

As if it had understood that now it could not succeed in pushing us ashore, the wind suddenly dropped to an almost instant calm and all the ice around us became stationary, with young ice forming quickly between the old floes and binding them tight together.

We lost no time in getting out our pickaxes and shovels and sinking two pieces of timber into the ground ashore, where we fastened stern lines from the ship to hold her in that position should the wind come up again. But all remained calm, and the next morning we had the most beautiful sunshine. After all we had been through, a clear sky was almost unbelievable.

From a slope on the land behind the ship we could look out over the bay and the long inlet where we were located. It was absolutely packed solid with heavy, blue polar ice shining in the sun. There was no doubt about it. This was to be our winter quarters.

Our further explorations revealed that there were deep ravines on both sides of the bay. In the bottom of these ravines we found old river beds running inland. At the bottom of the bay there was still a river of fair size, running from between two mountains we could see far in the distance. This was a good sign that indicated that we would have plenty of fresh water during the spring thaw and the summer. In turn, this would help to melt and wear down the heavy accumulation of old sea ice, which probably could not melt in the heat of the sun alone.

Although we were disappointed that we would not be able to complete the Passage that year we knew, at least, that we now had come so far that there would be no question of turning back.

One of the first things we did was to start to look around for Eskimos, but without success. However, we did get in touch by radio with the Hudson's Bay post at Fort Ross on the eastern side of Bellot Strait, some 150 miles away. The post manager there was Bill Heslop, who told us that his company's ship *Nascopie* had been to Fort Ross with a large party of government scientists, doctors and administrators. They had left again and had encountered no problems with ice. Somehow we had the feeling that the Master of the *Nascopie,* Captain Thomas F. Smellie, an old hand in the eastern Arctic, thought we were real fools for not making it.

47 A TRAGIC LOSS

In October, Bill Peters and I made a short exploratory trip north along the coast as far as Tasmania Islands. We saw that the heavy old ice had been pushed up along the shore and it was obvious that had we continued north instead of being stuck at Pasley Bay, this certainly would have meant the end of the *St. Roch*. This stretch of coast from James Ross Strait to Franklin Strait* can be classed as the key to the southern route of the Northwest Passage, in much the same way as McClure Strait holds the key in the west.

We also had established bi-weekly radio schedules with Coppermine, and pretty soon everybody in the Arctic knew where we were. Our old friend Learmonth, the Hudson's Bay manager at Gjoa Haven, some

*This body of water has since been named Larsen Sound by the Canadian government after Larsen's death in October 1964.

two hundred miles away, could hear our broadcasts, of course, but as he had no transmitter of his own he couldn't get in touch with us. We asked if he could send us a good Eskimo, who could accompany us on our travels that winter for the purpose of taking the Census at the various Eskimo camps on the eastern portion of Boothia. Late one evening around the middle of November our request was answered when a lone Eskimo arrived at the ship. It was none other than our old friend Ikualaaq, the same man who had shown me Niviassiaq's grave back in 1937. He had travelled over two hundred miles to reach us after Learmonth had asked him to join our party. The area we were in was known to the Eskimos as Qatigaujut, he told us. This was descriptive of the bay we were in, which had three arms.

Ikualaaq and I eventually reached Fort Ross on our Census patrol, and were given a warm welcome by Bill Heslop and his wife Barbara. Between Fort Ross and Pasley Bay we visited with many Eskimos, arriving back just in time for Christmas. Jack Foster greeted us on our arrival with the news of the Japanese attack on Pearl Harbor during our trip, which had covered some 320 miles.

Chartrand, Ikualaaq and I took off again on another trip on January 5. The main purpose this time was to establish a food cache at Gjoa Haven for longer Census patrols later on and also to collect some winter clothing the people there were making for us. While we visited Gjoa Haven, Chartrand stayed with Learmonth and Ikualaaq had a few days at the seal camp with his wife and family. When they returned, they reported that the Eskimos they had met all looked well fed and healthy and that they were doing well both hunting and trapping.

I knew that I could always rely on Chartrand: he was very conscientious, and I planned to take him along on the long patrol that was coming up. In the meantime we busied ourselves with more or less routine tasks when we returned to our ship. One of the more important jobs was to cook dog food. Oddly enough, this required a certain amount of skill and patience, and Jack Foster, Chartrand and I took turns doing this chore. The cooking was done in a ten-gallon drum on deck, where we placed the container on two primus stoves. After we had mixed a huge mass of rice, cornmeal and rolled oats with tallow and seal blubber added, there was quite a bit of stirring to do.

On February 13 it was Chartrand's turn to act as dog cook. Loving the dogs the way he did, he really enjoyed himself and looked forward to the job. At breakfast time everything was as usual, all of us sitting around the table chatting for a while. Chartrand complained that he had a slight headache, but nobody paid much attention to that. Shortly after, he went out on deck and lit the primus stoves, but when I got out on deck I found that he was far from well and he complained of feeling chilly. "You had better get down below for a while and take a rest," I said. "I'll be walking here on deck for a while anyway and will look after your dog food." Not too long after, Frenchy felt better. He got up and sat up in the fo'c'sle with the rest of the boys, listening to the radio. Suddenly he collapsed. I was called down and rushed below to see what was going on. To me this seemed like some kind of a seizure because he was soon back on his feet again, said, "Thank God that's over," and rolled himself a cigarette. When I asked him how he felt, he assured me that he was okay and I then returned to the deck.

Less than five minutes later, Pat Hunt shouted up to me: "Hurry down, Skipper, Frenchy is dying!" Chartrand was flat on his back, his hands flailing around. He was unconscious, and a moment or so later he died.

There was nothing any of us could have done to help him and we were completely stunned. During my fourteen years on the *St. Roch* we had been spared any form of human tragedy or even serious accidents. The sudden death of our friend grieved us all very deeply. I recalled that Chartrand had collapsed the previous summer at Tuk-Tuk and had complained of pains in his chest, but it was impossible to say whether or not this had been the first warning of a heart condition. Like all the rest of us he had passed a special medical examination before we left Vancouver and had been found fit for northern service. The incident at Tuk-Tuk had been forgotten, not the least because Frenchy himself had carried on in his usual cheerful way.

Chartrand had been extremely well liked by all in the North, both police and civilians. Behind him he had sixteen years with the Force, mostly in the North, which was the duty he preferred. Yet this was to have been his last trip in the Arctic. He had told us that he was engaged and planned to get married when we returned Outside. I had met his parents in Ottawa and recalled how proud they were of Albert, who was in the RCMP. After the first shock was over we sent word to the Ottawa Headquarters where Superintendent D. J. Martin, the Officer Commanding of "G" Division, personally went to inform Chartrand's family of the tragic death of our friend. At first they wanted to have the body shipped out or a priest flown in so he could be buried according to the rites of his own church. However, it was impossible to have an aircraft fly in to us during the winter, and to ship the body out was equally out of the question.

He had been the only Roman Catholic of the crew and all the others shared my opinion that the last rites of the Church should be administered, knowing as we did how much this meant to members of his faith. The nearest priest was more than four hundred miles away, down at Pelly Bay in the Gulf of Boothia, where Father Henri of the Oblates had a little mission. We decided that I would go down and get the Father to come up to bury poor Chartrand. In the meantime we made a coffin and buried it in a snowbank close by. This would have to do until spring, when we hoped to have the priest perform the real funeral.

On February 24 Constable Hunt, Ikualaaq and I left on our patrol with fully loaded sleds and provisions for the dogs and ourselves for two months. Near Cape Garry Ikualaaq pointed out a very ancient settlement to me. The houses had been built of whalebone and rocks on a ridge well above the present shore line, and had been abandoned centuries ago. Whether or not the people who had lived there had been similar to the present day Eskimos was hard to tell, but one thing was certain, they had been whale hunters, which the modern-day population of that area was not. Huge whale skulls, white with age, were standing upright in the ground and formed some kind of lanes and also supported the entrances to the abandoned houses. Ikualaaq said that we had passed a larger, similar settlement at Cape Esther a few miles back, and mentioned that the Eskimos of the area had visited these places for years to dig out the huge ribs and jawbones of the whales and split them up for use on their sleds. Such ancient dwellings were to be found all the way down the east coast of Boothia, and the Eskimos referred to the people who had lived in them as Tunits. According to legends the Tunits had been very tall and strong, almost giants, and this was plausible judging from the size of some of the rocks around the sites.

As we neared a large Eskimo camp on Athol Island, we were surprised not to see any people around, although there were several hundred well-fed dogs roaming about. Soon these dogs started to pick fights with ours, but in spite of all the racket, there were still no people to be seen. We had, however, spotted a large, new snow house a little away from the others, and when we moved closer we could hear noises from inside. I got down on my hands and knees and crawled in through the long narrow tunnel leading into the igloo, with Pat Hunt and

Ikualaaq hard on my heels. Then I heard a familiar hymn being sung in Eskimo to the accompaniment of what sounded like an accordion. Pushing the door open we crawled in and stood up to find the igloo packed with people, all of them standing around a giant of a white man dressed in a great pair of polar bear pants and a white Hudson's Bay duffle parka, which was trimmed with white bear skin so that it looked like a halo round his head. He was pumping away on a concertina, playing the hymn "Shall We Gather at the River." I could almost hear his jaw snap shut as the singing stopped, and there was no denying that the man looked concerned. Both Pat Hunt and I had quite long, bushy beards, and were no doubt taken for two Roman Catholic priests who were dropping in on this Anglican service. Quickly we introduced ourselves as policemen and the big man informed us that he was Canon John Turner, the Anglican missionary stationed at Pond Inlet on the northern part of Baffin Island. He was then on his annual tour of his enormous parish.

The Canon offered to stop the service, but we urged them to go on and told him that we would be glad to join in with the rest. This made the Eskimos very happy, for it was the event of the year, and they managed to squeeze together to make room for Pat and me on the large sleeping-platform. Ikualaaq had already vanished among the crowd in the igloo. So the service started all over again, first with a little prayer in Eskimo led fluently by the Canon. Each person had a prayer book with hymns printed in syllabics, a kind of shorthand alphabet invented years ago by the Rev. James Evans for the Cree Indians, adapted by the Rev. E. J. Peck for the Eskimos, and since adopted by both Anglican and Roman Catholic missionaries. There was no sermon as such, but every hymn in the book was sung, with each Eskimo being asked to select his favourite. The hymn we had heard when we came in must have been selected and sung at least fifteen times. The Eskimos, who themselves had been used to gather at rivers to get together to fish down through the centuries, could readily understand this hymn. The sweat was pouring down the faces of the members of the congregation, all of them dressed in heavy winter clothing. Many women had babies on their backs, some sleeping peacefully while others were peeking over their mothers' shoulders.

I stole a quick glance at my watch and could hardly believe my eyes when I saw that it was almost two o'clock in the morning, with still no sign of the end. Judging from the change in pace of Canon Turner's playing, I could tell that his arms were getting tired, but he kept on. Then there was a mighty surge as all the Eskimos joined in with powerful voices. The usual expression when people sing loud is that they raise the roof, but in this instance the entire domed section of the large snow house caved in, right on top of us! Out went the candles and we were in total darkness except for two tiny blubber lamps that flickered on. The crowd roared with laughter. This was the funniest thing that had ever happened. First their Ajurissuiji, or Minister, had arrived a couple of days ago on his annual visit, followed by a couple of bearded men they had taken for priests, or Attatas. To top it all, the roof had caved in on top of them. There was no need—nor any use—to try to rebuild the roof at this time of night, and the service was considered over. So it was time to eat, as was the custom after any Eskimo service. Canon Turner did the cooking and Pat and I gave him a hand. It didn't take long to get the feast under way.

The last guests left the igloo around five in the morning. Pat and I then lay down to get some sleep, with Canon Turner in the middle, but when we woke up a few hours later the Canon was standing in the middle of the floor again with his concertina, conducting a morning service. This time the singing really lulled us to sleep and we must have snored away for at least a couple of hours until Canon Turner woke us after the service was over. He had a steaming plate of food ready for each of us which we ate while he was busy getting in gear in order to leave for Fort Ross to conduct services for the Eskimos in that area. He would have liked to have come down to visit our ship too, but that would have been too far out of his way, so instead he invited us all to come and see him at Pond Inlet. When he left we felt richer for having met him and taken part in his service. He also had a brother, Canon Arthur Turner, who had also come out from England and taken up missionary work in the Arctic. They were two great Apostles of the North.

Then it was back to work for us, too. During the Census-taking, we gave the Eskimos small identification tags. The Northwest Territories had been divided into areas coinciding with the police detachments, and each of these areas had its own identification letter and number which was used on the tag. The Eskimos, who liked trinkets, were delighted to carry these tags around their necks. The number on each tag was then marked down in a book together with all the names the person was known by, including the white men's names which many now had. The missionaries were giving the Eskimos all kinds of biblical names when they baptized them. Personally, I don't think this was the right thing to do, for their own names usually had a specific meaning. Furthermore, the Eskimos never learned how to pronounce the foreign names properly so that they could be understood by a stranger. Yet they never failed to give their biblical names first, obviously to please us.

At Thom Bay, which forms a part of Lord Mayor Bay, we saw many Eskimos sitting out on the ice, waiting for the seals at the breathing-holes. We had to shake hands with each of them, young and old, and learned that Canon Turner had visited them the previous week. Many of these people were Roman Catholics and right away pulled out some small crosses and religious medallions they were wearing, thinking that we were Attatas, or Catholic Fathers, and colleagues of Father Henri, who lived farther south.

To Ikualaaq's great amusement, several men immediately picked out a clean patch of snow and started to build an enormous igloo. He had to explain to the crowd that we were not priests or missionaries, but two policemen from a ship frozen in at Qatigaujut. It was also explained to them that we had come to count them all and ask them questions about their families so that the answers could be put down in a big book. He stressed that we were neither Protestant missionaries nor Fathers and different from that kind of men. We were slightly amused to hear the Police described in that way, but it served its purpose.

48 THE STORY OF A CANNON

While we were at Thom Bay I made many inquiries about the Sir John Ross Expedition which had spent three years in the neighbourhood aboard the *Victory*, from 1829 to 1832, before they finally abandoned their ship at Victoria Harbour, only a few miles away. The older Eskimos had heard stories about this from their fathers and grandfathers. Felix Harbour, where Ross had spent his first winter, was a mile or two away from the camp we were visiting, and had been a real gold mine to these people for more than a hundred years. It was here that

Ross had put ashore his little steam engine, the paddle-wheels and his leaky steam boiler and much other equipment. The Eskimos called the place Qalunaarsivik, which meant something like "the place where the white men had arrived." Victoria Harbour was called Qilanaartuut, which I understood to mean "the place where it is easy to pick up things." Here the Eskimos had still a good deal of iron, obtained from Ross's remnants. Knives, seal spears and even blubber lamps were made of the light boiler plates. As for the *Victory* itself, the Eskimos didn't think it had been broken up by the people there, but had drifted out of the little harbour and had sunk near by, because one winter she had been there and when they returned the next summer it was gone.

I asked if there were any guns left from the ship. They knew about the old ship's cannons and said there was a big pitissie at Victoria Harbour. (Pitissie was the Eskimo word for any weapon, be it a bow and arrow, a rifle or a cannon.) As soon as I heard about the cannon I set out with some older men for Victoria Harbour. On the shore we found lengths of cable, hemp rope, large pieces of iron, and nuts and bolts, as well as two ice anchors. Most surprising of all, however, was a big beautiful bronze cannon of a wonderful blue-green colour after 110 years up there. There was very little snow around where the cannon was, or I would have been unable to see it. On closer examination I found that the Eskimos had not even scratched it. This was something I wanted, but it was very heavy, perhaps close to a thousand pounds. It could, of course, very easily be pulled on a sled, but not at this time of the year when our work was still only half finished. Anyway, the Eskimos said they would like to come and visit our ship in the spring when there would be lots of seal on the ice, and two brothers offered to pull the cannon on their sleds.

With many complications, it took ten years to get the cannon! The Eskimos did come to see us in the spring, but without the cannon. A great snowstorm had come up and the snow had completely filled the land around the river bank where the cannon was and covered everything. They told us that many men and boys had prodded around in the snow with their spears and even shovelled a lot of the snow, without finding the prize. All I could say was that it was too bad and ask them to pull it to Gjoa Haven for me some time in the future. I did not get back to that part of the world until 1946 and when one of the Eskimos came to Gjoa Haven and told me that the cannon was still in the same place I only could ask him to look after it for me. It was too heavy to pull, the Eskimos said, because the dogs were not as good as they used to be. It was not until 1950-51 that I had a chance to get back to Victoria Harbour, then as Officer Commanding of "G" Division inspecting the new police post a few miles away. I flew in, in a police aircraft, and met my Eskimo friends who still remembered their promise about the cannon; and that spring the two brothers hauled it to our post when I arrived there again the following summer. Although my pilot, Bill Heacock, said it might be just possible to fly it out on the Norseman aircraft as far as Cambridge Bay, we though that a little too risky, and decided to leave it. Then along came the Hudson's Bay Company's little supply schooner, the *Nigalik,* and offered to take it aboard and take it to Cambridge Bay. There the United States Air Force came to the rescue and took the cannon to Fort St. John in northern British Columbia, from where the RCAF plane took over and brought it in to Winnipeg.

My old friend Sam Bullard, who then was Officer Commanding of the Mounted Police at Winnipeg, one day received a phone call from the Air Force informing him that they had a large cannon addressed to the RCMP. What were they to do with it, the Air Force asked. Bullard didn't know anything about the cannon and was wondering what on earth was going on, but sent off a truck to pick up the artillery. Since the cannon had arrived from the Arctic, however, Bullard thought it just might have something to do with me and notified the Commissioner. The question therefore was what the Force was going to do with the thing. First of all a permit was required from the Department of Northern Affairs to remove archaeological relics from the Arctic. My argument was that Sir John Ross's cannon could scarcely be classified as an archaeological relic, but as there were no permits for the removal of old cannons an archaeological permit had to be issued. I had suggested to Commissioner Wood that since the cannon had been the property of the British Admiralty perhaps it should be sent to the British Maritime Museum in Greenwich, England. The Commissioner liked the idea and forwarded it to Major-General Hugh Young, whom I had first met on Herschel Island in 1924 when he arrived there to establish the first Army Signal Section in the Arctic. He had then been a young lieutenant but was now the Deputy Minister of Northern Affairs and as such had the final say on the disposal of the old cannon. In his opinion there could be no more fitting custodian of this very interesting relic than the Royal Canadian Mounted Police, and so it ends its days at the RCMP Headquarters at Regina, where it is displayed with other old guns near the parade grounds.

In the fall of 1952, when I landed at Rockcliffe Airport after my inspection trip to the North, I was immediately ordered to proceed to Regina. I hardly had time to get home for a bath and a change of clothes and had no idea what this was all about, except that it had something to do with a ceremony. On my arrival at Regina the cannon was the first thing I asked about, but was only told to wait and see. My old friend Tam Taylor then led me over to the flagpole and there to my dismay I saw my old cannon, but instead of the beautiful bluish-green sheen it had accumulated in the Arctic, it was now polished until it shone like burnished gold. The Sergeant-Major had used it for keeping his young recruits occupied by polishing it. It would be an understatement to say that I was disappointed. It had lasted for 110 years in the Arctic without polishing, I remarked to Tam Taylor, but if they kept on polishing it every day for the next 110 years, there wouldn't be much left of it in the end.

49 EASTER WITH FATHER HENRI

With the story of the cannon, I have jumped a bit ahead of myself. Much of that story took place in later years. In the meantime we were still at Thom Bay. Now Ikualaaq felt it was about time for him to get back to his family, so he decided to get us another good man as guide, before he left. He therefore picked a very good man to go with us, but then another man, by the name of Kinguk approached us and said he was very eager to go with us, as he, according to his own statement, "belonged to the Father at Pelly Bay" and he knew many Eskimos would be gathered down there for the Easter service. Ikualaaq was quite put out, as the man he had picked had been a professed Protestant. Kinguk, however, insisted that as we had beards just like the Father at Pelly Bay, we must be the same as Kayoo, which was his name for the Father. It meant Red Beard. An explanation seemed necessary and I corrected Kinguk, and said that we were the King's men, the men of the Isumataq, the Great Chief! We were neither Fathers nor missionaries, but above them, I said, for that was the only way I could make the point that we didn't take sides in the rivalry between the Protestants and the Roman Catholics. The fact that Kinguk was a local man from Pelly Bay made us decide to take him along regardless of what plans Ikualaaq might have had, and we then headed south with our Roman Catholic guide. On the last day of March we reached Father Henri's mission near Kellett River. The Father was outside and had seen us at a distance when we stopped to feed the dogs before our arrival. It was better to do it that way when one arrived late at night, because of all the loose dogs running around any camp.

Father Henri had, of course, expected Eskimos for his service and was quite surprised to see our dog team, which was hitched in a fashion he had never seen before. His curiosity rose when he spotted two white men with beards covered with ice from several days' travelling. After we had introduced ourselves he lost no time in making us feel welcome. He lived in a stone house, about sixteen by twenty-four feet long, which he had built all by himself. It was really a masterpiece. Hundreds of little stones had been fitted together with clay he had dug from the ground about two feet below the topsoil.

The Father was a charming man who lived almost entirely off the land, which undoubtedly kept him in excellent physical shape. He had partitioned off one part of the house with skins and pieces of wood and there he had a little heater where he burned chunks of seal blubber and moss. It was here he slept and ate, but he generously turned the room over to us and insisted on sleeping on the floor himself. As he had neither tea nor coffee, he offered us a glass of wine, but when the little keg was brought out, it was frozen solid. After a while he had it thawed out and tired as we were after our long trip, one glass was enough to put us soundly to sleep, while the Father was saying his Midnight Mass.

Next morning we woke after he had held the morning service and, like his Anglican counterpart further north, he was making breakfast for us. When we tried to apologize for sleeping through his services, the Father just laughed in his kind, humorous way and said that it only seemed right that we should sleep like good Protestants while he prayed for us.

The Eskimos had not started to arrive yet, but they would all be there on the night before Good Friday, when he would have a whole little village of snow houses around his house. He took us around and showed us his stores of frozen seal and fish, stacked up like cordwood in a large underground storage place he had dug out and topped with a heavy stone structure.

Originally Father Henri had come from Brittany in France where his ancestors had been fishermen, and he had known how to make nets and to fish since boyhood. This had all come in pretty handy in the Arctic. The respect and devotion the Eskimos showed him was testimony to his ability to look after himself in the North.

The time had come to tell him about Chartrand's death and to ask him to come to Pasley Bay, if at all possible, to conduct a funeral service. The Father replied that he appreciated our respect for our dead friend's faith and agreed to come during the latter part of May, when the seals would be on the ice, so that he and the Eskimos he would take along could hunt for food and dog food on the way. We also told him about our meeting with Canon Turner and the service we had attended. The Father liked Canon Turner and called him a good man and a good missionary, who was good for the Eskimos, and made it clear that as far as he was concerned that was all that mattered.

Just as the Father had predicted, the Eskimos soon started to arrive and the place became full of loose dogs running around so it was difficult even to answer the calls of nature. This didn't seem to bother the Eskimos, both men and women would squat just anywhere in a handy snowbank, often right outside the igloos! The scavenging dogs did the clean-up job. Fortunately the Father had pointed out to Pat and me a large empty snow house, calling it his "bathroom." He also had a long, stout stick standing in a snowbank for use when visiting the "bathroom." I picked it up and started to wander over towards the igloo, and soon was surrounded by dogs who felt that something was up. Familiar as I was with the nature and behaviour of Eskimo dogs I was glad to have the stick and backed up to the wall of the igloo, as far as I could get. Squatting down, I waved the stick at the dogs now sitting in a semicircle in front of me. A little bitch, bolder than the rest, seemed to think that I took my time with what I was doing and suddenly let out an impatient bark, with the result that I quickly pulled up my pants and stepped aside. With the bitch in the lead, the dogs forged ahead to the attack, but not on me. Life in the Arctic truly could have its problems.

On Easter morning we joined in the service attended by about eighty Eskimos of all ages. The little stone building was packed, and only the very old could sit down on the floor close to the priest in front of his little improvised altar. On one side of it the Father had a great pile of frozen fish that was thawing slowly. On the other was a big blubber lamp with a large pot of meat, which was simmering ready for the feast which was to follow the service. The Father had taught these people hymns and prayers, and the service was held in the Eskimo language. Father Henri looked impressive in his robes, being a tall, fine-looking man with his red beard. I had never attended a Roman Catholic service before and somehow shared the awe of the Eskimos.

A lovely cherubic-looking little Eskimo boy acted as altar boy, dressed in a robe. During the Mass the priest would take a couple of seconds off and with a "Dominus" give a stir in the meat pot, while with a "vobiscum" he would quickly adjust the flame on the blubber lamp. It was the most impressive service I have ever attended, bar none. It was all so very special, the little primitive church in the wilderness, the enraptured looks on the faces of the Eskimos as they followed the service and every movement of the priest, the holy sacrament and the chanting of the Mass. The women, in particular, joined in the hymn-singing with exceptionally good voices.

A young woman standing next to me fainted twice, but nobody paid any attention to her as they were too busy singing. Each time, I dragged her outside in the cold, fresh air, and when she came to she just smiled and shuffled back in. Afterwards I learned that she had just come about one hundred miles and had given birth to a baby a few hours before the service!

After the service all the participants gave themselves over to rejoicing and indulging in a great feast. Heaps of boiled meat from the pot Father Henri had tended during the Mass were laid out on a large wooden tray hollowed out from a piece of driftwood log, and all the people stood around with chunks of meat in their hands. Father Henri then introduced Pat Hunt and me as the King's men, and told the Eskimos to give us a hearty welcome. This they did with their mouths full of meat.

We stayed with Father Henri for six days. Our guide Kinguk returned with us to Thom Bay, while one of the Pelly Bay Eskimos came with us to Gjoa Haven to trade his fox furs. It was a good thing that we had an excellent guide with us, for it was a strenuous trip. Both Pat and I suffered from very bad head colds we had come down with at Pelly Bay. Pat ended up with a real bout of the flu and we were both pretty weak when we finally made it to Gjoa Haven on April 15.

Our friend Learmonth gave us a warm welcome and so did Ikualaaq, who was all smiles when he saw us again. Learmonth's radio, however, had been out of order for some time, so we were unable to get any news of our shipmates. The Hudson's Bay man was also concerned as he was waiting for the arrival of the mail plane from Coppermine, with the Company's District Inspector Paddy Gibson on board, and it was now well overdue. Four days later two Eskimos arrived from Sherman Inlet with news of a plane crash and the death of Paddy Gibson, who had been the only fatality. The mail also burned, but both the pilot and the engineer survived. It was a hard blow to all of us, as Paddy had been a dear friend, highly respected and well loved in the North.

50 AFLOAT AGAIN

After seventy-one days' absence we returned to the *St. Roch* on May 6, having covered twelve hundred miles with our dog teams. The very first thing we did was to have a bath, something we were in great need of. On a trip like the one we had behind us, cleanliness had largely to be dispensed with. Our next thoughts were of the war. We had had no news since we left Fort Ross and now we could listen to the radio again and find out what was going on in the world. We even got Hitler's propaganda in English.

Two weeks later Father Henri arrived with three Eskimos and on May 19 the priest conducted the Requiem Mass for Chartrand. It was held on deck and we all attended the service, of course. Then the little procession moved on to the hill where we had buried our friend, and the Father blessed the grave. Father Henri had shown Pat and me much hospitality and kindness and we tried to make his stay with us as pleasant as possible. We made a Latin cross of teakwood which we presented as a gift to his mission. I had noticed that the only cross he had was made of wood from a packing case, so I felt this offering would be appropriate.

During the summer we gathered rocks and built a fifteen-foot cairn. We also used large slabs of limestone and made sure that they were all well interlocked so there would never be any chance of their falling down. Situated on the little hill, we felt this was a fitting monument to our dead friend. We also built a pyramidical structure with several tons of rocks over the shallow grave to ensure that it would not be molested by animals. On top of this we placed a cross and a nameplate of brass, engraved with his name and regimental number, and the dates of his birth and death. Chartrand had always liked to have everything neat and orderly, and I think it would have pleased him to know of this lasting monument erected in his memory, not too far from the Magnetic North Pole.

Among the many Eskimos who came to visit us were also the young hunter Teeirkta and his sixteen-year-old bride Evalu. They had been married according to Eskimo customs, but now they wanted to be married by Canon Turner and asked if they could come with us to Fort Ross, where the Canon was expected aboard the *Nascopie*. The bay that had been our home for so long was still covered by ice on the first of August. The old ice-floes were as solid as ever, and it looked as if we had very small chance of getting away. Shortly after midnight on August 3, however, I noticed a faint movement in the ice. Without wasting any time, we gathered dogs and equipment in a hurry and also took on board the young Eskimo couple.

The large ice-floe that had been stuck on our anchor moved almost imperceptibly. We started up the engine and heaved anchor as soon as it had been freed. Very slowly, we began to move along the shore between the big ice-floes. It was completely calm, and the conditions were just about perfect. Now the various landmarks we had noted or placed along the shore came in very handy when it came to avoiding the most dangerous spots on our way out, and soon we passed the shoal we had almost stranded on the year before. In this manner we reached the entrance to the bay, but there we got stuck again. Only thirty hours later, a breeze from the east opened a little channel as an escape from the bay. I immediately decided to take it and cast loose from the ice-floe we had been moored to. In this way we managed to work our way about fifteen miles northward in the narrow lead between the heavy old floes before the wind dropped, then changed to northwest and stopped us completely. Closed in as we were, we were unable to move in any direction, but at least we were some fifteen miles from our winter quarter. The wind now increased from the north and from the masthead I spotted a huge floe with a little cove at its base. If only we could reach it, this would make a nice little harbour for us, less than two miles away. It took a couple of hours of twisting and turning, backing up and charging. Soon our protecting floe and the *St Roch* with it was forced southward and the ice behind us filled the little cove completely. With the heavy squeezing, the ship listed from side to side and two hours later the pressure increased alarmingly. The *St Roch* heeled over heavily to the port side, then righted herself, only to be lifted by the stern. When we examined the ship we found that a floe had been forced under our keel, the rudder was jammed hard over and the propeller hub, normally about eight feet under water, was exposed. We promptly went over the side to set off a few charges of gunpowder in order to break the ice close to the ship. The broken pieces were now forced under the schooner, forming a cushion against the force of the larger and sharper floes. The threat to the rudder and the propeller was our greatest concern, for should either of these be damaged, we would be in serious trouble. Some of us therefore got busy with axes and ice chisels and began to hack away chunks of ice as best we could from the rudder and the propeller.

Despite our efforts, the *St. Roch* was still held fast. Blasting had relieved some of the pressure, but the floe under our stern was still solid as a rock. The ship was canted forward at a sharp angle, the stern high in the air and the bow forced level with the ice ahead. It was now possible to walk straight from the top of the stern-post, the highest part of the hull, on to the ice pack. To dampen our outlook still further, it started to snow heavily.

The situation was so serious that I had all lashings and falls loosened from the boats, just in case the ship should sink. I also instructed each crew member to get out spare clothing and supplies of food in case we had to abandon ship. We knew, however, that if we had to leave the *St. Roch* our small boats would be quite useless and our only chance would be to try to walk ashore. Early on August 7 the wind increased and so did the pressure. For a moment I thought the end had come when a large floe ahead of us split from the bow with a tremendous crash and the *St. Roch* settled on an even keel and shot ahead three or four ship's-lengths into a small patch of open water. Contrary to our fears, she now floated, apparently undamaged. A check of the bilges showed no sign of water and the propeller turned when we started the engine. The rudder, too, functioned normally. A weaker ship never would have survived!

We were afloat again, but it was impossible to advance, and we remained in the same position for over two weeks. Occasionally we were favoured with pleasant, sunny days, but at other times we were wrapped in fog and rain. It was mostly calm; the ice had no chance of breaking at all and the floes would not separate enough to give us working space. As far as the eye could see it was one solid mass of white. We were also concerned by the fact that we were slowly being forced southward by the combined currents from McClintock and Franklin Straits. Soon we arrived in the area where Sir John Franklin had been stuck with his two ships, the *Erebus* and the *Terror*, in September of 1846, never to be released again. They had drifted perhaps less than fifty miles when they abandoned their ships on the northeast coast of King William Land in April 1848. Now it looked as if we were heading in the same direction. Our advantage, however, was that we had our little diesel engine which we could start up at a moment's notice and exploit every opening we saw. In comparison with the trials and tribulations of the men on those two ships, our own trip almost seemed like a picnic.

On August 12 we experienced what might have been a very serious affair. I noticed a large ice-floe a short distance away, and it looked like a good spot for us to secure a mooring as I could see a short lead. As soon as the engine was started up the number one cylinder head cracked, flooding the engine. This meant trouble, for we had no spare cylinder heads with us, but Jack Foster and Bill Peters took charge of the situation and succeeded in blocking out the cylinder. Still, after a bit of running, it was found that the piston had to be drawn and the cylinder blocked. Our power hadn't been all too great with the six cylinders; now we were reduced to five.

51 BELLOT STRAIT—THE LAST ORDEAL

That long period of time when we were fast in the ice could have proved quite a strain on our nerves. The frustrations were many, the watches seemed never to end and all the time we hardly moved ahead at all. The fact that the best part of the summer had already passed combined with all these difficulties to test the spirit of even the most optimistic among us. We had spent over two years trying to get through to Halifax and there was very little evidence that we would be able to get there before the third winter was upon us. In spite of all this, there was never any grumbling, not a sign of exasperation, and as far as I could see my colleagues were all cheerful and shared my confidence that we were going to make it. I attribute this to the fact that we were all enlisted men, members of the same Force.

On August 20 there was a slight slackening in the ice. Without hesitation we started up and actually covered a mile. This was not an advance to create great excitement or optimism, but at least we had moved forward. Then we were stopped again. The next day we made a few more miles, taking advantage of every drop of water we saw. After two more days of heavy rain and fog, the weather changed again and a strong wind came down Franklin Strait. It increased to gale force during the night of August 25, when I noticed a black stripe in the white expanse ahead. The ice had split in a line almost directly to the ship, and by daylight it extended northward as far as I could see from the masthead towards Tasmania Island.

We lost no time in starting up as the lead grew wider and wider and soon we were going ahead at our top speed of about five miles per hour on our five cylinders. It was almost like a miracle. The wind was against us, but never had a head wind been more welcome. The lead was not very wide, but it was almost completely clear of ice, perhaps owing to a combination of the wind and the current. By noon that day we had reached the end of the lead, right against the Tasmania Island group. This meant that we were almost clear of the influence of wind and current from the McClintock Channel. I managed to work the ship into the channel which brought down great chunks of loose ice. Finally we were able to drop anchor very close to the shore and quickly got lines fastened to some large rocks.

It was a very high island, perhaps five hundred feet to the top; and a few of us climbed to the top right away. There we had a good view to the north and across to Prince of Wales Island. But what we really wanted to see, water, was nowhere in sight. To the north all was still white. After twenty-three days of hard struggle we were now only sixty miles north of Pasley Bay.

Anyway, Tasmania Island was a great deal better than being out in the ice pack. Here, at least, we were not losing ground as long as we could hang on, even though our position was far from ideal. Finally, in the morning of August 29, a break appeared and we could see small pools of blue water among the ice-floes toward Prince of Wales Island. We got under way right away and worked various small leads towards the small Dixon Island, and from there on the ice conditions improved.

By seven o'clock that night we were abreast the entrance to Bellot Strait. To look into it was like peering into a huge tunnel. There was no ice in sight as the strong current made it travel back and forth with the tide. At Tasmania Island I had noticed that the tide was at least six or seven feet. My intention had been to go on up Peel Sound, which previously had been navigated by two ships besides Amundsen's *Gjoa.* Bill Heslop at Fort Ross had informed us by radio that the Prince Regent Inlet was jammed full of ice that summer, so we pressed right into Brantford Bay, the eastern approach to Bellot Strait. I fell for the temptation to go through the short cut provided by Bellot Strait and headed into it.

Bellot Strait is about eighteen miles or so long and less than a mile wide; like a huge canyon with high, steep, inaccessible cliffs on both sides. As far as I knew, the water was deep, except for one spot in the middle, but even that spot would be sufficiently deep to allow any vessel to pass, judging from the deep ice-floes finding their way over it. We had the current with us and I noted the ice following behind us. When we had almost reached the point where we were going to congratulate each other on our good fortune, the ice gods, frost giants, or whoever, decided to let us know that they were not through with us yet. Near the middle of the strait I sighted a solid white line right across the water. It was impossible to turn around. Behind us the ice from Peel Sound was practically pouring in with the strong tide and the current. Slowly I approached the barrier in front of us and found a huge old ice-floe aground on the shallow spot I knew would be just about in the middle of the Strait. There must have been thousands of tons of broken ice pressed up against the stranded floe. We were also being carried rapidly against a solid part of it. If we hit, it could only mean the end. I rang full speed. Standing at the wheel myself I swung it quickly in order to crash into the looser, floating ice at the southern tip of the floe and came to a stop near a projecting point of the ice. Here we could easily have been crushed like a box of matches. In no time at all we were cradled in the ice, completely stationary, the victims of a terrifying pressure. One could almost hear the timbers of the *St. Roch* groan. I ordered all hands on deck. It was getting near dusk, but there was still light enough to see. Huge cakes of ice spun and gyrated in large whirlpools. In some of the whirlpools we could see narwhals, lost and bewildered, with their long spiralled horns waving in the air as they stood almost upright in the water.

It turned out that the tides from the eastern and western ends of the Strait meet at this point and this caused these large whirlpools, which reminded me a great deal of the famous Ripple Rock in Seymour Narrows inside Vancouver Island. It certainly looked bad for the *St. Roch* for about fifty minutes, and I couldn't help but admire our two young Eskimo guests Teeirkta and his little wife Evalu. When things appeared at the worst, they both went up on the fo'c'sle head and began to sing, at the tops of their voices, hymns that Canon Turner had taught them. Only once in a while did they look over the side. I was quite intrigued and asked what they were doing. "We sing in prayer to the white man's God so that the ship won't sink," was the answer. At that I could only ask them to "carry on." These great and wonderful people with their simple faith could put many so-called civilized and Christian people to shame.

Eventually the projection of ice which held us broke under the pressure. The current started to run in the other direction, to the east, and moved us along. We had been in touch again with Bill Heslop, now only a few miles away, and the people at Fort Ross had climbed the hill behind the trading post, from where they could see our struggle. The last they saw of us before dark was that we had been able to get through and were heading for the eastern entrance of the strait. By this time it was midnight, but we still could make out the cliffs faintly, although it was difficult to estimate distances. When the Fort Ross people saw our lights at last they headed back to the settlement, and just as we spotted the lights from the building we noticed a number of rowboats heading towards us.

Bill Heslop and his wife were aboard before we had dropped anchor to congratulate us and invite us all to a hearty meal. All of a sudden our troubles and hardships were forgotten. Now we felt we had made it and were practically in Halifax. Our two Eskimos were very pleased when I told them that I was sure that their singing had helped us to get through.

52 RETURN TO CIVILIZATION

I realized how fortunate we had been in getting through Bellot Strait in time, when we continued on our way on September 2. Had we not made it, I suppose we still would have been stuck somewhere on the west coast of Boothia Peninsula, perhaps forever. There was much ice in Prince Regent Inlet, so I proceeded up close to the eastern side of North Somerset Island, almost skirting Creswell Bay. Past Fury Point and almost up to Port Leopold, I cut across for Cape York. The current was to the eastward now so I couldn't be driven down among the heavy ice in Prince Regent Inlet any more, and the ice in Lancaster Sound consisted only of a few scattered pieces. However, when the wind calmed down the young slush ice formed quickly and slowed us down considerably.

These were strange waters to me, and with the dark night we had to proceed very carefully. Two days later we sailed into Navy Board Inlet and saw no ice there, except for some icebergs in Eclipse Sound. Another two days took us to Pond Inlet where we anchored and immediately were boarded by the whole population. Constables Jack Doyle and Delisle were there and so was Canon Turner, who told us that he had remembered us in his prayers and had been certain that we would make the trip safely. Father Henri had said something similar when we visited him and had assured us that no harm would come to our little ship as he would pray for us. With men like these two missionaries interceding for us, I guess we never really had anything to worry about.

As a first step towards our return to civilization we put ashore our spare Arctic gear such as canvas, lumber for framework, our little barge and the sleds. Reluctantly we also left behind us our remaining dogs, who set up a frightful howl when they saw the ship leave without them. We, too, felt the sadness of the parting; in the Arctic one becomes as attached to these four-legged friends as to one's fellow human beings.

Being short one man on the ship, I was glad to have Jack Doyle with us for the rest of our voyage. Having spent four years at Pond Inlet, he was due to go Outside. No sooner had we reached the Davis Strait than a strong southeasterly gale came up and the visibility dropped to zero. The sea was studded with small fragments of broken-up icebergs, mixed with some larger ones called growlers. The smaller ones were almost submerged in the heavy swell and now and then bobbed up like giant sea monsters. With our low power, it was difficult to dodge them as the suction seemed to drag us towards every one. One dark night we were struck by one of these icebergs and it knocked out a piece of our hardwood guard rail. Had it struck us lower down it certainly would have gone right through the bottom of the ship.

The weather was bad, with even poorer visibility all the way down the coast of Baffin Island and Labrador. The first vessel we sighted was a Newfoundland fishing schooner, off Bateau Harbour in Labrador where she was heading for the harbour itself. I followed her in to the small fishing village and there we had a few days' well-earned rest. Because of the gale the fishermen were in port and they were surprised to learn who we were and the length of time we had been away from home, although I somehow had a feeling that they didn't completely grasp the fact that we had come all the way around the Arctic.

Late in the evening on September 30 we arrived at Cornerbrook, Newfoundland and tied up at the wharf of Bowater's Pulp and Paper Mill. While we were there we had the cracked cylinder head repaired temporarily and were given a wonderful reception by the local people. An old British Navy captain by the name of Campbell was particularly interested in our trip. He had been a member of Captain Scott's Expedition to the South Pole and had been in charge of one of the survey parties. I presented him with a few souvenirs we had picked up at Victoria Harbour from Sir John Ross's engine and the old man, long since retired, was full of gratitude.

A naval officer who was in charge of the port ordered us to proceed southward with one of the slow convoys that were expected to leave shortly. We left on October 5, but even the slowest convoy was too fast for the *St. Roch*, whose top speed was only five to six miles—in calm weather. Once outside the bay, we encountered a strong southwesterly gale with head winds and we came practically to a standstill. It was no use at all to try to keep up with the convoy, so I set the sails and headed offshore, and with the help of the engine made slow progress to the South. There had been reports of submarines in that general vicinity, but I doubt that any of them would have wasted a torpedo on us.

Three days later we were off Sydney Harbour on Cape Breton Island and were stopped by the Navy Examination Patrol. An officer hailed us and asked what ship this was and where we were bound as well as what port we had left. When I answered that we came from Vancouver bound for Halifax, the officer shouted back through the megaphone: "Well, you're a long way from your course, this is Sydney." The young man looked confused at first when I told him that we knew exactly where we were, and that we had come via the northern route. I don't think he believed us at first. The *St. Roch* looked a bit disreputable after the long voyage and could have done with a coat of paint to cover the now almost bare wooden sides. Although both bow and stern carried the name "R.C.M. Police St. Roch," I'm sure our little group of men, dressed in nondescript clothing, as always when we were at sea, looked like anything but Mounted Policemen to him. Anyway, the harbour pilot was signalled to take us in to the harbour, where we spent the night and were made very welcome by the Naval Officers Mess.

The next day we continued through Bras d'Or Lakes, a beautiful inland waterway, and through the little St. Peter's Channel, and arrived at Halifax at 3:30 P.M. on October 11. We had completed our voyage through the Northwest Passage, the first from the Pacific to the Atlantic!

All of a sudden everything seemed strange and uninteresting. We almost had a feeling that we had arrived in a world where we really didn't belong. Halifax Harbour was full of ships of all sorts, cargo ships, tugs, harbour craft and various types of warships as the pilot took the *St. Roch* in and we moored at Kings Wharf, a small one near the heart of the city. My old friend Assistant Commissioner Alec Eames, who was the Officer Commanding for Nova Scotia, came down to greet us with a few other RCMP officers and to convey Commissioner Wood's personal congratulations on the completion of our voyage. None of us had ever been to Halifax before and oddly enough nobody seemed very eager to go ashore, completely exhausted as we were. The harbour pilot, Captain Ogilvie, who had taken the ship in, kindly invited me to his house for dinner and a hot bath and also offered to let me sleep at his place. I certainly appreciated this and staggered to his house, practically sleep-walking.

It had not been an easy trip for our small ship with its very small crew and limited conveniences and facilities. The three seasons of the short Arctic summers from 1940 to 1942 had been extremely bad for navigation, the worst consecutive three I had experienced as far as ice and weather conditions were concerned, and in my remaining years in the Arctic I never saw their like. Without hesitation I would say that most ships encountering the conditions we faced would have failed. I also believe that had we missed the single opportunity we had to get out of Pasley Bay, we most probably would still be right there, in small bits and pieces. My crew had been just marvellous! All of them were regular, enlisted men of the RCMP with no previous experience or service aboard ships, yet at sea they had performed like veterans. I doubt very much that I could have completed the voyage with an ordinary civilian crew.

The next few days we had a hard time getting the ship in shape again. This was left to some of us, while others were transferred to duty elsewhere or given a few weeks' leave, the first in two and a half years. *St. Roch* was finally ordered to Lunenburg, Nova Scotia, for the necessary repairs and docking. Lunenburg was a busy little fishing port about sixty miles from Halifax with a shipyard and a foundry busily working on corvettes and minesweepers for the Navy. The fishing fleet consisted of graceful schooners, and alongside these the *St. Roch* looked like an ugly duckling, short and squat and different from anything ever seen along this coast.

For me these were busy days, writing all the records and observations we had noted during the voyage. Among these was the Navigation Report pertaining to the depth of water along our course, harbours and anchorages, outstanding landmarks, weather conditions, and so on. In fact, we had to report on anything that had to do with the Arctic from the living conditions of the Eskimos to the game situation. Many different government departments were, of course, interested in all this information.

In December I was instructed to report to Ottawa for discussions with Commissioner Wood regarding the future commitments of the *St. Roch*. I also met with numerous government officials and military people concerned with the defence of the Arctic. Following this "debriefing," as it probably would be called, I obtained leave of absence and left for Vancouver and Victoria, where Mary and the children were waiting for me. After a pleasant stay at home for a few weeks I returned east for duty and had to report at Ottawa. In the capital I received word that I had been promoted to Staff Sergeant, and some weeks later we were informed that His Majesty King George VI had awarded the Polar Medal to each member of the crew. The inclusion of our late comrade, Albert Chartrand, on the list brought me a special feeling of satisfaction.

53 A SUMMER VOYAGE TO THE EASTERN ARCTIC

My winters in civilization, when the *St. Roch* was laid up, were usually uninteresting and tedious, and this winter in Lunenburg was no exception. Only one of our old crew, the Second Engineer, Bill Peters, now promoted to Corporal and Chief Engineer, remained with me. The others were spread all over the place. Jack Foster had decided to remain ashore for the rest of his service and was stationed in Vancouver, as were Dad Parry and Fred Farrar. Pat Hunt and Hadley had gone to one of the prairie provinces, where Hadley joined the communications branch of the Force.

Finally the plans for the 1943 season were made up and I was instructed to take our ship on a patrol and inspection trip to the eastern Arctic during the summer, and then return to Halifax. This was a good assignment. By then the eastern Arctic had become quite important, with both the United States and Canada building airstrips and weather stations at various strategic locations, including Ungava Bay, Fort Churchill and on Baffin Island. With the transportation and shipping facilities strained to the utmost because of the war, I was also instructed to carry all the supplies we could handle and to provide the police detachments in the eastern Arctic with all their needs.

One disappointment was that Headquarters informed me that they would be unable to spare any men for this trip and that I had to pick a crew in Lunenburg to act as deck hands. Apart from myself, the police force would be represented by Constable Bill Marshall, who was a communications man, and by Corporal A. S. Wilson. I had known Art Wilson for many years when he served in the Arctic at Baillie Island in 1924 and at many other locations in the North and was very glad to have him with me. The rest of the crew, however, was difficult to assemble. I therefore considered myself lucky when I was able to obtain the services of an old-timer from the Arctic who was well known to many RCMP people from the Commissioner on down. Rudolph Johnson, an old Dane, became my Second Engineer. He had been in turn trapper, trader and engineer of various Hudson's Bay ships through his years in the Arctic since 1900. It was more difficult to get the deck hands. Because of the war a manning pool had been formed in Halifax for merchant seamen, but after a visit to their office I wasn't any too keen on picking up any of the men I had seen. I doubted that a sailor who was used to larger steamers, regular meals and good accommodation would be suitable for our kind of work. In the end I picked a young lad of about seventeen from Dartmouth, Nova Scotia. John Boutillier was the type of lad one felt would make out. I also located three Lunenburg fishermen, who decided to take a chance with me to see what this was all about. One was an old-timer, Willis Parkes, who was used to fishing schooners. The other two were younger: Ted Mayo and Lohnes. All three were good men, used to long hours and hard work on deck in all kinds of weather. It was more difficult to get a cook, and we ended up with a man from the manning pool. He was from France, had a crippled leg and limped very badly. I had certain reservations about this young fellow and wondered what he would be like in our tiny, smoky galley, but cooks were scarce and few would care to join us voluntarily. We had tried out one who left us after only a few days while we were still in Lunenburg Harbour.

We got under way on July 17 and immediately ran into extremely dirty weather in the Cabot Strait. The ship was standing on her tail and head alternately, rolling at the same time. Our French cook was in despair. Trying to do his best on a stiff leg in a heavy sea was no joke, and as soup, hot water, kettles, ketchup bottles and slices of bread mixed with broken dishes on the little galley floor, he swore in French and several other languages that the manning pool had shanghaied him aboard this so-and-so tub where he couldn't stand on his feet let alone do any cooking. Even my Lunenburg fishermen weren't any too sure that their stomachs were in the right place at all times.

By the time we reached Halifax, we had patrolled about eight thousand miles and, though there was general agreement that it had been an interesting trip, my entire crew deserted me with the exception of old Rudolph, who stayed aboard throughout the winter with a Corporal Peters and myself.

54 WESTWARD THROUGH THE NORTHWEST PASSAGE

During the winter that followed our trip to the eastern Arctic we had a new and much more powerful diesel engine installed. With its three hundred horsepower, it was twice as powerful as the one we had before and many other changes were made to the ship at the same time. Among other things, I recommended the removal of the heavy mainmast, which we had had little use for, and we had it replaced by a short mast near the stern. In this way we could carry a small riding, or storm, sail there. This was an alteration I had had in mind a long time, ever since our stay at Pasley Bay when I had measured up the space and drawn a rough plan of what I had in mind.

I made a couple of trips to Ottawa that winter and received new orders to return to the Arctic during the summer of 1944 to carry out specific duties and if possible try to return to Vancouver by a different route of the Northwest Passage. This time I said I would like to try the more northerly route, through Lancaster Sound and west to Melville Island and then across McClure Strait to Prince of Wales Strait. This was the real Northwest Passage, I felt, and it had never before been navigated. These waters were free of reefs and shallow spots and would be suitable for ships of any size. The only hazard, of course, was ice, but with the help of powerful modern icebreakers, like those used by the USSR, I was sure this would become the northern route of the future. The main thing was for someone to try it, and if it could be proved that a small ship like the *St. Roch* could make it, then others would surely follow.

Again our mission was kept secret and we had a great deal of trouble getting all the work on the ship completed in time. With a new deck-house the *St. Roch* had a new look and certainly was more efficient than before.

My main problem, again, was to assemble a crew. Of my old crew, Corporals Peters and Hunt both volunteered for the voyage. Again the Police had no additional regular members to spare, except one young constable unknown to the rest of us, a James Diplock, who became our fourth regular police member. Commissioner Wood, who never forgot his old friends from the Arctic, suggested to me that I try to get Ole Andreassen and give him a job for as long as he wanted. He was around sixty-five years old, and was far from well off, having given all his profits as a trader away, mostly to needy Eskimos. I was very glad to have him, having met him on my very first trip to the Arctic. It was this man who had been with Stefansson and Storker Storkerson on the famous trek across the Beaufort Sea during the Stefansson Expedition, and who had originally come from the same part of Norway as I. Commissioner Wood had Ole flown out from Coronation Gulf to Halifax, where he joined our little company together with Rudolph, who was to be my Second Engineer on this trip.

I still needed a few men and managed to get two young fellows, just released from the Air Force. L. G. Russill became my radio man and G. B. Dickens turned out to be a good cook. A seventeen-year-old boy, William Cashin, who was working at the Dartmouth Shipyard, also joined us, as did two hardy fishermen from Port Aux Basques, Newfoundland, Stanley McKenzie and Frank Matthew.

There were very few trials before we headed north, and those we had were really too short to bring out any serious shortcomings. We knew that we had to get away as quickly as possible and had to trust to luck. As soon as possible, we started to load our stores. A day or so before our departure I decided to sample some of the canned food. There were several cases labelled "Lamb Stew" and others marked "Boiled Dinner"; I instructed the cook to try the stew for lunch. This was the kind that only required heating, and he opened a couple of cans. We had all been busy as stevedores all morning and were famished when we sat down to eat in the little messroom next to the galley. The appetizing smell of the stew gave us high hopes, but when the plates full of stew were placed in front of us we almost gagged, each and every one of us. The most prominent ingredient seemed to be potatoes and some thick, watery stuff mixed with pieces of dark meat. We did not mind this so much, but the trouble was that the whole concoction was in a salty brine. One mouthful was all it took before the protests were heard. I asked the cook whether he had emptied the salt shaker into the stew, but he assured us that he hadn't used any salt at all, nor had he tasted the stew. He had only followed the instructions on the label and heated the contents of the cans. The meat certainly wasn't lamb. We opened several more cans, but they were all the same. We had no better luck with the "Boiled Dinner" we decided to try out; it was only another name for the same so-called "Lamb Stew." This was not funny. Here we were ready to leave for the Arctic on a voyage which might take perhaps only a few months, but might possibly last for as long as two years, and our canned-food supply was unfit to eat. I telephoned the Officer Conmmanding at Halifax, who sent over Inspector Peacock and the Quarter Master, Sergeant Beale. The food was sampled, but it was too late, we were due to sail the next morning. When our two visitors left they carried a couple of tins as "exhibits," promising to do everything possible for us even if the outlook was far from promising. The nearest source of supply was far from Halifax. It turned out that there was nothing they could do and we left with the briny canned goods. Our only consolation was that soon, perhaps, we would come across bears and seals and perhaps even fish. The most annoying, and at the same time amusing, part of the whole affair, was that each and every can was clearly labelled "Prepared Especially for the Royal Canadian Mounted Police."

Never before, I thought, had anyone prepared so badly for an Arctic voyage. I had appealed to our Headquarters at Ottawa repeatedly, but the people there had seemed to be as helpless as myself in getting things done for our ship. It had been an almost continuous fight to get anything at all done and we were already late when we sailed out of Halifax Harbour and through the gate of the submarine nets.

During the night, we noticed that the deck had become so hot that the pitch in the seams around it was melting and had started to run. We even had to run our water hose on the deck to prevent it from catching fire. The cause of this was the new cooling pipe, which had started to leak. Joints in the pipe had started to squirt water all over the place and the exhaust silencer became so hot that the iron plates it was placed on heated up the deck. Obviously we couldn't carry on like this. I had warned the people who installed the engine that such a thing could happen, and here we were on our way to the Arctic. Instead we made for Sydney, Nova Scotia, where the Navy lost no time in helping us to repair the leaky joints, pipes and the exhaust system.

Icebergs and fog hampered our progress along the Labrador coast, but at least the new engine was working properly. The bad weather continued and as we really couldn't afford to lose any more time, I decided to bypass Frobisher Bay and continue northward. On August 3 we saw Cape St. David on Baffin Island on the south side of Cumberland Sound. We were now in broken, but tight-packed, ice and were hardly moving at all, in spite of burning a lot of our precious fuel. There was no other way to take but the long route and we headed for the Greenland coast, skirting the edge of the ice pack. On the eastern side of the pack the weather was fine and clear and we had open water except for the giant icebergs. It was the first time I had seen the big, beautiful mountains of the Greenland coast, some fifty miles off. Keeping offshore as far as the ice pack permitted, we proceeded northward until things started to look a bit better just north of Disco Island. Then we cut westward again across Baffin Bay, heading for Pond Inlet. Had it not been for the fact that we were to call in there, I would have gone much farther north along the Greenland side of the bay and then cut across to Devon Island.

While we drifted for a while in the ice pack again, we shot a great polar bear which suddenly loomed out of the fog, heading for the ship. The members of the crew who had never seen a polar bear before were all excited and were soon on the ice skinning the animal, butcher knives flying in the air. A couple of the boys even managed to cut each other's fingers. To save any serious loss of fingers, Ole and I finished skinning the bear, which weighed well over one thousand pounds. At first some six of the men were in doubt whether or not the meat would be fit to eat, and our cook made it quite clear that he had had no experience in cooking polar bears. However, old Rudolph, who, among many other qualities, was an excellent cook, soon had some wonderful juicy tenderloin bear steaks coming up, to everybody's great enjoyment. Some of the tougher parts of the meat were ground up into bearburger and the rest was hung up in our rigging where it would last indefinitely in the cold air. With this our disappointment over the canned-food tragedy was soon forgotten.

Our arrival at Pond Inlet coincided with that of Canon Turner, who had come to conduct a Sunday service, which he immediately offered to postpone so we could get our cargo unloaded and be on our way. We took advantage of the kind offer, and Pat and I later went ashore and joined in the late service, which included lengthy prayers for a safe voyage by the *St. Roch.*

Before we left we took aboard an Eskimo by the name of Panippakussuk and his family, including his mother Panippak. They were seven people in all, with seventeen dogs. They were quite willing to sail with us and made themselves comfortable in a tent on top of our deck-house, where they lived until we reached Herschel Island. Jo, as the man of the household liked to be called, was a natural sailor although he had never had anything to do with a ship the size of the *St. Roch*, and so was his fifteen-year-old son, Arrea. None of them spoke any English but they soon picked up the odd word, especially the children, nine-year-old Anne Palluq, eight-year-old Mary Pannikkussuk and the "baby," four-year-old Sophy. Jo, who was a good hunter, added to our meat supply when he shot a bear right near the edge of an iceberg near Navy Board Inlet.

Late in the afternoon on August 20 we crossed Maxwell Bay and found a good anchorage at Beechey Island, where we dropped anchor in six fathoms of water in Erebus Bay. (The bay is named after one of Sir John Franklin's ill-fated ships, which spent its first winter there in 1845-46 in search of the Northwest Passage.)

On Beechey Island, we went immediately to the cenotaph erected in memory of those who perished in the British Naval Expedition of 1852 under Sir Edward Belcher. At the base of the stone a marble tablet had been placed by Captain McClintock on behalf of Lady Franklin. It reads:

TO THE MEMORY OF
FRANKLIN,
CROZIER, FITZJAMES
AND ALL THEIR
GALLANT BROTHER OFFICERS AND FAITHFUL
COMPANIONS WHO HAVE SUFFERED AND
PERISHED IN THE CAUSE OF SCIENCE AND
THE SERVICE OF THEIR COUNTRY
THIS TABLET
IS ERECTED NEAR THE SPOT WHERE
THEY PASSED THEIR FIRST ARCTIC
WINTER, AND WHENCE THEY ISSUED
FORTH TO CONQUER DIFFICULTIES OR
TO DIE.
IT COMMEMORATES THE GRIEF OF THEIR
ADMIRING COUNTRYMEN AND FRIENDS;
AND THE ANGUISH, SUBDUED BY FAITH,

OF HER WHO HAS LOST, IN THE HEROIC
LEADER OF THE EXPEDITION, THE MOST
DEVOTED AND AFFECTIONATE HUSBAND
"AND SO HE BRINGETH THEM UNTO THE
HEAVEN WHERE THEY WOULD BE."
1855.

Above the Franklin tablet was a smaller tablet inscribed in memory of "Joseph René Bellot, Lieutenant in the French Navy". A few hundred yards away were the graves of some of Franklin's men, with weathered oak monuments.

We also examined the remains of a cache known as Northumberland House, established in 1854 by Commander W. S. Pullen of HMS *North Star.* All that was left was a broken stone wall, a bit of lumber from the house and thousands of barrel staves and lumps of coal. Near by we came across pieces of the keel, stem and planking of the yacht *Mary,* a small vessel of twelve tons left at Cape Spencer on Devon Island by Sir John Ross in 1850 in the hope that it would serve any survivors of the Franklin Expedition if they ever reached it. Two years later Commander Pullen moved it to Beechey Island. Captain Bernier, who visited the spot in 1906, also left a record of that occasion, which we found in a cairn on an elevated plateau. We added our own, with a report of our activities.

We ran into more history a bit later when we reached Dealy Island off the southern coast of Melville Island, nearing the eastern approach to McClure Strait. The weather had been bad and continuous snowfall had made navigation rather difficult for several days as both the land and the sun had been obscured. The magnetic compass had been bafflingly unresponsive for days, often with its north point fixed on the ship's head regardless of the direction we were travelling. Then the weather cleared and we spotted a cairn on top of Dealy Island. It was a huge pile of rocks with a large spar surrounded by three barrels and could be seen from a great distance. We anchored close inshore and set out to examine the massive cache which, like the cairn, had been built in the spring of 1853 by Captain Henry Kellett, who had spent the winter there with HMS *Resolute.*

The cache was partially destroyed and its contents had been scattered all over by marauding bears. Originally it had been built in the shape of a house, but only the sturdy stone walls remained, the roof having long since fallen in. At one end were iron tanks of what had been hard, square biscuits. The tanks were rusted through and the biscuits were wet and soggy. By rummaging around, however, we did find a few that were still hard as rock, stamped with a broad arrow, indicating that they were the property of the British Navy. Canned meats and vegetables, stacked up and covered with sod, formed part of one wall, and the centre of the building was a hodge-podge of broken barrels of flour, clothing, coal, rope, salt beef and broken hardwood pulleys for ships' blocks. It was amazing to see the various items left here. Much of it was frozen in ice, but leather sea boots, broken barrels of chocolate, peas and beans and other items were spread around outside. No doubt the bears had had many a good picnic there down through the years. On the beach we found two broken Ross army rifles and some boxes of ammunition, left behind by Captain Bernier.

We picked out a few good tins of "Ox Cheek Soup" made in 1850 by a manufacturer located opposite East India House in London. They bore the following directions for opening: "Take a hammer and chisel and cut out one end while being careful not to let flakes of the paint which cover the cans get into the soup." We also selected some cans which seemed to contain preserved carrots and some marked as containing "Normandie Pippins," whatever they were. When we opened one we found that it was a form of small dried apples. These items all were turned over to our Headquarters for analysis when we returned outside. I doubt that our modern canned food would have lasted so well if placed out for such a long time under similar conditions.

On the beach we also found an eighteen-foot boat turned bottom-up. It had been left by Captain Bernier, too, and was built of light oak planking. Two steel runners, like those on a sleigh, were fastened to the bottom, and these made the boat useful on the ice as well as in the water. It was far superior to our own skiff or rowboat built for us in Victoria in 1940, which was heavy, clumsy and leaky, so we decided to trade ours for Captain Bernier's.

Regardless of how fascinated we were by all this history we had to push on, as it was already getting late in the season. After a brief examination of Bridport Inlet, a fine harbour on Dealy Island, well protected and seemingly big enough to hold a fleet of ships, we left on August 28. While we had a wide expanse of completely ice-free water along the shore, we could see the ice tightly packed a few miles to the south in Melville Sound. When we passed Cape Bounty, I recalled that Lieut. William Edward Parry, R.N., had passed here too in 1819 with his two sailing-ships, the *Hecla* and the *Griper*. It was he who had named the Cape, and most appropriately, for by reaching that spot on the 110th Meridian he won a sum of five thousand pounds. It had been offered by the British Admiralty to the first man to pass that Meridian, in the quest of the Northwest Passage.

At Winter Harbour we visited the Parry Rock, where the names of the explorer's two ships and several of his men were carved. They had been almost within grasp of the Northwest Passage, but at Cape Providence they ran into impenetrable ice, had to return to spend the winter at Winter Harbour and went back to England in 1820. Thirty-two years later Captain Kellett got almost as far and wintered on Dealy Island. While some of his men were mapping the coastline they discovered that a party from the HMS *Investigator*, McClure's ship, which was frozen in the ice north of Banks Island, had visited Parry Rock and left a note giving the position of their ship. Captain Kellett immediately dispatched a party of men across the strait now known by McClure's name. On the other side they found the crew of the *Investigator*, most of them in pretty bad shape from scurvy and apparently with little hope of ever getting out of the ice after two years at Mercy Bay. As a senior officer, Kellett ordered them to abandon ship and to proceed over the ice to the *Resolute* at Dealy Island. Captain McClure thus became the first to discover the Northwest Passage and to navigate it by ship, apart from the sixty to seventy miles he and his party covered on foot.

On Parry Rock we also saw a large copper plate. It carried an inscription of the Union Jack and the Canadian Coat of Arms with the following words:

> "THIS MEMORIAL IS ERECTED TODAY TO COMMEMORATE TAKING POSSESSION FOR THE DOMINION OF CANADA, OF THE WHOLE ARCTIC ARCHIPELAGO, LYING TO THE NORTH OF AMERICA, FROM LONG. 60 W TO 141 W, UP TO LAT. 90 NORTH. WINTER HRB. MELVILLE ISLAND, C.G.S. "ARCTIC." JULY 1ST 1909, J. E. BERNIER, COMMANDER, J. V. KOENIC, SCULPTOR."

Thus, thirty-five years before our visit, on Dominion Day, this doughty and great Canadian skipper recorded Canada's claim to the vast Arctic region north of her mainland to the North Pole. We realized the significance of this declaration and before we left we deposited the record of our call together with various papers and ordinances in a brass cylinder and placed it on top of Parry Rock.

Some thirty miles to the west we struck heavy ice about the same place where Captain Bernier, who had returned there the year after his visit to the Island, had been forced to turn around because of the same ice-floes that had stopped Parry in McClure Strait in 1819. But there was no turning back for us, as I began to negotiate the narrow passages between the gigantic floes of old blue ice from the Polar Sea itself. All went well for a while until the weather became very thick with fog, mist and heavy rain and we were forced to moor to a large ice-floe. There we took the opportunity to replenish our fresh-water supply from a large pool of sweet water on it.

We were now in waters never before sailed by any vessel, the eastern entrance to McClure Strait! Taking advantage of every little break, we gradually worked southward alternately tying up to the ice and drifting and then moving ahead a little again.

At noon on August 31, the fog lifted briefly and I caught a glimpse of the entrance to Prince of Wales Strait, but the ice was solid in front of us. I couldn't decide whether we were near Russell Point on Banks Island or Pell Point on Victoria Island, and we continued up what turned out to be Richard Collinson Inlet on Victoria Island, a bit east of the strait. As soon as we realized our mistake, we turned about and followed the coast back and soon were in Prince of Wales Strait. There were only a few pieces of ice there, and we were greeted with wonderful clear weather and sunshine. It was, in fact, the only real fine day we had during the entire passage! That night we were at the southern end of the strait and shut down our engine so that we drifted until daylight.

Shortly afterward we passed the entrance to Walker Bay, our winter quarter of 1940-41, wondering what our Eskimo friends there were doing. We anchored at Holman Island on September 4 and I recognized Andrew and Jorgen Klengenberg's boats tied to the beach by the Hudson's Bay warehouse. I blew the whistle a couple of times but no sign of life, and this I found very strange. The reason for this "cool" welcome turned out to be the fact that the Hudson's Bay ship *Fort Ross* had been in port busily unloading cargo for the settlement, and everybody had worked around the clock and had just gone off to sleep. This was a little bit of history: two Canadian ships had met after a complete circumnavigation of the North American continent, for the *Fort Ross* had left Halifax three months before and gone through the Panama Canal, up the west coast to Vancouver and then continued until it reached the point where we now anchored, having come from Halifax via the northern route!

For the rest of the trip we were in familiar waters, but the welcome was a rather frigid one as we ran into a blinding snowstorm just out of Holman Island. This weather stayed with us right to Tuk-Tuk, where the wind rose to a full gale, long to be remembered there. We rode out the storm in that harbour, which we had reached just in time to save the ship, there could be no doubt about that. We had yet another enemy to face before the Arctic was to give up its grip on us—the ice. An aircraft from Aklavik reported that unbroken ice blocked the passage between Pull Island and Herschel Island and for a while it looked as if we would have to winter at Tuk-Tuk. Then suddenly the weather changed and I decided to try to get at least as far as Herschel. It became a race with the ice and we barely had time to land our Eskimo family at the now completely deserted settlement. Once a thriving Arctic metropolis, Herschel Island had been abandoned and not a soul was to be seen. We could almost feel the ice closing behind us as we headed west as quickly as we could. The Eskimo family stayed behind in one of the abandoned warehouses, well supplied with everything we now didn't need. But we hung on to one item, the infamous Lamb Stew in Brine.

The closer we got to Point Barrow, the worse things looked as far as the ice was concerned. On top of everything else, I received a message from Point Barrow saying that the little lead that had opened there was rapidly closing with the changing wind. We could only go ahead, however, and I ordered the engineer to give her all she had. We simply had to make it, having come this far. The water shoaled alarmingly near the point when all of a sudden the leadsman, who had been kept busy without let-up, shouted "We've lost the bottom!" That was the call I had been waiting for; I now knew we had passed the point itself. Shortly afterwards we saw the welcome lights of the settlement, but there was no time to stop this time. We had to content ourselves with radio contact with the shore and all lights were lit up so that we could see where they were.

On September 27 we passed through the Bering Strait and docked in Vancouver on October 16 at 6 p.m. Behind us were 7,295 nautical miles, which we had covered in 86 days!

There was nobody to meet us at the wharf. Canada was still at war and had no time for frivolous things. I was just about ready to go ashore with the rest of the crew to find a restaurant with a good meal when an old-time friend, Superintendent Jim Fripps of the RCMP, arrived to greet us together with Captain Smith of the Royal Canadian Navy. After a short while other friends started to arrive as well. A few reporters who showed up later were very generous in their articles on us in the Vancouver newspapers, just as they had been in the past on our returns from the North.

Again I must pay tribute to all the members of my crew. Tribute is also due to those early explorers whose sacrifices and exploits blazed most of the trail we followed. Their successes and failures taught me much. It is true that many of the pioneers were defeated by the North, but I feel that this was mostly because of the slow ships of those days, rather than because of the ice and the hard country. In spite of their lack of facilities many of these men also set out on foot to explore and to claim the land for the old Empire. This is the very spirit which we must never allow to die in Canada. In my opinion, the Royal Canadian Mounted Police, in its own way, is doing its best to continue these great traditions. I recall particularly the long, overland journeys of former Assistant Commissioner C. D. LaNauze and of Assistant Commissioner T. B. Caulkin, who, in the early days, covered by sled the territory which later was to become the area of Operation Muskox.

At the time I made certain reflections and put my thoughts down on paper. Looking through my notes in later years, I found that I expressed my belief that before long the Arctic would become better known. Large, powerful steel icebreakers driven by diesel motors would ply the Arctic waters and during the summer they could carry supplies to the North, while planes would maintain regular flights over the area all year round. As for the Northwest Passage, I felt that the icebreakers would be able to navigate it, probably by the route we took. But the Arctic would always remain the Arctic. On occasion planned voyages would run behind schedule, delayed perhaps by the heavy ice in Melville Sound and along the Alaska coast. Some ships, I thought, would find it easy, others more difficult, and some were bound to meet with disaster. But one thing I firmly believed: modern ships would have the advantage in power and strength, and if they were forced to winter, they would only have to wait for the next season. The young ice which forms in open water, and which stopped us so many times, would present no obstacle to future Arctic vessels; they would plow right through it.

I also took some time out to look back on our latest voyage. It had been an eventful trip and the *St. Roch* had nobly upheld the traditions she had established during the past fifteen years. Yet the Arctic guards her secrets well. Some of her mysteries have been solved, but many remain. Among them, the greatest mystery, perhaps, is still the whereabouts of Sir John Franklin's grave. It had been a lifelong ambition of mine to find the grave of this great man, but this was not to be. I firmly believe, however, that at some future date the grave will be found, for in my opinion this outstanding explorer must have a resting place somewhere on land in the heart of the Northwest Passage. No British Navy explorer of that day would have buried his beloved leader at sea, when land was so near. And what about Franklin's records? Where are they, and what story can they tell?

55 HONOURS AND PROMOTION

The next couple of weeks were busy ones, as I prepared the various reports required. A civic luncheon was given for the crew at Vancouver City Hall and we were welcomed and congratulated on our accomplishment by the mayor and officers of the three armed services.

The port of Vancouver was very busy in those days, with several ships leaving and arriving daily. Among them were some Soviet icebreakers and cargo ships, some of which were using the Northeast Passage or, as the USSR called it, the Northern Sea Route. They had a trade commission in Vancouver and numerous liaison officers looking after the interests of the Soviet ships. One of these officers was a young lieutenant named Pavlov. As the Russians perhaps knew more about the Arctic and its problems, particularly as far as shipping is concerned, than anybody else, they showed great interest in our voyage and asked the RCMP Liaison Officer for permission to visit us. I had the distinct feeling that they were rather taken aback when they saw the ship's small size and the small crew. There was no hesitation, however, in their warm congratulations and admiration.

The greatest honour bestowed upon me was undoubtedly a letter of congratulation from the Royal Geographic Society of London, England, informing me of the award of the Patron's Gold Medal of the Society as well as an Honorary Fellowship. This pleased me immensely, as I knew that very few people received this medal, except for outstanding geographical achievements in the field of exploration. I also received a telegram signed by Christmas Moller, the head of the Free Danish Committee in London, congratulating us on the Northwest Passage trips.

After our duties in Vancouver had been completed, the *St. Roch* was again moved to the Naval Dockyard at Esquimalt and laid up for the winter. This gave me an opportunity to enjoy a bit of home life for a change and again to get acquainted with my family. In December I was ordered to proceed to Ottawa to attend various meetings and discussions dealing with the Arctic, its problems and its future. One of the highlights of my life was when Commissioner Wood instructed me to go to Washington, D.C., to meet with the Director of the FBI, J. Edgar Hoover. I was delighted to meet the head of this famous law enforcement body and spent almost a week exchanging views both with the Director and a number of Assistant Directors and Agents. As their guest I was shown their methods of work, laboratories and the training establishments. One day I spent some time with their men on their firing range, and tried out several types of hand guns and sub-machine guns. Having read a lot about the famous G-men, I had never dreamed that I would some day be a guest of the famed J. Edgar Hoover himself.

Commissioner Wood also wanted me to call on his friend, the Arctic explorer Vilhjalmur Stefansson, who lived in New York City. It was my first meeting with this great man whom I had always admired, and I was warmly greeted. Stefansson was very pleased that we had been able, over the years, to prove many of his Arctic theories in practice. He was particularly interested in our recent Northwest Passage voyage through Lancaster and Melville Sounds and Prince of Wales Strait, which he himself had travelled by dog teams while supporting his small party by hunting. Many changes had taken place since his time, both with regard to the people, their way of life and the dwindling game resources brought about by indiscriminate killing, and not the least by the introduction of modern fire-arms and the disappearance of the old taboos. I was also able to give him some recent information on the Eskimos on Victoria Island, the so-called Blond Eskimos at Walker Bay and Prince Albert Sound.

I just couldn't resist, and had to go across the Brooklyn Bridge while I was in New York. There had been many changes here, too, since my visits as a young sailor, the last in 1919. The old barque the *Indian Girl* came back to mind, and I recalled how she had sailed up the Hudson River and anchored close to the Brooklyn Bridge.

It was getting close to Christmas and I was anxious to get home.

There were thousands of travellers, both civilians and servicemen, and transportation was quite a problem. I had my return ticket, but no reservation on the train for Montreal. It was almost impossible to get on the train, but I was lucky to have with me Stefansson, who knew his way around Grand Central Station. Here it was I who felt almost as lost and bewildered as an Eskimo in a strange place. Finally, I got on the train, where I met a Canadian Army Medical Officer from Montreal. He was returning from some duty in the United States and very kindly invited me to his house when we reached Montreal, where I had to wait for another train until some time in the afternoon. When we got to the doctor's house he woke up his wife, who gave us a good breakfast. While I was waiting, I picked up a Montreal newspaper and noticed my own photograph. The paper announced that I had been promoted to the commissioned rank of Inspector a couple of days before. This was news to me and I showed it to the doctor, who was quite amused by the fact that I had learned of my promotion through a newspaper. This, he felt, called for a special celebration.

Naturally I was elated. Officers of the RCMP are commissioned in the same manner as those of the armed services, and the only way to the senior positions is through enlistment and prior service in the ranks. Less than three per cent of the entire strength are commissioned officers, so I really appreciated my good fortune. As with my earlier promotions, this one too, I realized, was due to my serving aboard the *St. Roch* in the Arctic. I felt a deep sense of gratitude, having come to Canada as a young Norwegian sailor inspired with the desire to join the Royal Canadian Mounted Police and to serve it in any capacity. The Arctic had been my particular dream, but I never thought that I ever would reach the position of a commissioned officer.

In Ottawa I was congratulated by Commissioner Wood and my many friends among the NCO's and men who had served with me. True to the traditions of the Force, these latter now addressed me as "sir," which I at first found very difficult to get used to. After another round of talks with my superiors, I finally managed to get away and spend Christmas with my own family.

56 THE LAST ARCTIC VOYAGE WITH THE ST. ROCH

The story of the later years of the *St. Roch* can be told briefly. Our last voyage through the Northwest Passage brought to an end a notable phase of her career, and the routine duties that followed seemed rather tame in comparison. Arctic transportation was still scarce, and 1945-46 saw us back in the western Arctic. This time Peters and Hunt were the only Mounted Policemen in the crew, which also included old Rudolph. The other members of the crew were civilians who, except for L. G. Smith, our young Department of Transport radio operator, and Billy Cashing, a young fellow from Dartmouth, Nova Scotia, were flown out before the vessel froze in for the winter at Cambridge Bay. This was another voyage with a happy message for me from the south. My youngest daughter, Beverly, was born in Victoria only a month or so after we had headed north.

Our Eskimo friends from Pond Inlet, Panippakussuk and his family, whom we had left at Herschel Island, were all happy and in good health and had enjoyed a good winter with plenty of game. They had made a trip to Aklavik, where they aroused quite a bit of curiosity with their eastern Arctic dress and the way they drove their dogs. In the east they were used to a fan formation of dogs, but Jo told us that this was hardly suited for this type of country where the dogs got tangled up in every stump of tree and all the willows from Shingle Point to Aklavik.

The family came back with us to Cambridge Bay where we again were greeted by many old friends who assured us that we had been missed. Young Kinmeuk remarked that since we had left there had been "no Umiarjuaq (ship), no Santa Claus, no Hanorie, no nothing!" Old Quarlilaak was still alive and on hand to greet us, a bit stooped now, but still an impressive figure. The news had travelled that I now was an Inspector, and the Eskimos, who by then were quite familiar with the various ranks, seemed to be pleased. "You Spector now," Quarlilaak said, looking at the gold braid on my cap. I said that that was right, but the old man shook his head in disbelief. How could this be when I still looked the same as before?

The big happening that winter at Cambridge Bay was Operation Muskox, a combined operation by Canadian and United States Army and Air Forces. It was a trek from Churchill, Manitoba to Baker Lake, across the Barren Lands to Perry River in Queen Maud Gulf and then on to Cambridge Bay and Coppermine. There the men headed south again to Great Bear Lake, along the Mackenzie River and finally on to Edmonton, Alberta. All told, this was a very creditable performance by the troops, who used small tracked vehicles, which I think were called Penguins. The party arrived at Cambridge Bay in late March and stayed for about a week, changing engines and tracks on their vehicles.

The men were a fine, interesting group, and in a way they started a new era in the Arctic, particularly in aviation and transportation on land. Hundreds of barrels of gas and other supplies were dropped by parachute all the way across their route for the advancing party. At Cambridge Bay we were busy collecting supplies dropped all over the place, and the Eskimos stared in disbelief at the wastefulness when the military party helped themselves to only part of this "loot" and just left the rest behind. Following in the wake of the tracked vehicles with their dog teams, the Eskimos made a windfall. For the first time in their life, Eskimo women wore silk and nylon underwear made of the dozens upon dozens of parachutes lying everywhere in the snow. On a trip I made somewhat later to King and Perry River, I noticed that almost all the women wore white and red striped clothing made of these parachutes, while other parachutes were made into summer tents.

Soon the huge military aircraft started to land on the bay itself at Cambridge, and among the many experts in weaponry, communications, supplies and so on was my old friend Frank Riddell, who had been at Herschel Island in the old days, and on our last meeting at Tuk-Tuk in 1937 had been a sergeant. He was now a Major in the Canadian Army Signal Corps and was certainly one of the most versatile and practical men on that undertaking.

The Eskimos were quite amused by watching the military clothing experts who had lots of boots, underwear, socks and outside clothing to try out. Some wore one kind of boot on each foot and really did look funny. I maintained that these men could hardly make true evaluations of their equipment travelling as they were in heated vehicles, and only rarely exposed to the weather either while they made or broke camp. Their tents were overheated and they had plenty of food and fuel. I therefore suggested to one of the Majors of the U.S. Quartermaster Corps that he should take a trip with our dog team for about thirty to forty miles, build a snow house and spend the night there. I further suggested that he wear my Eskimo-made footwear on one foot and his own on the other to be able to compare their relative merits. The Major gladly accepted, and I told one of my Eskimos to take eleven of our fastest dogs and the big sled with only a night's dog food and go out with the American. When they returned, having had a nasty grounddrift of snow and head wind, the Major had some trouble telling me which foot had been the coldest. "I feel like an icicle all over and have no idea what part of me is the coldest," was the answer. This and other similar practical tests, however, had great importance for the future development of Arctic equipment and clothing.

In the end, all the experts and military men left, but Cambridge Bay never went fully back to normal again. During the summer several large Catalina aircraft landed with more experts to examine the area in order to establish airstrips and find sites for Loran Towers and all kinds of things. The next winter, huge cargo aircraft started to fly in steel and other building material and landed tractors and caterpillers. When I saw the place again in 1949 all these installations had already become obsolete and had been abandoned. A huge Loran Tower remained, however, as a reminder of the brief period of "civilization." To me the most painful thing about it all was that many Eskimos had given up hunting and trapping to work for the white men, and many of them had become plain hangers-on. The once fine and independent Eskimos of Cambridge, who to my mind had been far superior to almost any other Eskimo group I had ever met, had started on a downward route. I was glad that I had seen them as they were during my four years when I lived among them and during my many summer visits. While the march of progress cannot be stopped, these had been steps in the wrong direction, at least for the Eskimos.

The winter of 1945-46 also marked a watershed for me. It was my last aboard the *St. Roch*, and a sled patrol to King William Island to see my old friends turned out to be my last long trip with a dog team. It covered about eight hundred miles.

In July I went along on a flight in an RCAF Canso, which had come up to Cambridge Bay in connection with the Air Force "Operation Investigator." We flew over Victoria Island and did a great deal of low flying over the Geographical Islands before heading over the northern part of King William Island. Among other things we were looking for possible spots where aircraft could land, but there was ice everywhere and not enough open water for us to set down. At Thom Bay I spotted several tents belonging to the Eskimos whom Hunt and I had visited in 1942. This was really travelling in comfort in comparison to fighting one's way with a heavy sled and a team of dogs. We also flew low over Chartrand's grave. When we returned to Cambridge Bay, we had covered around twelve hundred miles and I had learned a good deal about the surface and outline of the country I had previously seen only from the ground.

It was with deep sorrow that I later heard that Patsy Klengenberg's little schooner *Aklavik* had had a fire in her engine and gas tank and that Patsy had died of burns. This happened only a few days after I had said good-bye to him before we left Cambridge Bay on August 12.

On our way back to Vancouver I had one of the strangest experiences of my life. We had run into a heavy southerly gale with pouring rain and fog after leaving Point Hope and when we finally reached the Bering Strait we were all exhausted from lack of sleep. Suddenly I saw land looming up ahead and I knew we were near one of the Diomede Islands located in the middle of the Strait. The Large Diomede—or Ratmanoff Island, as it is called by the Russians—belongs to the Soviet Union, while Little Diomede, close by, is part of the United States. I had seen these islands several times in the past and had sailed past them on both sides. There was a fair-sized Eskimo community and a mission station on Little Diomede, but the settlement was a little bit inland, and because of the fog and the gale I decided not to take any chances, but only to go in close by Ratmanoff Island and drop anchor there so we could get ourselves a meal and some sleep.

We left a watchman on deck and the rest of us turned in and after a couple of hours the fog lifted. The first thing we saw was an armed soldier, and then several others on a knoll and in a small ravine on the island. Soon they started to signal, using flags and semaphore and we tried to read these signals with the aid of the International Code Book, but without too much luck. There was no boat on shore, so we assumed that they wanted us to land, but the surf along the shore was too strong to risk that. We therefore decided to stay where we were to await any further developments. Our ship was flying the Blue Ensign and the name of the vessel was plainly shown, both bow and stern, with the legend "R. C. M. Police." To have weighed anchor and left would have been foolish as the *St. Roch* certainly was not built for speed and it would have taken us hours just to get out of sight of the island.

Around two in the afternoon a Soviet naval or coastal patrol vessel hove in sight and anchored close by. A motor launch was quickly lowered and sent ashore to pick up a well-armed party from the beach. Within a few minutes the party had boarded our schooner. It was an impressive display of both military and naval efficiency. The group, all carrying sub-machine guns, was under the command of a young, good-looking Army captain and none of the Navy officers or sailors took part in the actual boarding. Immediately we were faced with a problem: none of the Russians spoke a word of English and we, of course, spoke no Russian. The captain repeated the word "Karta" again and again and I took it to mean that he wanted to see our charts. He also indicated that he wanted to see our log-book, and all this was produced. The captain looked at this and by the use of sign language made it clear to me that they wanted me to accompany them ashore. I therefore went off in their launch with an armed escort while the crew remained aboard under surveillance of the Soviet patrol boat.

This was a new experience and one that I must confess I didn't enjoy. To be detained by armed Russians at a time when international relations had already started to deteriorate was far from promising. Without an interpreter I had a hard time trying to explain to the Army captain that we were on our way to Vancouver from the Arctic where we had spent a year, and tried to use both the charts and the log to illustrate what I was saying.

In spite of the fact that I also seemed to get across the point that I had only anchored that close to the shore to seek protection from the gale, I was made to understand that I would be detained until the captain had communicated with Moscow. Pointing to his watch and repeating the word Moscow he indicated that this might take until six in the evening, some three and a half hours away. Next I was escorted to a small room which was furnished with a cot, a chair and a table. Pointing to the bed, the captain told me to lie down and sleep and I was handed a pack of cigarettes.

Alone in my "prison" I cursed myself for anchoring here instead of off the American island, but it was too late now. Through my window I could just see the business end of a bayonet fixed to the equally business-like gun of my sentry.

Shortly after six, the captain called on me and, with the aid of a printed questionnaire asked my full name, rank, age and place of birth as well as the name of our ship and her call letters. He also wanted to know our official duties in Canada and seemed satisfied with the explanation that we looked after the Canadian Eskimos in our own Arctic territories. I was then told that I would have to spend the night with my hosts until final word had been received from Moscow. The weather was still as dirty as ever, and I pointed to the *St. Roch* which was rolling heavily at anchor, suggesting that I be put back aboard and be guarded there, but to no avail. Drawing his finger in a suggestive fashion across his throat he said "Molotov" and then "Stalin." From this I gathered that if he allowed me to get away either one of these two gentlemen would order his immediate execution.

In spite of the uncomfortable situation, I was well treated. A tall, blue-eyed woman, who I think was the captain's wife, brought me some food and smilingly said something in Russian, which could have been an apology for the simple fare of fish, bread and tea. Somehow I couldn't eat; my only thoughts were when and how I would be able to get away. A few minutes later the woman returned for the dishes, and noting that most of the food was left, she took off again and then returned with a plate full of tasty little pancakes and another big glass of tea. I understood this to be a friendly gesture and ate it all, to her obvious pleasure when she returned.

Early next morning I was served breakfast and then brought to the captain, to find my charts and the log book on his desk. All of this was returned and I was asked to sign a document detailing the names of our crew, our general route and our destination. The document was printed in Russian, so I was reluctant to sign it, but the captain kept nodding his head saying "Goot, Goot," more or less telling me not to worry. On my way down to the shore where I was taken by the captain, I noticed around twenty men, four or five women and three children, and some buildings which I made out to be part of a weather station. The captain then shook hands with me, as did his lieutenant, the guards and the woman. One of the soldiers who helped me aboard a little boat that was to take me back to the *St. Roch* presented me with a pack of cigarettes. He was without doubt a Siberian Eskimo, the only one among these men.

Back on my own ship I found that no guard had been posted there, nor had she been boarded, but a searchlight had played on the ship all night. We lost no time in getting our anchor up and getting under way.

It had been an unnerving experience, but it had been handled with efficiency and dispatch.

On September 26 we arrived in Vancouver, where the crew again was dispersed and the *St. Roch* moved to the Naval Dockyard and laid up for the winter, while I was instructed to report to Ottawa Headquarters.

St. Roch's last Arctic voyage took place the following year, in 1947. After nineteen years in the Force this had become routine to me. However, many important changes were taking place. Our assignment that year was to proceed to Melville Island and there rendezvous with the big, powerful United States Coast Guard icebreaker the *North Wind* coming from the east, which was to land men and equipment there to build an airstrip. We were to winter there to act as a police detachment and generally look after Canadian interests. Owing to very difficult ice conditions that year, it proved impossible for us to reach Melville Island. Our only consolation was that the American icebreaker with its 10,000-h.p. diesel engine did not make it either. The airstrip, instead, was built at Resolute Bay on Cornwallis Island and I was instructed to return west and winter at Herschel Island, where it was the intention to reopen the detachment which had been closed for eleven years.

Not needing all the men there for the winter, I radioed for the police aircraft to be sent in to fly most of the crew out, leaving only two constables, and myself as well as Rudolph Johnson and Bill Cashin, who had been with us right from Halifax. Shortly before Christmas I travelled to Aklavik by dog team and from there was flown out to Edmonton, managing to get home to Victoria just in time for the holidays. After a month or so I flew back to Herschel Island. The police plane brought in a new crew in April. My last spring in the Arctic was very enjoyable and I was glad to spend it at Herschel, where my Arctic experiences had started back in 1924. Now, twenty-four years later, it was quite different from those early days.

It was by then no longer necessary for the RCMP to maintain a floating detachment in the North nor to have people winter in out-of-the-way places in order to emphasize Canada's claim to the Arctic Archipelago. The region was soon to become important in the area of defence with communities springing up in places which until then had been known only to the Hudson's Bay Company, the missionaries and the men of the Mounted Police. The Arctic, in short, was becoming "civilized," and the *St. Roch* was out of her element in such surroundings.

During the winter several Eskimos from the Barter Island area in

Alaska arrived and asked if they could remain on the Canadian side. Their claim was that there were getting to be far too many white people in their own district and that the construction work was scaring off the game. Another thing that I am sure attracted them to Canada was that the Canadian government was paying family allowances for each child up to the age of sixteen. There was also an old age allowance and other benefits, which the Alaska Eskimos didn't have. In the early days, the Eskimos could come and go as they liked on either side of the border, but this had been changed, the main reason being that these people no longer could be classified as nomads. Anyway, I was of the opinion that we were short of Eskimos in the huge Mackenzie area and recommended that they be allowed to stay. The request was granted by the authorities.

By August 29 our work was completed and the Eskimos came aboard, for the last time, for tea and biscuits. The little ship had become a symbol of goodwill to all the Eskimos, this I know. They knew we could be trusted to lend a helping hand, and no Eskimo, no matter what he had done, was ever afraid of coming to confide in us. They all knew that they would get fair treatment. Ours was not a police force to be afraid of.

Our return to Vancouver on October 18, 1948, marked not only the last voyage to the Arctic for the *St. Roch*, but also the end of an era in the history of Canada's North. The ship was moored at the Naval Dockyard and temporarily laid up, and my own days of sailing in the western Arctic waters came to an end too. I was assigned for temporary duty at Vancouver and Victoria that winter and inspected various detachments throughout British Columbia. Knowing very little about the interior of that province, I found this most interesting. The beauty of the country, with its huge mountains and forests and long, narrow fiords made a deep impression on me.

But I was by no means through with the Arctic yet. In July of 1949 I was ordered to Edmonton, Alberta, from where I was to fly into the Arctic with two men. Our assignment was to fly over the area between Cambridge Bay, King William Island, the Adelaide Peninsula and the Chantrey Inlet and make several landings to collect data of possible future interest. I was thrilled at the prospect of getting back to this part of the North which I knew so well and looked forward to this adventure with the RCMP Norseman aircraft.

In Edmonton I took the opportunity to visit the new Charles Camsell Hospital for Indians and Eskimos. It was a lovely new hospital staffed by doctors and nurses from the Department of National Health and Welfare and I was taken on a tour to visit the many Eskimos I knew. Most of them were suffering from tuberculosis and some were almost beyond recognition. Seeing so many Eskimos in the hospital, I obtained a film projector from our headquarters and made up a program of films from the Arctic, most of them shot by myself. The hospital staff arranged for a large room and we had the satisfaction of seeing the Eskimos come back to life when they recognized the well-known landmarks and many of their own friends.

When I arrived at Coppermine with my two colleagues, I was informed by Canon Webster and Father Delalande of the Oblate Fathers that the Eskimos had had a very bad winter that year. It was easily seen in the faces of the people. It was strange, however, for Coppermine had almost always been a land of plenty. With Sergeant Heacock at the controls we continued to Cambridge Bay and later to King William Island. No sooner had we started to approach the coast than thick fog came down and forced us to turn about and head for the Royal Geographical Island to wait there for improved weather. Our next attempt to get to Terror Bay was met by more fog and a terrible storm. We finally landed, and rode out the storm on the water after having dropped a little anchor. That was a most uncomfortable night and I couldn't help thinking again of old Niviassiaq's curse. There was no doubt about it, it seemed to be as powerful as ever.

Near the end of August I headed back for Vancouver and again took up my duties in British Columbia.

57 "THE MEN WHO SPEAK THE TRUTH"

I could hardly believe my own ears when I received instructions to report to the Commissioner of the RCMP in Ottawa and to prepare for taking command of "G" Division, which controls the police work in all of northern Canada. Superintendent H. H. Cronkite, who was filling the post, was gravely ill and a replacement was urgently needed. He had served in the Force for thirty years and had been promoted to his present rank only a few months before. His death a few weeks after my arrival in Ottawa was a great loss to the RCMP.

To be given the command of this Division, which is directed from its own headquarters in Ottawa, was indeed an honour. It controls the largest area within the Force, covering the entire Northwest and Yukon Territories with the remoter parts of the Province of Quebec and the James Bay district of Ontario thrown in for good measure. The Yukon and the Northwest Territories alone constitute an area of one and a half million square miles, roughly forty per cent of Canada. I had to take on a large volume of administrative responsibilities which up to then I had been spared. While my predecessor had served in some parts of the North for short periods, I did have the advantage of knowing almost every corner of the region. It was twenty-one years since I had enlisted in the RCMP and now I was to assume command of the same Division I had served in continuously since I had been a green recruit. I had indeed a great deal to be thankful to my adopted country for.

In my twenty-five years in the Arctic I had become familiar with its numerous problems. The decline both in health and in economic resources of the Eskimos and the Indians was particularly serious. The men in my Division were responsible to me for the administration on behalf of many departments of the federal government, and I decided right from the beginning that I was going to do all I possibly could to correct all the shortcomings and mistaken policies I knew from experience to be in existence. Commissioner Wood welcomed my suggestions. He had a deep affection for the North, having spent a good deal of time there as a youngster in the Yukon and as Commanding Officer of the Western Arctic from 1919 to 1924. He retired in 1951 and was succeeded by Commissioner L. H. Nicholson, who was equally sympathetic to my recommendations. The new Commissioner could see the pattern of the Arctic development and was able to bring many matters, which I considered to be of utmost importance, to the attention of the Northwest Territories Council, the legislative body for the Territories.

During the 1950's it was fascinating to watch the increased interest in the future of the Far North. Only the northern part of the Soviet Union has conditions similar to those of our Canadian Arctic. The problems of frequent communication between the main population centres in the South and the Arctic had always been the greatest obstacles to the full development of the North. This handicap had now been overcome. The old-time bush-pilots, who wrote a glorious chapter in the history of Canadian aviation in the 1930's, were now replaced by a new breed of airmen, both military and civilian. In the fifties, flights started between the Old and the New Worlds seeking the most direct route, and these also crossed the skies of the polar regions of Canada. Soon long-established concepts of northern transportation and communication became obsolete and as I watched these developments I thought that in a not-too-distant future well-constructed highways and railroads would certainly penetrate the North, bringing the Territories within comfortable reach of our southern cities.

The changes, both those that already were taking place and those yet to come, would drastically change the duties and responsibilities of the RCMP in the North. I knew, of course, that I would be out of the service before the new era was fully ushered in, but it was my job, I felt, to prepare for that day by shaping the policies of the Division I now commanded. My experience in attending committee meetings had been limited, but as Commanding Officer of "G" Division this form of activity became very familiar to me. After a life devoted to practical tasks in the field, the lengthy discussions often seemed frustrating. The Arctic was no longer an area where the administration was left solely in the hands of the Mounted Policeman. Other government agencies were moving in. The only way to solve many of the problems appeared to be to gather around the conference table. I was not a member of the Northwest Territories Council, but my presence was necessary at groups functioning under the council, to advise my Commissioner and keep him informed of developments so that he could speak with knowledge of the problems at the council meetings.

When I took over my new post there were approximately ten thousand Eskimos, a similar number of whites and about five thousand Indians in the region under my command. Thirty-seven per cent of this total lived in the Yukon, leaving a mere sixteen thousand people scattered across the million and a quarter square miles of the Northwest Territories. There were no signs of impending civic developments in the Northwest Territories to match those of the Yukon with its comparatively large city of Whitehorse, which now is its capital. But several mining towns were springing up and Yellowknife, on the north shore of Great Slave Lake, was booming.

The strength at my disposal was far from impressive, considering the challenges. All told, "G" Division had forty-one detachments scattered throughout the North, staffed by 140 men of all ranks. Twenty-five of these were special constables—interpreters, guides and so on. It was obvious that in order to cover an area slightly less than half the size of the United States with a mere 115 trained policemen, we would have to continue the long-extended patrols I myself had been used to.

The administrative duties of the Division affected not only the native residents, but the entire population in the North. As our men were serving often in isolated posts, they had to act as the government's representatives in such matters as income tax problems, customs, vital statistics, and so on. The reason for this arrangement was mainly a question of economics. It would have been impractical to send representatives of all the various agencies concerned to the North, so the lot fell to the Mounted Policemen. Our people collected poll taxes, customs dues, and looked after fur licensing and taxation. They issued family allowances and old age assistance, organized voluntary fire brigades and supervised life-saving equipment. In addition to these duties, our men logged the currents and recorded the levels of the rivers, acted as inspectors of weight and measures, as meteorologists, registrars of shipping and commissioners of oaths. In short, they represented the public administration. When professional services were not readily available they became the family physician and often the local midwife. The Deputy Sheriff of the Territories is usually a Mounted Policeman and so is the Immigration Officer. All this and much more was reflected daily in the volume of mail which started to reach my desk in Ottawa, and needless to say much of my time was spent on this variety of problems.

Another problem that concerned me much was the maintenance of traditions in an organization such as ours. With all the rapid changes taking place, I felt nevertheless that tradition was of the greatest value. There were few university graduates in the RCMP, mainly because the pay scale was too low to attract such men. But the Force did try to secure men who would bring with them an attitude of understanding and common sense to their tasks. To me this was in keeping with the tradition started by the Originals of 1874, when a handful of pioneering policemen met and dealt with thousands of restless Indians in a friendly way, thus paving the way for a peaceful settlement of the prairies. I strongly feel that many of our contemporary historians often have chosen to ignore this fact. The men of the Original Force set the pattern on the prairies; those who first penetrated the Arctic continued the tradition. Among the many northern Indians I met in my days, we were still known as "The Men Who Speak the Truth."

58 BUDGET PROBLEMS AND WORDS OF CAUTION

My first long inspection trip as Commanding Officer of "G" Division took me into both the Yukon and the Northwest Territories. I found that by then white women truly had made their entrance in the Arctic settlements in large numbers. There were teachers, nurses and the wives of various officials and trading post managers. It seemed only right that the RCMP should follow suit and provide our men with attractive quarters to make this possible. I knew, from experience, that our men were among the best housekeepers in the North, but that few had the opportunity to get married because of the lack of suitable accommodation.

In all I visited thirty-eight detachments, travelling some 12,300 miles by aircraft, aboard the new Canadian Government Arctic ship the *C. D. Howe* and by police car. A lengthy list of recommendations and requisitions resulted from the observations made by our Quartermaster-Sergeant W. C. Dodsworth and myself. I was far from pleased with all I had seen. In particular, I was saddened by the plight of the Eskimos. For many years I had been a champion of their cause, and now things were going in the wrong direction.

Commissioner Wood received QMS Dodsworth's and my recommendations and agreed that many improvements were needed. It was more difficult to convince our supply officer and the purchasing department, whose responsibility it was to deal with the Treasury Board of the government. This board is never eager to increase budgetary allotments from year to year, and this is a contagious attitude which quickly affects all those who have any connection with the preparation of the annual estimates for the government. This had also affected the RCMP Supply Department and when my ambitious plans reached the people there, all concerned seemed shocked. This was a period when the government was displaying an unaccustomed degree of generosity towards other departments branching out in the Arctic. For years, the RCMP had been carrying out its duties with a minimum of cost both in material and manpower. Consequently, when we asked for more money, we became the object of intense scrutiny and examination. Further difficulties stemmed from the fact that for years the same unchanged requests had been made to the supply officers of the Force and that these had only covered the bare essentials and little more. We had put up with this over the years, but now, when all these new agencies and departments obtained first-class housing and equipment, I felt our time had come as well. Certainly our men should not be treated like stepchildren. We flooded our supply officers with requests for new power boats, improved dwellings, oil-burners, refrigerators and furniture and, above all, more adequate rations.

To the guardians of the purse-strings this was near anarchy. One or two die-hards suggested that I was ruining the Arctic Service. But I was far from wasteful or extravagant and I knew that our men in the North looked after their equipment and supplies much better than the other organizations in the North. They were subject to very strict semi-annual inspections by an officer of the Force, who would permit no slackness or wastefulness. Only gradually, at times painfully slowly, did my representation start to bear fruit. I also tried to post my men to places where they were best suited and to keep them as long as possible. Above all, I tried to get them interested in the welfare of the Eskimos and the Indians. Among the men serving under me were some outstanding people, both in the field and at Headquarters. Without their zeal, energy and loyalty I could not have accomplished all we did during my eleven years at Ottawa Headquarters.

In May 1952 I was invited to attend a meeting with representatives of the Department of Resources and Development, dealing with problems affecting the Eskimos. It was perhaps the biggest meeting of its kind ever held, and I must say it was about time. Here people from the Department of National Health and Welfare, the Wildlife Service, heads of the trading companies, the Department of Indian Affairs, heads of the two churches and many others could put forward their views. The views of the RCMP were clearly stated by our Commissioner and were based on many years of observation and detailed reports on the deterioration of the conditions of the Eskimos. He even went so far as putting forward my request for a royal commission. Such a commission should be composed of competent and unbiased men who had never had anything to do with the Arctic and consequently were not influenced by any agency, to be sent in to investigate and report on conditions in the North. My men in the field and I were beginning to get a bit discouraged by continuously sending reports without getting any results, without seeing any improvements.

It was a long and disappointing meeting: to me it seemed that very little progress was made. One result, however, was that in a way it was the beginning of the formation of a new Northern Affairs Branch, the so-called Arctic Division, with the appointment of a large staff in Ottawa and in the field. The new Northern Affairs officers were to travel throughout the North in order to study Eskimo conditions in various areas and to make recommendations, the very same things we had been doing for years. Our reports had always been available to any concerned member of the administration, but few had shown any great interest. At any rate, we welcomed this new branch even if it meant a further delay while new reports were being produced. Somehow it seemed that our representations were finally beginning to have some effect. There was a new awareness of the problems and that was something. I could not resist feeling how ironic it was that it took the fear of a war to accomplish almost overnight the very things we had advocated for half a century. With the sudden revelation of the strategic importance of the Arctic, the attitude of unconcern that had characterized reactions to the needs of the North was soon swept away. Regardless of the motives, I was glad that my friends the Eskimos would soon benefit from this new interest.

With the beginning of the DEW Line project to warn of aerial attack from the north, the influx of people to the North was fantastic. Whole communities, large and small, mushroomed. It took but little imagination for anyone who knew the mentality of the Eskimos to realize that the sudden and sweeping changes would bring problems as well as benefits to these fine, but socially backward native sons and daughters. Few Eskimos could speak English and most had no idea at all of the white man's life. The improved medical and hospital facilities, the establishment of schools and the introduction of a civilized way of life, as I had foreseen it, should have been beneficial to the Eskimos. But the new townsites brought stores, restaurants, pool-rooms, movie theatres, hotels and even cocktail lounges. The voice of the juke-box was heard in the land, as was the musical fare of the new radio stations. Such old-time essentials as the kerosene lamp and the box stove quickly became obsolete. The Eskimo, lured by these exctiing new things, gazed with wonder as he drifted into these communities with his family. Then followed far-reaching changes in the administration. The days of the Mounted Policeman as a general handyman for all federal departments were gone forever and new specialized organizations were required to handle the administration. It was with great satisfaction that I learned that steps were taken in this direction. In 1953 a new department, that of Northern Affairs and National Resources, was set up to deal with Arctic administration. For some years following, the work of the RCMP and the reliance on its members continued as before, but then we were gradually relieved by other agencies.

The establishment of the new department was heralded with much publicity, much of it centred on the sins of omission and commission of the past, as far as the neglect of the Eskimos was concerned. With easy access to the Arctic, newspapermen, writers and armchair explorers now arrived in droves, all full of ideas and self-righteousness. Now things were going to be done for the Eskimos. Loud cries were heard, and many who never had given a single thought to the plight of the Eskimos were setting themselves up as some kind of collective guilty conscience. The government and, surprisingly enough, every single agency in the North was blamed for the conditions. Books, magazine and newspaper articles attacked the Force, the missionaries and, to a certain extent, the traders. Across the country many people joined in the outcry and editorials and letters to the editor alike criticized the RCMP for having allowed this to happen. We were cited as unfit, both by temperament and training, to carry out administrative duties. But our critics forgot, or were unaware of the fact, that the Mounted Police had been the only government agency in the area for over fifty years and over the years had compiled report upon report recommending improvements. In this the Police had been ably assisted by missions of both the Roman Catholic and Anglican faiths, the very same that now were branded as the villains who had completely demoralized and ruined the Eskimos. I and many of my old northern friends could hardly believe our own ears. Certain people in the government joined in the lamentation and hastened to absolve themselves of the omissions of their predecessors. There was an amazing amount of chest-thumping in Ottawa in those days.

Yet nobody could escape the question why some of the very same people who now were criticizing had failed to do something about the conditions while there still had been time. The conditions had not been a state secret. Stefansson and Jenness had produced almost a library on this some forty years earlier, describing in detail the Eskimo, the land he occupied and its resources. The Mounted Police had kept its records up to date with able support from missionaries and traders.

In order to fully appreciate the difficulties the changing world around him presents for the Eskimo, it is well to examine the characteristics of the people themselves. At heart the Eskimo is an improvident soul and his tendency to drift into the new townsites is of little help in overcoming this trait. He possesses some attributes similar to those of the white man, a fact that is too frequently overlooked, particularly by armchair critics who know little about the real conditions. There are ambitious Eskimos, and happy-go-lucky types. Over the years I have seen many of both. It is common knowledge to all who have lived with these people that hardships and want are not always due to poor economic conditions. I have visited camps where the people seemed to be really in trouble, yet they made little or no effort to secure food despite the fact that they lived close to good sources of fish and game. On the other hand I have seen communities where a team spirit had been developed and every effort was made to subsist.

All this must be taken into consideration. The plans to provide employment for the male Eskimos are excellent, for they will soon learn to copy the white man in most fields. But construction work is not continuous in the North. It seems that years may pass before there will be sufficient work in the new townsites to keep everybody employed. If these communities are attracting more Eskimos than they can absorb, and I fear this is often so, the natives will lose all desire to support themselves. They will end up being charges of the government, living on available welfare schemes. Idleness and hand-outs, combined with the removal of ambition, could spell disaster. No doubt this process will be accelerated if we permit the Eskimos to copy the white man's less commendable features. While applauding the rehabilitation of the Eskimos I must record keen disappointment, for instance, in the decision to permit them free and legal access to the newly-established liquor outlets. I have heard all the arguments in defence of this policy, that there should be no discrimination against the Eskimos. Many of those who scream the loudest about "discrimination" know nothing about the very people they claim to defend. I am as anxious as anyone to see the Eskimos given the full benefits of our civilization as quickly as possible, but in my opinion, shared by many others who know the true conditions, the extension of liquor privileges is an unfortunate step.

Canada's stand on racial discrimination is well known. Most of us feel that restrictive practices are repugnant, but when we are dealing with the Eskimos, we must remember that we are dealing with a race that is centuries behind us in development. A lifting of all restrictions now may prove a threat to their existence.

If today we sit in judgment on those who failed to help the Eskimos during the past half-century, I shudder to think of the criticism which will be levelled at us in another fifty years' time. The Eskimo may have taken a great step forward towards his assimilation into the culture of the white man by his presence in the cocktail lounge, but I fear the consequences will be grave. It both hurts and annoys me to think of my old friends among the Eskimos, with their meagre earnings, wasting their money and sacrificing their dignity in this fashion.

As I see it now, it is unfortunately too late to change established policies or to withdraw privileges already granted the Eskimos. I am sure, however, that we could have found a happier method of helping these people so that they might have accepted our way of living and become first-class citizens.

Not all Eskimos are ignorant or uneducated. There have been some gratifying cases of distinct success in the field of education. And yet, I am afraid, it will be a slow process before all youngsters are brought into the sphere of complete education.

The Department of Northern Affairs has gone about its tasks with considerable zeal, backed by generous financial support of the government. On formation it was confronted with the problem of securing the large staff needed for its projected operations. Most of these people had to come from the slender ranks of those with previous Arctic experience. There were few men available who knew the North, but such men will emerge as new officials gain experience. The new department will come to realize, as we did, that the best men are those dedicated souls who really love the Arctic and its people and who are prepared to devote a lifetime to its service.

59 THE *ST. ROCH* ENDS HER CAREER

The *St. Roch*, which had been laid up at Esquimalt since 1948, almost got another chance to visit the Arctic in 1950. Some thought had been given to reopening the detachments at Craig Harbour and Bache Peninsula, both on Ellesmere Island. Both places, which are right opposite Etah, on Greenland, had been closed since 1932, mainly because of the problems of supplying them by ship. We knew that the Etah Eskimos had been in the habit of crossing over to kill muskox, which in the early years had existed in great numbers. Now they had been practically exterminated by explorers and Eskimos. The idea, therefore, was to move in some people from Pond Inlet, which was already overcrowded with many on permanent relief. The matter had been carefully looked into. We had no intention of having anything to do with settling a new group of Eskimos in that area unless we were certain such a move would be in their best interests.

It seemed to me that the *St. Roch* was ideally suited for this moving job and the Commissioner gave his permission to transfer the ship to the Marine Division at Halifax. In early summer of 1950, therefore, a skipper, two or three mates and a crew of fifteen in all, I think—twice the number of men I had in my days—were sent to Esquimalt where the ship was fitted with an echo sounder, radar and various other modern navigational aids. Also, for the first time in the life of the ship, she was fitted with a large ice-box in the hold to keep fresh food for the voyage through the Panama Canal to Halifax. When the *St. Roch* arrived there in September of that year, she became the first ship in history to have gone completely around the North American continent, although it had not been a continuous trip!

However, the people of the Marine Division came to the conclusion that the brave little ship was unfit for them to go to sea in with her poor accommodation, slow speed and her lively habit of rolling and pitching in a bit of sea. "G" Division did not have any men to spare to man the ship for summer trips in the eastern Arctic, and professional sailors apparently did not want to go on her. The ship, therefore, was laid up at the Naval Dockyard in Halifax, unloved and unwanted, to gather barnacles. It was obvious that the *St. Roch* was surplus. The question then arose as to what her fate would be. To sell her for scrap was unthinkable, yet she had little commercial value and there were few who could have found any use for her services. In Halifax she was an alien, in spite of the Maritimers' love of the sea, and while a few people came down to visit her once in a while, she was far from her place of birth. In Vancouver, on the other hand, the *St. Roch* was almost a legend, for although registered in Ottawa, Vancouver was her home port and a warm welcome had always awaited her on her return there from the Arctic.

As the time for her disposal drew near, many west-coast citizens felt that she should be taken back to Vancouver and there be placed ashore in a place of honour to become an historic reminder of Canada's contribution to Arctic exploration and a permanent tribute to the work of the Royal Canadian Mounted Police.

The RCMP, with the consent of the government, therefore offered the *St. Roch* to the citizens of Vancouver for five thousand dollars, the approximate cost of taking her back there. The offer was gladly accepted and instructions were issued for the ship to be sailed back to the Pacific port. This gave me great satisfaction, and I was highly honoured when I heard that the good citizens of Vancouver had insisted that I should take her back on her last voyage and officially present her to the City. I had passed through the Panama Canal several times, but in this way I would actually personally have navigated the little vessel completely around the North American continent.

I had come to love this ugly duckling of a faithful little ship over the years. We had come through a lot together, and now the last run of her eventful career was in my charge. On that nostalgic voyage, I alone remained of the small company that had formed the original crew in 1928. Of the others, I knew that two had died, and the rest no longer were members of the RCMP. With my new crew and all the modern devices on board, I actually found time long on my hands, as we sailed from Halifax at the end of July, 1954, and visited Bermuda,

Jamaica, Acapulco, San Diego and San Francisco before arriving at Vancouver in early October.

In San Francisco I had a moving experience when I met with old Captain Pedersen, the now long-since-retired skipper I had raced so many times in the Arctic.

The welcome given the *St. Roch* when she reached Vancouver was truly thrilling. The huge new Royal Canadian Navy icebreaker *Labrador* had arrived a few days previously from Halifax. We were given the honour of leading her into the harbour itself with two helicopters from the icebreaker hovering over us while craft from the Royal Vancouver Yacht Club manoeuvred into position, dipping their ensigns as we passed. The Navy Band was on hand and a large crowd of citizens was on the wharf for the event. One could almost feel the *St. Roch* quiver at the royal reception.

Perhaps my greatest pleasure came from the presence of former crew members who were there to meet us: Olsen, Parsloe, Kells, Foster, Dad Parry and Sealey, all veterans of the maiden voyage of twenty-six years before. Then followed greetings from His Worship Mayor Hume and several aldermen, and the next day an official welcome was extended to us at City Hall. Major J. S. Matthews, the City Archivist, formally related the history of the vessel, and the moment had come for a unique transaction. The Mayor handed me a cheque made out to the Government of Canada for $5,000 in payment for the ship and in turn received from me the Certificate of Registry. Thus the schooner passed into the care and keeping of the City of Vancouver. The event was due largely to the unflagging interest of Major Matthews and of the late Mr. Tom Howarth, who previously had been connected with the Burrard Drydock Company which had built the ship. The maintenance of the ship is now in the hands of the Maritime Museum authorities at Vancouver and she is in a very favourable location, resting in a concrete basin. Unfortunately, however, she is exposed to wind and weather.

It can only be hoped that one day she will be placed under a roof similar to that given Nansen's and Amundsen's ship the *Fram* in the Oslo Harbour in Norway.*

During an inspection trip to the Arctic in 1953 I received a telegram

*(Some months after Supt. Larsen's death the Canadian government declared the *St. Roch* a national historic monument and provided seventy thousand dollars for the building of a closed shelter near Vancouver's Maritime Museum.)

from Commissioner Nicholson informing me that I had been promoted to the rank of Superintendent, and the occasion was duly celebrated aboard the ice-breaker *D'Iberville.*

60 THE LAST YEARS IN THE FORCE

Two events stand out in my mind when I think of the years that followed until my retirement on February 7, 1961.

In July 1957 I returned to Norway for the first time in more than thirty-four years. It seemed incredible that I now was a Canadian and an officer in the Royal Canadian Mounted Police and that I was about to represent my adopted country in my native land. The Canadian government had made a contribution to the erection of a monument of the Norwegian Arctic explorer Otto Sverdrup at Steinkjaer, Norway, as a tribute to the man who had done so much for the exploration of Canada's Arctic. As Chief of the Arctic Division of the RCMP and as a former Norwegian I had been selected to be present at the ceremony.

On my way to Norway, I first flew to London, where I called at the headquarters of the Royal Geographical Society, which once had awarded its Royal Medal to Otto Sverdrup. Mr. L. P. Kirman, the Secretary of the Society, asked me to present a tribute from it to the memory of the explorer, and to me this was a singular honour.

It was a coincidence, of course, that the British European Airways aircraft which took me from London to Oslo was called *Sir John Franklin,* and yet I felt it only appropriate that I should return to Norway aboard an aircraft named for one of my greatest heroes. As we flew up the Oslo Fiord, after having passed my birthplace, I spotted the famous ship *Fram* in her specially built tent-shaped house and made a mental note to visit her before leaving Norway. When I later did, I considered it a great experience.

After a brief visit to my birthplace I went north to Steinkjaer, where a distinguished group led by the then Crown Prince, now King Olav V, had assembled for the unveiling of the monument. Also present were some ten thousand people who had turned out to honour their great native son, Otto Sverdrup.

It was a clear, beautiful day and it was with great emotion that I concluded my official remarks with the following words:

"The names of Sverdrup and Norway will forever be linked with that of Canada through the islands in Canada's Arctic carrying his name and the names of those who assisted him in his work there. This is an additional tie linking our two countries so closely and devotedly together."

Three years later I was honoured by the award of the Royal Canadian Geographical Society's Massey Medal. As the first recipient of this medal I received it from His Excellency the Governor General himself, one of his last official acts in that office.

On the day of my retirement the following year I looked back over the years and felt that I had been given the opportunity to live a rich and active life. I was filled with deep gratitude to my native Norway, which had given me the ideals, the dreams and the ambitions, and towards my adopted country, Canada, which had given me these many opportunities and honours.

EPILOGUE

During the summer of 1964 Henry Larsen made a second, and last, visit to Norway, this time accompanied by his wife Mary. He had lived the past few years since his retirement at Lunenburg, Nova Scotia, near his beloved sea, but decided to move to Vancouver on his return from Europe.

When he arrived at Vancouver in September of that year, he was a man marked by death and went straight to a hospital, where he died on October 29, 1964. Aware that death was near, he wrote to a friend that he "soon will be setting out on that last, great sled patrol." His only regret and unrealized dream was that he never would see his "ugly duckling" the *St. Roch*, properly housed and cared for.

Larsen's last dream was fulfilled some two years later when his widow cut the ribbon inaugurating the beautiful *St. Roch* House near the Maritime Museum in Vancouver on June 23, 1966. The ceremony was attended by the Minister of Northern Affairs, the Hon. Arthur Laing, senior RCMP officers, and civic dignitaries led by His Worship Mayor Rathie. The *St. Roch* had finally been named a national historic monument by the federal government.

Far to the north, where the McClintock Channel joins the Franklin Strait, a body of water has been named the Larsen Sound, while some one thousand miles inland from the *St. Roch*, "Henry with the Big Ship" or "Hanorie Umiarjuaq," as his countless Eskimo friends called him, is buried in the RCMP cemetery at Regina, between the two coasts he had come to love like the one he had grown up on across the ocean.

INDEX